Simply Shakespeare

Weekly Reader's Read *Magazine Presents*

Simply Shakespeare
Readers Theatre for Young People

Edited by Jennifer Kroll

2003
Teacher Ideas Press
361 Hanover Street
Portsmouth, NH 03802-6926

British Library Cataloguing in Publication Data is available.

Copyright © 2003 by Weekly Reader Corporation

All rights reserved. No portion of this book may be
reproduced, by any process or technique, without the
express written consent of the publisher. An exception
is made for individual librarians and educators, who
may make copies of activity sheets for classroom use
in a single school or library. Standard citation information
should appear on each page.

ISBN: 1–56308–946–7

First published in 2003

Teacher Ideas Press
361 Hanover Street, Portsmouth, NH 03802
www.lu.com/tips

Printed in the United States of America

The paper used in this book complies with the
Permanent Paper Standard issued by the National
Information Standards Organization (Z39.48-1984).

10   9   8   7   6   5   4   3   2   1

Copyright Acknowledgment

Illustrations used courtesy of Getty Images.

Contents

Introduction vii
As You Like It 1
Hamlet: Prince of Denmark 17
Julius Caesar 33
King Lear 51
Macbeth 69
A Midsummer Night's Dream 91
The Merchant of Venice 107
Much Ado About Nothing 121
Othello 139
Romeo and Juliet 161
Taming of the Shrew 179
The Tempest 199
Twelfth Night 213

Index of Scripts 233

Introduction

 Introducing Shakespeare to Young Readers

Effective and appropriate early encounters with Shakespeare's classic stories and characters can create a positive feeling about the Bard and his works that will remain with students throughout their school years and the rest of their lives. The play adaptations in this volume are designed to provide just such a positive introduction to the works of Shakespeare. These adaptations, culled from the pages of *Read* magazine, have been favorites with our teacher subscribers—and their students—for years. Every year, teachers write to tell us how well these adaptations work in the classroom and to ask us to print more. Here, finally, are thirteen *Read* adaptations of some of Shakespeare's greatest and best-known works, collected conveniently in one volume. In these adaptations we've modernized Shakespeare's language so that young readers, as well as older readers with comprehension difficulties, will immediately be able to grasp and appreciate plot developments and characters' motives. We've worked to preserve the flavor of Shakespeare's wonderful originals while providing age-appropriate, simplified versions that your students can read or perform in just one or two class periods. These adaptations can be used independently or as a useful precursor to a classroom reading or viewing of one of Shakespeare's plays in its original version.

 ## The Role of Readers Theatre

Readers theatre plays have been a favorite feature of *Read* magazine for years. In readers theatre, the primary focus is on an effective reading of the script rather than on a dramatic, memorized presentation. Students are thus able to enjoy participating in play presentations without needing to attend lengthy practice sessions beforehand. Generally, only minimal props or stage movements are involved, although adding such touches does tend to enliven the production and invite more active participation.

Readers theatre can easily be incorporated into any language arts program. It provides teachers with an exciting way to enhance the program, particularly in today's classrooms that emphasize a variety of reading and listening experiences. Readers theatre encourages strong oral skills and promotes active listening for students in the audience. Perhaps most important, readers theatre is enjoyable for students and teachers and promotes interest in and enthusiasm for literature.

 ## Vocabulary in Scripts

Before using the scripts, assess each one for difficulty and appropriateness of content and for vocabulary that might be challenging to your particular students. Prior to beginning a classroom reading with a group of students, you may wish to have individuals pre-read their own parts, looking for words they don't understand or know how to pronounce.

 ## Preparing the Scripts

Once a script is chosen for reading, make a copy for each character, plus an extra set or two for your own use and a replacement copy. To help readers keep their place on the page, highlighter markers can be used to designate a character's lines within the copy.

Photocopied scripts will last longer if you use a three-hole punch (or copy them on pre-punched paper) and place them in inexpensive folders. The folders can be color coordinated with the internal highlighting for each character's part. The title of the play can be printed on the outside of the folder, and scripts can be stored easily for the next reading. Preparing the scripts and folders is a good task for a volunteer parent or a student helper. The preparation takes a minimum of initial attention and needs to be repeated only when a folder is lost.

 ## Presentation Suggestions

For readers theatre, readers traditionally stand—or sit on stools, chairs, or the floor—in an informal presentation style. The narrators may stand slightly off to one side with their scripts placed on a music stand or lectern. The readers may hold their scripts in folders.

The position of the reader can indicate the importance of his or her role. For example, in *Romeo and Juliet* the two title characters could be positioned in the front center of the stage area, with the minor characters to the sides and slightly behind them. Suggestions for possible placements are given for each individual play.

To keep the stage area from becoming overly crowded, you may wish to have readers of brief parts enter or leave the area prior to and following the reading of their parts. Alternatively, readers may stand up for a reading and sit down for the remainder of the script.

Because these scripts are appropriate for developing and remedial readers, it is important that the students be comfortable with the physical arrangement. Students may have their own ideas about presentation strategies, and their involvement should be fostered.

Props

Readers theatre traditionally has few, if any, props. However, you may wish to add simple costuming, such as hats and scarves, as well as a few props, to lend interest to the presentation. Suggestions for simple props or costuming are included with each play; however, students should be encouraged to decide how much or little to add to their production. The use of props or actions may be overwhelming to some readers, and in such cases emphasis should remain on the reading rather than on an overly complicated presentation.

Delivery

Some suggestions for the delivery of lines are included in parentheses within the plays. Students should be encouraged to respond to these suggestions and to brainstorm delivery strategies for all lines. A variety of warm-ups can help students feel more comfortable with the idea of dramatic delivery. For example, you might have the entire class respond to the following Shakespearean situations:

- Seeing a ghostly figure appear before you
- Suspecting that others are plotting against you
- Learning that you have been the brunt of a joke
- Discovering that a long-lost family member is still alive
- Basking in the admiration of others after an accomplishment
- Refusing to give others the information they desperately want

During their first experiences with presenting a script, students are tempted to keep their heads buried in the script, making sure they don't miss a line. Students should learn the material well enough to look up from the script during the presentation. They can learn to use onstage focus—to look at each other during the presentation. This is most logical for characters who are interacting with one another. The use of offstage focus—where the presenters look directly into the eyes of the audience—is more logical for narrators or for characters who are speaking to themselves.

Simple actions, such as hand gestures or turning, can easily be incorporated into readers theatre. Generally, the audience should be able to see the readers' facial expressions and any of their actions during the reading. On occasion it might seem logical for a character to move across the stage, facing the other characters while reading. In this event the characters should be turned so that the audience can see the reader's face.

The Next Step

Once students have enjoyed the process of preparing and presenting these *Simply Shakespeare* scripts, you may find you want to capitalize on their enthusiasm and interest by extending the learning experience. Following are some possible extension activities that you might wish to try:

- Have students read, listen to, or watch at least part of the play in its original version.
- Attend a live Shakespeare production with your students.

- Embark with your students on a historical exploration of Elizabethan times and the theatre in Shakespeare's day.

- Introduce students to the structural elements of Shakespearean comedy and tragedy. After students are familiar with these forms, have them write their own comedic and tragic plays or stories.

- Introduce more sophisticated students to the Shakespeare authorship controversy. Allow them to research the issue, then stage their own authorship debate within the classroom.

- Have students add stage directions to one of these readers theatre scripts and create a stage play from the script.

However you choose to use these scripts, we are sure you will find them a valuable addition to your language arts curriculum. Curtains up!

Read magazine staff:
Suzanne I. Barchers, Managing Editor
Jennifer Kroll, Senior Editor
Jennifer Peters, Associate Editor
Robin Demougeot, Art Director
www.weeklyreader.com

CHAPTER 1

As You Like It

By William Shakespeare

Adapted by Jennifer Kroll

 Summary

Duke Frederick has overthrown and ousted his older brother. The old duke now lives in exile in the Forest of Arden, accompanied by a number of his loyal followers. The old duke's daughter, Rosalind, remains at court because of her close relationship with Frederick's daughter, Celia. While attending a wrestling match, the two cousins meet a handsome young nobleman who has decided to test his luck in the wrestling ring. The young man, Orlando, takes a liking to Rosalind, just as she does to him. However, he feels too flustered to respond to Rosalind's flirtation and fails to express his feelings. When Duke Frederick's anger turns against Rosalind, she and Celia escape together to the Forest of Arden, disguised as a peasant brother and sister. Not long afterward, Orlando also flees to the forest. But when Rosalind and Orlando meet up there, the young man doesn't recognize Rosalind, who is disguised as a boy. She offers to tutor the hapless Orlando in the ways of love, and much silliness results.

Presentation Suggestions

Place the narrators, Adam, Oliver, Charles, Monsieur Le Beau, and the courtier in standing position or on high stools or chairs. Place the remaining characters in a front row on lower chairs or cushions. Make sure Rosalind, Orlando, and Celia are front and center.

 Props

Duke Frederick can wear a crown or royal robe. Orlando, Oliver, Lord Amiens, Jacques de Boyes, and Courtier can wear nice clothes. Phebe and Silvius can hold a stuffed sheep or a shepherd's staff. They can tie their hair back in bandanas or kerchiefs, wear flannel shirts, or in some other way denote their working-class status. Celia and Rosalind can dress in long skirts or other nice clothing and can throw on flannel shirts or bandannas when they disguise themselves in Scene 3. To transform herself into a boy, Rosalind could put on a false mustache or pull her hair up under a cap.

Cast of Characters

(main parts in boldface)
Narrators 1, 2, 3
Orlando de Boyes, *youngest son of Sir Rowland de Boyes*
Adam, *an old servant in the de Boyes household*
Oliver de Boyes, *Orlando's older brother*
Charles, *a wrestler*
Celia, *daughter of Duke Frederick*
Rosalind, *daughter of the exiled duke*
Duke Frederick, *usurper of the throne*
Monsieur Le Beau, *a courtier in Duke Frederick's court*
Exiled Duke, *older brother of Duke Frederick*
Lord Amiens, *companion to the exiled duke*
Courtier, *at Duke Frederick's court*
Silvius, *a shepherd*
Phebe, *a shepherdess*
Jacques de Boyes, *brother of Oliver and Orlando*

As You Like It

By William Shakespeare
Adapted by Jennifer Kroll

Scene 1

Narrator 1:	In the orchard of Oliver's house, his youngest brother, Orlando, stands talking with a servant.
Orlando de Boyes:	In his will, my father left his money to my oldest brother, Oliver. He charged Oliver with the task of raising and supporting my middle brother Jacques and I. That's where my problems started. Oliver hates me. He sent my brother Jacques to school, but he won't send me.
Adam:	Here comes my master, your brother, now.
Orlando:	Stay here and listen to the horrible way he speaks to me.
Oliver de Boyes:	*(gruffly, to Orlando)* What are you doing?
Orlando:	I'm doing just what I've been trained to do—nothing.
Oliver:	Well, make yourself busy doing nothing elsewhere.
Orlando:	If you don't want me around, you could always send me to school.
Oliver:	I wouldn't waste my money on such as you.
Orlando:	On "such as me"? I'm the son of Sir Rowland de Boyes, just as you are.
Adam:	*(interrupting)* Masters, be patient! For the sake of your dear father, don't quarrel with each other.
Oliver:	I won't listen a minute longer to this nonsense.
Narrator 2:	He turns to go.
Orlando:	Stay where you are and hear me out. My father instructed you to give me a good education. Instead, you have brought me up as a peasant. But now my father's spirit grows strong in me. I will no longer endure this life. Either pay for my schooling or at least give me a little of my father's money so that I can go out and seek my own fortune.
Oliver:	*(sarcastically)* And what will you do when that's spent—beg? *(changing tone)* I tell you what. I'll think about giving you some

	cash. But for the time being, go away and don't bother me. *(to Adam)* You go with him, too, you old dog.
Adam:	*(to Oliver)* Is this my reward for a lifetime of good service to your family? Your father would not have spoken to me in this way.
Narrator 3:	Adam and Orlando leave. Oliver returns to the house. About an hour later, he receives a visit from a wrestler named Charles, a man who often entertains at court.
Charles:	Good morning, my lord.
Oliver:	Good morning, Charles. What's new at court?
Charles:	There's no new news, just the same old news. The old duke has been banished by his younger brother Frederick, who has taken over his position. The old duke and some of his most loyal followers have gone into exile.
Oliver:	Is Rosalind, the duke's daughter, in exile with her father?
Charles:	No. She stayed at court with her cousin Celia, the new duke's daughter. Those two are inseparable. They're like sisters.
Oliver:	Where's the old duke now?
Charles:	They say he's off in the forest of Arden, living like Robin Hood.
Oliver:	Do you wrestle tomorrow in front of the new duke?
Charles:	Yes. And that's why I've come to see you. I've heard that your younger brother, Orlando, wants to try to wrestle me and win the prize money. You have to dissuade him from doing this. He's sure to get hurt if he goes against me.
Oliver:	To tell you the truth, I couldn't care less whether Orlando gets hurt. In fact, I'd just as soon he broke his neck as broke a finger. Please, by all means, wrestle my brother.
Charles:	Well, if that's how you feel, I'll be sure to give him a good thrashing. Good day to you, sir.
Narrator 1:	Charles departs.
Oliver:	*(to himself)* Why do I hate my brother so much? He's a gentle, noble soul. He's never been to school, and yet he's well read and knows as much as many who have schooling. I think I hate Orlando because everybody loves him so much. He makes me look bad by comparison. Well, I must go find him now. I want to make sure he appears in that wrestling ring tomorrow.

Scene 2

Narrator 2:	A day later at court, Duke Frederick's daughter, Celia, sits talking with her cousin Rosalind.
Celia:	Rosalind, you look so down. Cheer up!

Rosalind:	I'm already acting cheerier than I actually feel. With my father banished, it's hard for me to feel very cheerful. Yet I'll try to rejoice in your good fortune and forget my own misfortune.
Celia:	Remember, Rose, I am my father's only child and heir. When he dies, I promise I'll give you back everything you've lost. So please, cheer up, dear cousin!
Rosalind:	I'll do my best, for your sake, Celia.
Celia:	I know what you need—some pastime to distract you from your problems. I heard that Charles the wrestler is going to entertain the court today. Do you want to go watch?
Rosalind:	Watch wrestling?
Celia:	Sure—why not? Charles is supposed to be pretty much unstoppable. Just last week he took on three brothers, one right after the other, and badly injured them all.
Narrator 3:	The two young women head over to the site of the wrestling match. When they are ringside, they immediately spot a big, brawny man who is strutting around, looking anything but nervous.
Rosalind:	That must be Charles.
Narrator 1:	Rosalind also spots Orlando warming up near the ring. She notices that he is extremely handsome and looks to be about seventeen, her own age. She gawks.
Rosalind:	*(to Celia)* Is *that* the challenger?
Narrator 2:	Celia's father, Duke Frederick approaches the two girls.
Duke Frederick:	Hello, daughter and niece. Are you girls sneaking in to watch the wrestling?
Celia:	We are.
Duke Frederick:	I'm warning you—you're not likely to take much joy in it. That young man is never going to make it out of the ring in one piece. I've told him as much, but he won't be dissuaded from competing. Perhaps you girls would have more luck talking him out of his foolhardy plan.
Narrator 3:	The duke summons Orlando over so that Rosalind and Celia can try to talk him out of wrestling.
Rosalind:	Young man, haven't you heard what became of the others who wrestled Charles?
Celia:	We pray you to look after your own safety and to abandon your plan.
Rosalind:	Please, sir. Your reputation does not have to be harmed if you back out of this match. We can have it announced that the duke canceled the match at the last minute.
Orlando:	I thank you, dear ladies, for all your kindness and concern, but I still intend to wrestle. I hope you'll send your good wishes with me as I enter the fight.

Rosalind:	Whatever strength and luck we have, we send it with you.
Narrator 1:	Orlando heads back to the ring. Rosalind and Celia gaze after him.
Rosalind:	What an incredible young man!
Celia:	I wish I were invisible. I'd jump in there, grab Charles by the leg, and help that young fellow out.
Narrator 2:	The wrestling match begins. Despite Charles's larger size and seemingly superior strength, the match turns out to be very exciting. The crowd oohs and ahhs as Orlando is nearly thrown a number of times. Each time, he manages to wrestle his way free. Orlando finally manages to throw Charles, who is taken out of the ring on a stretcher.
Duke Frederick:	(*excitedly, to Orlando*) Well done, young man! What is your name?
Orlando:	Orlando, my lord. I'm the youngest son of Sir Rowland de Boyes.
Duke Frederick:	(*seriously*) Alas. I wish you were somebody else. Your father was my enemy. Good day.
Narrator 3:	The duke turns and abruptly departs.
Rosalind:	(*to Celia*) My father thought the world of Sir Rowland de Boyes. If I had known that this young man was Sir Rowland's son, I would have tried even harder to keep him from harm.
Celia:	I feel bad that my father was so rude to him. Let's go and have a few words with him.
Narrator 1:	The two women approach Orlando. As they do, Rosalind unclasps a chain from around her neck. She holds it out to Orlando.
Rosalind:	Please, sir, wear this for me. I am out of favor with fortune, or I'd offer you more.
Narrator 2:	Orlando takes the chain but stands speechlessly staring at Rosalind. He has little experience with women and romance, and he feels awkward. Although he wants to say something to this attractive young woman, he suddenly can't think of a thing to say.
Rosalind:	Sir, you have wrestled well and have overthrown more than just your enemy.
Narrator 3:	Orlando blushes and remains unable to speak.
Celia:	Shall we go, cousin?
Rosalind:	(*reluctantly, to Celia*) Yes, all right. (*to Orlando*) Fare you well.
Narrator 1:	After the two women leave, Orlando turns to Monsieur Le Beau, who stands beside him.
Orlando:	She wanted to talk to me, but I couldn't think of a thing to say! What an idiot I must have looked. Who *was* that beautiful woman?
Monsieur Le Beau:	The tall blond one? She's the daughter of the exiled duke.

Orlando:	And she remains at court?
Le Beau:	Her uncle keeps her here as company for his own daughter. But I can tell you that lately he has grown more and more impatient with the girl. I don't think that she'll be safe here very long. And you'd better leave as well. duke Frederick is dangerous to his enemies—and their sons.

Scene 3

Narrator 2:	The next day, Celia and Rosalind sit talking in the duke's palace.
Celia:	You're really smitten with this Orlando fellow, aren't you?
Rosalind:	Yes. I think he's amazing.
Narrator 3:	Rosalind looks up and notices her uncle coming.
Rosalind:	Here comes your father. His eyes look full of anger.
Celia:	Uh-oh.
Duke Frederick:	*(to Rosalind)* Mistress, get gone from my court at once.
Rosalind:	*(in surprise)* Me, uncle?
Duke Frederick:	Yes, you. If you are caught within twenty miles of my court, you die.
Rosalind:	*(shakily)* Please, sir. Can't you at least tell me what I've done to deserve this? I can think of nothing that could have angered you so much.
Duke Frederick:	All traitors claim their innocence, just as you do now.
Rosalind:	Your mistrust doesn't make me into a traitor.
Duke Frederick:	You are your father's daughter—that's enough.
Celia:	*(to Duke Frederick)* Dear Father, let me speak.
Duke Frederick:	*(angrily, to Celia)* It's for your sake I've kept her here. Otherwise she'd be long gone already, as she ought to have been.
Celia:	But, Father, I can't live without my dear cousin! She is my best friend!
Duke Frederick:	*(to Celia)* You are a fool, child. You don't know what's good for you. *(to Rosalind)* You had better leave quickly.
Narrator 1:	The duke departs, and Rosalind bursts into tears.
Celia:	Oh, poor Rosalind! What are we going to do?
Rosalind:	*(crying)* I don't know.
Celia:	I do. We'll go and seek out your father, my uncle, in the Forest of Arden.
Rosalind:	But two young women like us, traveling alone together—we'll be in great danger on the long road.

Celia: We'll have to disguise ourselves. We'll put on tattered clothing and dirty our faces. Then nobody will take much interest in us.

Rosalind: I know how we can make ourselves even safer. I can dress up as a man and pretend to be your brother. I'm tall enough to pass for a man.

Celia: That's a great idea. What shall I call you, dear brother?

Rosalind: My name will be Ganymede. What will yours be, sister?

Celia: You shall call me Aliena.

Scene 4

Narrator 2: In the forest of Arden, the exiled duke and his companions are hunting for deer.

Exiled Duke: Brothers in exile, this isn't such a bad life. These woods are less full of danger than court was.

Lord Amiens: You are such a balanced person, Your Grace. You see the good and the bad in all things. That's why everyone respects you, and so many of us left court to be with you.

Narrator 3: Meanwhile, back at court, the departure of Celia has just been noted by Duke Frederick.

Duke Frederick: *(raving angrily)* Didn't anybody see them leave?

Courtier: Not a soul, my lord. But it seems possible that those girls have run off with Orlando de Boyes. Celia's maid overheard the two girls speaking of him. They seemed quite impressed with the lad.

Duke Frederick: Send some men to the de Boyes house and have them bring Orlando here! If they can't find the youth, have them bring his brother. Celia must be returned to court!

Scene 5

Narrator 1: Meanwhile, Orlando is returning home to his brother's house. On the road leading up to the house, he meets Adam, who seems very upset.

Orlando: Adam, what's the matter?

Adam: Oh, you poor boy! I would be devastated if anything were to happen to you!

Orlando: What are you talking about? What's going to happen to me?

Adam: It's your brother, sir. I've heard him talking. I think he wants to see you disgraced or dead. Your life is in danger if you return to that house.

Orlando: Where else can I possibly go? All the money I have in the world is this prize money I've just won.

Adam: Please, I beg you—don't go in there! I have some money that I've saved up over the years. I was going to use it to support myself in my old age. But I will gladly share that money with you, sir. Use it to travel to the Forest of Arden. There perhaps you can find the exiled duke, your father's dear friend.

Narrator 2: Orlando departs for the Forest of Arden. Later that day, Oliver is brought before Duke Frederick.

Duke Frederick: What's this I hear? You say you don't know where your brother Orlando is? How can this be?

Oliver: I swear it's true, sir. He's disappeared. Believe me, I would turn him over to you if I knew where to find him. I have no love for my brother.

Duke Frederick: Whether you love him or hate him is your own business. But this brother of yours had better be found. I give you one year to find Orlando. If you do not come up with the lad by then, I fully intend to seize all of your family's lands and possessions. *(to guards, standing nearby)* See this man out!

Scene 6

Narrator 3: Rosalind and Celia, disguised as a sheperd and sheperdess, travel through the countryside. They reach the border of the Forest of Arden. There, they purchase a small cottage. From the cottage, they make regular journeys into the forest in search of the exiled duke, Rosalind's father.

Narrator 1: At first, they do not find the duke. One day, however, they come upon something odd while walking in the forest.

Rosalind: What's this?

Narrator 2: Rosalind pulls down a piece of paper that is nailed to a tree. She is amazed to find that it's a love poem written to herself.

Rosalind: *(reading)* Whose worth is spoken in the wind?

That of dearest Rosalind.
Let no face be kept in mind
but that of fairest Rosalind.

(to herself) What a bad poem! And it goes on like that. Is this written to me?

Narrator 3: Just then, Rosalind spots Celia. She too is reading another bad poem aloud.

Rosalind: What's that you're reading, cousin?

Celia: It's a declaration of love for you. There are dozens of poems like this one, nailed to the trees throughout this forest. Haven't you seen them?

Rosalind:	I was just reading one. I wonder who the poet might be.
Celia:	I know who the poet is, for I saw him nailing up his poems. He is none other than Orlando de Boyes.
Rosalind:	*(excitedly)* Orlando de Boyes is here? In the forest?
Celia:	Yes, and wearing the chain you gave him. I can take you to him.
Narrator 1:	Celia and Rosalind approach the clearing where Orlando stands, looking melancholy and reciting one of his poems.
Rosalind:	Hello, young sir! What is it you are reading?
Orlando:	It's a poem I wrote to the woman I love.
Narrator 2:	Rosalind can see that Orlando doesn't recognize her in her costume. She decides to keep her identity a secret so that she can play a game with him and test the extent of his devotion.
Rosalind:	Surely your love cannot be so very great. In fact, I don't see any of the marks of love on you.
Orlando:	The marks of love? What marks do I lack?
Rosalind:	Well, you look well rested. You don't have any bags under your eyes. Your shoes aren't untied. Your hair's not a mess. I don't believe you really know true love at all.
Orlando:	But I do! My love is true!
Rosalind:	No woman would ever believe that, from looking at you. Clearly you are inexperienced in the ways of love. You need practice.
Orlando:	It's true that I don't know how to speak to a woman or how to act around one. But how can I get practice at love, here in the forest?
Narrator 3:	Rosalind gets a mischievous glint in her eye.
Rosalind:	You can practice on me.
Orlando:	Practice on you? What do you mean, young man?
Rosalind:	If you'll come to our cottage tomorrow, I'll begin training you in the arts of love. I'll pretend to be your Rosalind, and you can practice saying romantic things to me. Why don't you start right now? Call me your sweet Rosalind and ask me to marry you.
Orlando:	*(awkwardly)* Sweet Rosalind! Will you . . . be my wife?
Rosalind:	There! That's pretty good. With a little practice, you'll be a pro at love in no time.
Narrator 1:	The appointment scheduled with Orlando, Rosalind and Celia return to their cottage. They have not gone far when they overhear two local shepherds talking in a clearing.
Silvius:	Sweet Phebe, why do you scorn me? I'm dying little by little from my love for you.

Phebe: *(scornfully)* I don't want to be your executioner. Why don't you go and love somebody else?

Narrator 2: Rosalind and Celia step into the clearing.

Rosalind: *(to Celia)* There's nothing but love troubles in these woods today. *(to Phebe)* What's wrong with you, girl? You're nothing much to look at. Yet this man is obviously crazy about you. You should feel honored. Why don't you return his love?

Narrator 3: Phebe looks at Rosalind, dressed as Ganymede. She obviously likes what she sees.

Phebe: *(to Rosalind)* Handsome youth, I'd rather hear you say such rude things to me than hear any more of that man's ridiculous declarations of love.

Rosalind: *(to Celia)* Ahh! I've seen this type before. This woman loves only men who scorn her. *(to Phebe)* Please, miss, I pray you, don't fall in love with me. I am bound to disappoint you, for I am quite a deceiver.

Narrator 1: As Rosalind and Celia walk past Phebe and Silvius and out of the clearing, Phebe stares after Rosalind with a dreamy, love-struck expression on her face. Silvius looks at Phebe with a miserable, pained expression.

Scene 7

Narrator 2: During the next few weeks, Rosalind meets regularly with Orlando to "coach" him in the ways of love. Although it becomes clearer and clearer that Orlando's love for Rosalind is true, she continues to keep her identity a secret.

Narrator 3: Meanwhile, Phebe has also fallen in love with Rosalind—or, rather, with Rosalind's male alter ego, Ganymede. The more Rosalind attempts to discourage Phebe's attraction, the more devoted Phebe becomes. Phebe begins following Rosalind around, usually with Silvius trailing after her.

Narrator 1: Weeks go by. Then one afternoon Orlando fails to arrive at the cottage for his love lessons.

Rosalind: Celia, what time is it?

Celia: It's after two. Isn't Orlando here yet? He's late.

Narrator 2: Suddenly the two girls hear a knock on their cottage door, expecting to see Orlando. Rosalind opens the door. She is surprised to see a man in his late twenties who looks like an older version of Orlando.

Oliver: Good day, fair young people. I believe you are just the folks I'm looking for. I was told to bring this . . .

Narrator 3: Oliver pulls out a bloody handkerchief.

Oliver:	. . . to the youth Orlando calls his Rosalind. *(to Rosalind)* Are you the lad?
Narrator 1:	Rosalind turns pale as she looks at the handkerchief.
Rosalind:	*(shakily)* I am. But what am I supposed to make of this?
Celia:	*(worriedly)* Please, sir, tell us what the handkerchief means.
Oliver:	I will tell you the story of what happened to Orlando. When last Orlando parted from you, he promised to return quickly. But then, as he was passing through the woods, he came upon a strange sight.
Rosalind:	What did he see?
Oliver:	Under an old oak tree, a ragged man lay sleeping on his back. Around the sleeping man's neck, a green and gold snake had curled itself.
Celia:	How horrifying!
Oliver:	As soon as the snake saw Orlando, it slid off under a bush. Orlando followed the snake with his eyes, and saw that under the bush a lioness was lurking, ready to pounce on the sleeping man. Just then, Orlando realized that the man was none other than his elder brother.
Celia:	The brother who hates him?
Rosalind:	We've heard Orlando speak about that brother many times. Did Orlando leave his brother to be eaten by a lioness?
Oliver:	Twice he turned his back, ready to do so. But finally kindness, which is nobler than revenge, overtook Orlando, and he began to do battle with the lioness. The beast quickly fell, and Orlando managed to save me.
Celia:	You are Orlando's brother!
Oliver:	I am, although I feel unworthy to be. I only hope that I can be a better brother in the future.
Rosalind:	And Orlando—is he OK?
Oliver:	He has a large wound on his arm. He is resting now at the cave where the exiled Duke lives.
Rosalind:	The duke! And poor Orlando! You must bring us to him at once!

Scene 8

Narrator 2:	It is twenty-four hours later. Rosalind has been reunited with Orlando and has met the duke, her father, who has failed to recognize her.
Narrator 3:	In that short span of time, Oliver has fallen in love with Celia and has asked for her hand in marriage. Still posing as Aliena, Celia has agreed to the marriage. The two plan to be married by the exiled duke.

Orlando:	*(to Oliver)* It seems impossible that you should fall in love on such short notice, much less win the lady's hand.
Oliver:	It seems impossible, yet it's true! I have never been so happy! Dear brother, you can have our father's house and all his possessions. I am happy just to live and die a country peasant with Aliena at my side.
Orlando:	Well, I'm very happy for you. Go and help Aliena get ready for the wedding. Look! Here comes my Rosalind.
Rosalind:	Good day, sirs.
Oliver:	Good day.
Narrator 1:	Oliver tips his hat and leaves.
Rosalind:	*(to Orlando)* You look depressed. What's the matter?
Orlando:	Tomorrow my brother will be married. He will have the very thing I wish for but can't have.
Rosalind:	I'd be happy to play the part of beloved Rosalind at the wedding tomorrow, if you wish.
Orlando:	*(in a gloomy voice)* It's no good. I can't go on just pretending that you're Rosalind anymore.
Rosalind:	*(mysteriously)* Maybe you won't have to pretend. If your heart is truly set on Rosalind, then, when your brother marries Aliena, you shall marry Rosalind.
Orlando:	How can that ever happen?
Rosalind:	Didn't I tell you? I'm a magician.
Narrator 2:	Orlando and Rosalind are approached by Silvius and Phebe.
Rosalind:	Look, here comes an admirer of mine and one of hers.
Phebe:	*(to Rosalind)* Ganymede, I adore you. Why don't you return my love? Just look at this man.
Narrator 3:	Phebe gestures toward Silvius.
Phebe:	He'll show you what it truly means to love.
Silvius:	To love is to be all sighs and tears, as I am for Phebe.
Phebe:	And I am for Ganymede.
Orlando:	And I am for Rosalind.
Rosalind:	And I am for no woman.
Silvius:	To love is to be all full of fantasies, passion, and wishes, all full of adoration and humbleness, patience and impatience—as I am for Phebe.
Phebe:	And I am for Ganymede.

Orlando:	And I am for Rosalind.
Rosalind:	And I am for no woman. Listen to me, everyone. I have a plan that will secure the happiness of all of our miserable selves. Tomorrow let us all meet here again. *(to Phebe)* Tomorrow I will marry you, if ever I marry any woman, for I plan to be married tomorrow. Will you be here?
Phebe:	I will!
Rosalind:	*(to Orlando)* I intend to make sure that your dream is answered and that you are married tomorrow. Will you meet me here?
Orlando:	I will!
Rosalind:	*(to Silvius)* I intend to make sure that your wishes come true and that you are married tomorrow. Will you meet us all here?
Silvius:	I will!

Scene 9

Narrator 1:	It is an hour before Oliver and Celia's wedding. The old duke stands talking to Orlando.
Exiled Duke:	Do you really think that Ganymede the shepherd is going to bring my daughter here today?
Orlando:	I pray he will. I wish for nothing so much as to marry her.
Narrator 2:	The duke and Orlando are approached by Silvius, Phebe, and Rosalind in her shepherd costume.
Rosalind:	*(to the duke)* Good day, sir. If I can bring your daughter Rosalind here, do you promise me that you'll marry her to this youth, Orlando?
Exiled Duke:	I would like to be able to give my daughter the gift of marriage to this fine young man. I have little else to give her.
Rosalind:	Very well. *(to Phebe)* And you, shepherdess, you'll marry me, if I'm willing?
Phebe:	Of course!
Rosalind:	But if you refuse to marry me, do you promise to give yourself in marriage to Silvius?
Phebe:	I would never refuse to marry you. Sure. Fine. You have a deal.
Rosalind:	*(to Silvius)* And you'll take Phebe as your wife, if she's willing?
Silvius:	Of course!
Rosalind:	Then please excuse me. I'll be back soon.
Narrator 3:	Rosalind hurries off to change out of her costume.

Exiled Duke:	*(to Orlando)* You know, that boy Ganymede bears a remarkable resemblance to my daughter.
Orlando:	It's true. When I first met him, I thought he must be Rosalind's brother. But I knew that couldn't be true.
Narrator 1:	A few minutes later, Rosalind returns with Celia. Both have changed out of their costumes.
Exiled Duke:	*(to Rosalind)* If my eyes aren't deceiving me, you *are* my daughter.
Orlando:	*(to Rosalind)* If my eyes aren't deceiving me, you *are* my Rosalind.
Phebe:	*(to Rosalind)* If my eyes aren't deceiving me, my love for you is over!
Rosalind:	*(to Phebe)* Then you refuse to marry me. Will you keep your agreement and marry Silvius?
Phebe:	My word is good. I will.
Narrator 2:	Phebe takes Silvius's hand, and the three couples stand before the Duke. He is about to perform the triple wedding ceremony, when all of a sudden, Orlando and Oliver's brother Jacques comes riding up on horseback.
Jacques de Boyes:	I come bearing great news! The old duke can return to court and resume his position!
Oliver:	What do you mean, Jacques? What's happened?
Jacques:	Duke Frederick became increasingly jealous and fearful as more and more of his men came out to live in the forest with the old duke. Recently, he became so jealous and nervous that he set out for Arden with the intention of killing his brother. As he neared the edge of this forest, however, he met a religious man, an old hermit. He was converted to the hermit's religion and decided to give up his wicked ways and live the life of a monk. He has given his crown and lands back to his banished brother.
Lord Amiens:	Can it be true?
Jacques:	Yes, it's true. You can all return to court.
All:	*(shouting)* Hooray!
Exiled Duke:	What wonderful news! There's so much to celebrate. Let's begin these marriage rites. I know that they will end in many true delights.

Simply Shakespeare: Readers Theatre for Young People is from *Read* magazine, a Weekly Reader publication, in collaboration with Teacher Ideas Press. Edited by Jennifer Kroll. www.weeklyreader.com. www.lu.com/tips. 1–800–541–2086.

CHAPTER 2

Hamlet: Prince of Denmark

By William Shakespeare

Adapted by Jennifer Kroll

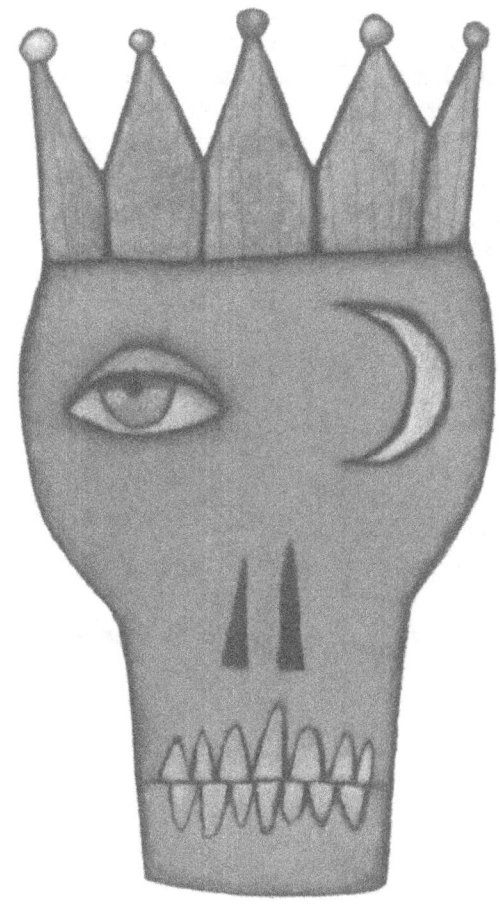

 Summary

Hamlet, the Prince of Denmark, is upset over the recent death of his father, the king, and over his mother's speedy remarriage to his uncle, Claudius. When the ghost of Hamlet's dead father appears on the castle battlements, Hamlet learns that Claudius is his father's murderer. The ghost not only shares this information but also commands Hamlet to avenge the murder. Hamlet broods about this order rather than carrying it out immediately. Soon his odd mood swings and depression become obvious to everyone in the castle, a source of concern to his mother and stepfather. After Hamlet commits a murder, killing a man he has mistaken for Claudius, he is sent away to England. But a twist of fate soon brings Hamlet back home to Denmark, where he must face both his uncle and the angry son of the man he killed.

Presentation Suggestions

Place Hamlet a little apart from the other main characters and partially facing them. Seat or stand other main characters—Horatio, Claudius, Gertrude, Laertes, Polonius, and Ophelia—in a row or group. Place the minor characters—Francisco, Bernardo, Marcellus, Ghost, Rosencrantz, Guildenstern, Actor, Gravedigger, Osric, and Ambassador—behind the major characters. Place the narrators off to the side or behind Hamlet.

Props

The ghost can wear a spooky mask or white sheet. Gertrude and Claudius should wear crowns. Rosencrantz, Guildenstern, Hamlet, Laertes, and Horatio are all college-aged boys and might wear college or university hats or sweatshirts to represent this idea. Ophelia might have papers or jewelry in her hands to give back to Hamlet. If a plastic skull is available, Hamlet can hold it up during the graveyard scene. Rulers or other substitute weapons may be used by Hamlet in Scenes 8 and 12 and by Laertes in Scene 12. A poison cup of some kind can be used by Gertrude, Hamlet, Claudius, and Horatio during the final scene.

Cast of Characters

(main parts in boldface)
Narrators 1, 2, and 3
Francisco ⎫
Bernardo ⎭ *soldiers*
Horatio, *a college student, Hamlet's friend*
Marcellus, *a soldier*
Claudius, *king of Denmark*
Gertrude, *queen of Denmark, mother of Hamlet*
Hamlet, *son of the late King Hamlet and nephew of the current king*
Laertes, *son of Polonius*
Polonius, *a high-ranking lord at court*
Ophelia, *the daughter of Polonius*
Ghost of Hamlet's father
Rosencrantz, *a courtier*
Guildenstern, *a courtier*
Actor, *leader of an acting troupe*
Gravedigger
Osric, *a courtier*
Ambassador

Hamlet: Prince of Denmark

By William Shakespeare

Adapted by Jennifer Kroll

Scene 1

Narrator 1: It is midnight at Elsinore Castle in Denmark. On a cold, windy platform outside the castle, a guard hears a sudden noise.

Francisco: *(nervously)* Who's there? Show your face!

Bernardo: It's just me, Francisco. It's time for my shift. Have you had a quiet night, so far?

Francisco: Not a mouse stirring.

Narrator 2: Francisco leaves. A few minutes later, Horatio and Marcellus arrive.

Horatio: Hello, Bernardo. Has the thing appeared again tonight?

Bernardo: Not yet. But it has come every night for the past week.

Narrator 3: The men suddenly freeze as a ghostly figure passes before them.

Marcellus: Look! There it is!

Bernardo: It looks just like the king who died.

Horatio: *(to the ghost)* What are you and why are you here? Speak to us!

Narrator 1: The ghost looks straight at the men, then silently vanishes.

Bernardo: It will not speak to us.

Horatio: No. But there may be somebody else to whom it *will* speak. I'd better tell Prince Hamlet about this.

Scene 2

Narrator 2: The next morning in the castle, King Claudius speaks with his family members and courtiers.

Claudius: It was with equal amounts of delight and sadness in our hearts that my one-time sister-in-law and I celebrated our recent wedding. Despite the sadness we all feel, we must keep our chins up and look to the future.

Narrator 3: King Claudius turns to his nephew, Hamlet, who stands off to one side, staring at the ground with a dark, brooding expression on his face.

Claudius: Hamlet, my nephew and now son, why do you still look so down in the dumps?

Gertrude: Please, Hamlet. Don't keep looking for your noble father in the dust. You know that all lives must someday end and all souls pass into eternity.

Hamlet: Yes, I know.

Gertrude: Then why do you continue to appear so depressed?

Hamlet: I don't merely *appear* depressed, madam. How I look on the outside is nothing compared to how I feel on the inside.

Claudius: You mourn your father, and that is right. But remember that your father lost a father and that father's father lost one, too. It's not manly to grieve too much. Stop brooding over your father's death and start thinking of me as your father. After all, you are the next in line for the throne, and I feel all the love for you that a father feels for his son.

Narrator 1: Later, as the room empties out, Hamlet stands alone, still looking depressed and upset.

Hamlet: *(to himself)* Oh, how I wish this too, too solid flesh would just melt away. Nothing in this world seems worthwhile to me anymore. This world is an untended garden where weeds grow out of control.

Narrator 2: He sighs and begins to pace.

Hamlet: I can't believe my mother married my uncle so soon after my father's death!

Narrator 3: Horatio enters the room.

Horatio: *(brightly)* Hello, Lord Hamlet!

Hamlet: *(cheering up a little)* Horatio! It's good to see you! When did you get back from the university?

Horatio: Not long ago. I came for your father's funeral.

Hamlet: *(sarcastically)* I think you came to see my mother's wedding.

Horatio:	Indeed, my lord, it followed soon after the other event.
Hamlet:	*(joking darkly)* Well, we're very thrifty people around here. My mother didn't want to waste any leftover cold meat and appetizers from the funeral. *(more serious)* You know—I would rather have fought my worst foe than attend that wedding. All I could think of was my father....
Horatio:	*(in a serious tone)* My lord, I think I saw him yesterday night.
Hamlet:	*(confusedly)* Saw whom?
Horatio:	The king, your father.
Hamlet:	*(in a faint voice)* My father?
Horatio:	Please, let me explain....
Narrator 1:	Horatio begins to explain to Hamlet about the ghost that has been appearing before the guards.

Scene 3

Narrator 2:	Meanwhile, in another part of the castle, Hamlet's girlfriend, Ophelia, bids farewell to her older brother, Laertes, who is about to head off to college in France.
Laertes:	Ophelia, I'll be worrying about you while I'm away. I want you to watch your step with Prince Hamlet. I know he's said some sweet things to you in the past, but—
Narrator 3:	Their father, Polonius, enters the room.
Polonius:	*(to Ophelia)* What is it, Ophelia, that Hamlet has said to you?
Ophelia:	He has expressed his love and made many promises.
Polonius:	Hamlet's out of your league and will be trouble for you. I command you to break off your relationship with him at once.
Ophelia:	*(sadly)* Yes, father.

Scene 4

Narrator 1:	That night, Hamlet accompanies Horatio and Marcellus out on the guard platform, hoping to catch a glimpse of the ghost. Just before one A.M., the ghost appears. The three men quake with fear.
Hamlet:	Ghost of my father! Why have you come? What is it that you want us to do?
Narrator 2:	The ghost begins to move down the platform, beckoning Hamlet to follow it.
Hamlet:	It wants me to follow it.
Marcellus:	Don't go after it, I beg you!

Narrator 3: Horatio and Marcellus try to hold Hamlet back, but he struggles free from their grip and runs after the ghost, following it until he is high atop the castle's battlements.

Hamlet: *(trying to catch his breath)* Speak to me here, ghost. I can go no farther.

Ghost: *(in a spooky, ghostly voice)* If you ever loved me, revenge my foul and most unnatural murder.

Hamlet: *(in a faint voice)* Murder?

Ghost: Yes, my son. I was napping in my garden, as I often did. Your uncle came with a vial of deadly poison. He poured the poison into my ears. Almost instantly, it swept through my body. Thus, my life, my crown, and my queen were all stolen at once.

Hamlet: That horrible, wicked man! I knew it! I'll avenge you!

Ghost: But I command you—whatever you do, do not lay a hand on your own mother.

Narrator 1: The ghost vanishes.

Scene 5

Narrator 2: The next day, Ophelia follows her father's instructions. She returns Hamlet's letters and tries to avoid him. Eventually, though, he comes looking for her. After his visit, Ophelia runs to see her father.

Polonius: Ophelia—you look upset. What's happened?

Ophelia: I'm so frightened! As I was sewing in my room, Hamlet came in to see me. His jacket was all unlaced and his clothes were all dirty. He was so pale and his knees were shaking so hard that they knocked against each other. He acted like a crazy person!

Polonius: Maybe his love for you is driving him mad. What did he say?

Ophelia: He just grabbed me hard by the wrist and, for long moments, studied my face. He kept sighing. He seemed so changed, so odd.

Polonius: What has caused the change, do you think? Have you said any harsh words to him lately?

Ophelia: No, my lord. But I have refused to accept his letters, and I've tried to stay away from him, just as you asked me to do.

Polonius: That is driving him mad. I will go and talk to the king about this.

Scene 6

Narrator 3: In the castle's assembly hall, King Claudius and Queen Gertrude speak with two young courtiers named Rosencrantz and Guildenstern, who have recently arrived from England.

Claudius:	Thanks for making the trip to Denmark so quickly. We have much need of your help here. It's Hamlet, you see. He seems so depressed. We'd like you to find out what's been bothering him.
Gertrude:	Hamlet has often spoken fondly of you two. We are hoping you can cheer him up and take his mind off his troubles.
Rosencrantz:	Anything we can do for Your Majesties . . .
Narrator 1:	Polonius enters the room.
Polonius:	Your highnesses, I believe I know what's been troubling Hamlet. He is being driven mad by his love for my daughter, Ophelia.
Narrator 2:	Claudius and Gertrude look over love letters and poems that Polonius hands them.
Gertrude:	*(to Claudius)* Do you think Polonius could be right?
Narrator 3:	Hamlet appears at the far end of the hall, his face buried in a book.
Claudius:	Here he comes now. Let's leave him alone with his friends and see what they can learn.
Narrator 1:	The king, the queen, and Polonius sneak off.
Rosencrantz:	*(to Hamlet)* Lord Hamlet!
Narrator 2:	Hamlet looks up from his book.
Hamlet:	*(cheering somewhat)* My good friends! How are you, lads?
Rosencrantz:	Not too bad.
Hamlet:	You must be a little out of fortune's favor, or else you wouldn't be here in this prison.
Guildenstern:	Prison?
Hamlet:	Yes. Denmark's a prison.
Rosencrantz:	Why do you say that?
Narrator 3:	Hamlet refuses to answer. Instead, he asks Rosencrantz and Guildenstern about their travels. As they describe their voyage, they mention the fact that they recently passed a theater troupe on the road.
Guildenstern:	One of the best troupes in all of Europe. They'll be here soon. Won't it be fun to see them perform?
Narrator 1:	Not long afterward, a flourish of trumpets can be heard, and the theater troupe enters the castle. The prince and his friends go to meet them.
Hamlet:	Welcome, actors!
Rosencrantz:	Will you be putting on a show for us in the next few days?
Actor:	Yes, indeed.
Hamlet:	What shows do you perform?

Actor:	*Julius Caesar, The Fall of Troy*—we can do pretty much any story you'd like.
Hamlet:	How about *The Murder of Gonzago?* Do you know that story?
Actor:	Yes.
Hamlet:	Good. I'd like to see you perform that one tomorrow night.
Narrator 2:	A little later, Hamlet paces in the library, alone, talking to himself.
Hamlet:	Am I a coward? a villain? Well, those titles probably fit me well enough. Here I am—the son of a dear murdered father. I've been ordered by his ghost to avenge his death. And instead of acting, I stand unloading the grief in my heart with words!
Narrator 3:	Hamlet pauses for a moment.
Hamlet:	But, what if that ghost were really a demon, sent to test me? I'd better make double sure my uncle is guilty before I act. That's where this theater troupe will come in handy. I'll watch Claudius's reaction to their performance tomorrow. Then I'll have better proof of his guilt. Yes, indeed. The play's the thing wherein I'll catch the conscience of the king.

Scene 7

Narrator 1:	By the next day, Hamlet's mental health—or lack thereof—has become the talk of the castle.
Claudius:	*(to Rosencrantz)* When you talked to Hamlet yesterday, did he tell you what's been bothering him?
Rosencrantz:	He wouldn't say.
Gertrude:	Have you managed to get him interested in some kind of lighthearted activity?
Guildenstern:	A theater troupe arrived at the castle yesterday. Hamlet seemed very eager to see the players perform. In fact, he wanted to make sure that Your Majesties attended their performance tonight.
Claudius:	I'm relieved to hear that Hamlet's taking an interest in such things. Go and keep working on cheering him up.
Rosencrantz:	We will, my lord.
Narrator 2:	Rosencrantz and Guildenstern leave.
Claudius:	*(to Gertrude)* My dear, will you leave us also? Polonius and I are going to set up a meeting between Hamlet and Ophelia in order to see how he responds to her.
Gertrude:	As you wish.

Narrator 3:	The queen leaves. The king and Polonius get Ophelia to stand in the hallway, pretending to read a book. They duck out of sight when they see Hamlet coming.
Hamlet:	*(talking to himself)* To be or not to be—that is the question. Is it nobler to quietly suffer the stones and arrows that fortune flings at me? Or should I fight back against this sea of troubles? To die, to sleep—that would end all this heartache and pain. Part of me wishes that I could die and be done with this world, but I also worry about what happens after death.
Narrator 1:	Hamlet spots Ophelia.
Ophelia:	Good day, my lord. How are you today?
Hamlet:	Well, well, well.
Ophelia:	I have some things here that I've been wishing to return to you.
Narrator 2:	She holds out a bundle of love letters, poems, and trinkets. Hamlet looks at her blankly.
Hamlet:	I never gave you such things.
Ophelia:	You know you did. You said many sweet words when you gave these things to me.
Hamlet:	You should never believe sweet words in this sour world.
Narrator 3:	Hamlet begins to rant and rave at Ophelia.
Hamlet:	Get thee to a nunnery! Why would you wish to marry anyhow and bring new sinners into this world?
Narrator 1:	Eventually Hamlet runs out of steam and shuffles off. Ophelia stares after him with tears streaming down her face.
Claudius:	*(to Polonius)* I don't think love is the cause of Hamlet's behavior. And I also don't think he's insane. But I do think he is dangerous. I think I had better get him away from here. I'll send him to England. We owe the English king a visit and some tribute money. Hamlet can deliver that.
Polonius:	As you wish, my lord. But before he leaves, why don't you have the queen talk with Hamlet privately one last time? Perhaps she will be able to get some real answers out of him.
Narrator 2:	Claudius agrees. A message is sent to Hamlet, saying that he is to see his mother after the evening's entertainment has ended.

Scene 8

Narrator 3:	That night, the king and queen and all the courtiers attend the theater troupe's performance of *The Murder of Gonzago*. The play is the story of a woman who conspires to have her husband poisoned. Once he is dead, she marries the poisoner. At the moment in the play when the poisoner is pouring his deadly potion into a sleeping man's ears, King Claudius suddenly rises, looking shaken.

Claudius:	*(shouting)* Give me some light! Stop the play! Everybody out! Lights! Lights!
Narrator 1:	The lights are lit. In confusion, everyone files out of the room.
Narrator 2:	A little later, King Claudius stands in his private chambers, talking to Rosencrantz and Guildenstern.
Claudius:	I don't think it's safe to keep Hamlet here, given the way he's been acting lately. Therefore, I am asking you to return to England and bring him with you. I will give you papers that you can deliver to the English king, introducing Hamlet and explaining our situation.
Guildenstern:	Your safety and the safety of your people are our greatest concerns, Your Highness.
Narrator 3:	Rosencrantz and Guildenstern depart, leaving Claudius alone, looking frightened and shaken.
Claudius:	*(to himself)* The offense I committed stinks to high heaven! To kill my own brother! And now, guilt and fear hound me every minute.
Narrator 1:	Claudius falls to his knees, attempting to pray.
Claudius:	*(to himself)* I want to pray, but what words can I use? How can I ask for, or be granted, forgiveness when I continue to wear this ill-gotten crown? How can I ask for forgiveness when I continue to be married to the queen? I'm stuck in a pit of corruption and sin, and I can't get out of it.
Narrator 2:	Hamlet enters the room quietly, with his sword drawn.
Hamlet:	*(to himself)* Now I should do it. I should kill him.
Narrator 3:	He raises his sword, then pauses.
Hamlet:	*(to himself)* But look at him. He's praying. If I kill him now, he might go straight to heaven. My father had no chance to confess his sins before he was killed. No—I ought to kill Claudius when he's in a rage, or swearing, or drunk—not when he's praying. I'll wait.
Narrator 1:	Hamlet puts his sword down and sneaks away.

Scene 9

Narrator 2:	Later that night, Queen Gertrude stands in her private chamber, speaking to Polonius.
Polonius:	You must tell Hamlet that his behavior of late has been unacceptable to the king.
Gertrude:	I will. But hide now. I hear him coming.
Narrator 3:	Polonius hides behind a tapestry.
Hamlet:	Why did you want to see me?
Gertrude:	Hamlet, you have offended your father.

Hamlet:	*(laughing darkly)* Mother, *you* have offended my father!
Gertrude:	*(sounding hurt)* You have a wicked tongue, my son.
Hamlet:	I think the wickedness is all your own.
Gertrude:	*(with anger and shock)* Hamlet, have you forgotten to whom you're speaking?
Hamlet:	No, I certainly haven't. You're the queen, your husband's brother's wife. And you're also my mother. I wish it were not the case!
Narrator 1:	She rises to leave, looking both indignant and scared.
Gertrude:	I'll not speak to you, if you're going to be like this.
Narrator 2:	Hamlet grabs his mother by the arm, holding her back.
Hamlet:	No—you'll sit down and listen to me.
Narrator 3:	Gertrude struggles against Hamlet's grip. She looks very frightened.
Gertrude:	What are you going to do? Are you going to kill me? *(shouting out)* Help! Help!
Polonius:	*(in a muffled voice)* What's going on?
Narrator 1:	Hamlet hears a voice. He turns and sees that someone is hiding behind the tapestry.
Hamlet:	Ah! I smell a rat!
Narrator 2:	Hamlet draws his sword and runs the blade through the tapestry. Polonius shrieks and falls to the ground, dead.
Gertrude:	Oh, Hamlet! What a rash and bloody deed!
Hamlet:	Yes, a bloody deed—almost as bad, good Mother, as to kill a king and marry with his brother.
Queen:	*(with shock)* Kill a king!
Hamlet:	Yes. That's what I said.
Narrator 3:	Hamlet pulls the tapestry aside and discovers Polonius's body.
Hamlet:	Oh—it's Polonius. That intruding fool. *(to Polonius)* Farewell, old man. I did not intend to kill you. I mistook you for your better.

Scene 10

Narrator 1:	After Polonius's murder, the king and queen hurry Hamlet off to England. Rosencrantz and Guildenstern accompany him, carrying papers to deliver to the English king.
Narrator 2:	Although no official pronouncement of Polonius's death is made, Ophelia soon finds out the truth. Badly shaken and afraid that she's losing her grip on reality, she writes to her brother, Laertes, begging him to return from France.

Narrator 3:	By the time Laertes has returned to Denmark, Ophelia has gone mad. Laertes longs to avenge his father's death and his sister's mental collapse by killing Hamlet.
Narrator 1:	It becomes clear that he may soon have the opportunity after two letters arrive from Hamlet. Horatio receives the first one....
Horatio:	*(reading)* We were on our way to England and had been sailing for two days when our ship was attacked by pirates. In the skirmish, I was taken prisoner. Fortunately, the pirates were willing to release me with the understanding that I would repay the favor someday. As you read this, I'm on my way back to Denmark. Rosencrantz and Guildenstern continue on their way to England. I have much more to tell you, but it can wait until I see you next. Your friend, Hamlet.
Narrator 2:	The king receives a different letter. He shares the contents with Laertes.
Claudius:	*(reading)* Your Majesty, I am about to arrive back in your kingdom. I am unarmed and without any money or possessions. I ask you to show mercy toward me. As soon I see you, I'll explain the circumstances of my sudden, strange return. Hamlet.
Laertes:	He's coming back! Now he'll have to face me and face what he's done!
Claudius:	Laertes, your desire for revenge is natural, and I don't intend to stop you. However, I ask you to go about it *my* way—OK? I have a scheme in mind through which you can get your revenge without taking any blame for your actions.
Laertes:	What do you propose?
Claudius:	I'll coax Hamlet into fencing with you. During the match, you can kill him and pretend that it was an accident.
Laertes:	I'll put some poison on the tip of my sword, so that even a small cut will do him in.
Claudius:	And just in case that fails, we'll also have a cup of poisoned wine at the sidelines for him.
Narrator 3:	Just then, Claudius and Laertes hear an anguished cry. The queen rushes into the room.
Gertrude:	Laertes, your sister has drowned!
Laertes:	*(sounding stricken)* Drowned? Where?
Gertrude:	In the brook, down by the weeping willow. She wandered down there, covered herself in flower chains and garlands, and then lay down in the water, singing. Eventually, the water pulled her under.
Laertes:	Ophelia? Drowned? Alas!

Scene 11

Narrator 1: When Hamlet returns to Denmark, the first person he goes to see is his trusted friend Horatio. The two talk as they stroll through the local churchyard.

Hamlet: When Rosencrantz and Guildenstern weren't looking, I stole a peek at those documents they were carrying. I'm glad that I did. In one of them, Claudius had requested that I be beheaded as soon as I reached the English court.

Horatio: So what did you do?

Hamlet: I made some changes to the documents and put them back where I'd found them. I guess those papers are still on their way to England, along with Rosencrantz and Guildenstern.

Narrator 2: Horatio and Hamlet come upon a gravedigger, singing as he digs.

Hamlet: How can he sing like that when he's digging graves?

Horatio: He's dug so many that he can do it now without thinking about it.

Narrator 3: Hamlet leans down and picks up a skull that's been exposed during the digging.

Hamlet: This skull had a tongue in it once, and could sing, too. *(to the gravedigger)* Whose was it? Do you know?

Gravedigger: That skull was Yorick's. He was the king's jester.

Hamlet: Alas, poor Yorick! I knew him, Horatio. In fact, when I was a little boy, he carried me on his back a thousand times.

Narrator 1: A funeral procession enters the churchyard. Hamlet and Horatio stand back, watching as the king, the queen, Laertes, and a number of lords and ladies approach a newly dug grave. A body is lowered down. The queen throws petals into the open grave.

Gertrude: Sweets to the sweet! Farewell, Ophelia! I hoped you would be my daughter-in-law. I thought I'd be putting flower petals on your bridal bed, not on your grave.

Hamlet: Ophelia! Dead? Oh no!

Laertes: I hope doom falls heavily on the head of the man responsible for this!

Narrator 2: Hamlet steps forward.

Hamlet: *(to Laertes)* I fear I may be the man of whom you speak. Laertes, please know that I never meant this to happen! I loved Ophelia!

Laertes: Hamlet! You're back! Now you'll pay!

Narrator 3: Laertes lunges for Hamlet. They wrestle until they are forcibly parted.

Gertrude: *(to Laertes)* Please, don't hurt him! He didn't mean to cause your sister's death. He was out of his head when he killed your father.

Narrator 1: Eventually, Laertes is calmed. But as Hamlet and Horatio exit the churchyard, Claudius leans over and whispers in Laertes's ear.

Claudius: Just be patient. You will have your revenge yet.

Scene 12

Narrator 2: The next day, a message comes for Hamlet as he stands speaking to Horatio.

Osric: His majesty wanted me to tell you that he has made a wager with the king of France. Laertes, who is newly returned from France, is known there to be a very good fencer. King Claudius has wagered that in a dozen fencing passes between you and Laertes, he shall not exceed you by three hits.

Hamlet: What's riding on this wager?

Osric: Six Barbary horses and six fancy, expensive French rapiers.

Hamlet: Well, it's the time of day when I usually take some exercise. If someone will bring the foils, I will see if I can win this bet for the king.

Narrator 3: Osric departs. Soon, servants come in carrying seating cushions, fencing foils, and wine. They begin setting up for the match.

Horatio: *(worried)* If you feel at all uncomfortable or threatened, just say the word, and I'll do what I can to stop or stall this match.

Hamlet: There's no way to stall one's fate, Horatio. If my time has come, my time has come.

Narrator 1: Laertes, Claudius, Gertrude, and other lords and ladies arrive.

Claudius: Come, Hamlet—shake hands with Laertes before the match.

Narrator 2: Hamlet takes Laertes's hand.

Hamlet: Give me your pardon, sir. I have done you wrong. But I did not intend to. It was my madness, not I.

Laertes: I pardon you.

Hamlet: Come then, let's fence. Your talent should shine here today, when matched against my lesser ability.

Narrator 3: Hamlet and Laertes begin to fence. Hamlet scores a hit.

Claudius: You look thirsty, Hamlet. Here, have a drink.

Narrator 1: Claudius holds a cup out to Hamlet.

Hamlet: I'll finish this bout first. Set my drink over there.

Narrator 2: The fencing match continues. Hamlet scores another hit.

Claudius:	*(to Gertrude)* Our son is going to win!
Narrator 3:	Gertrude picks up the cup that Claudius has offered to Hamlet.
Gertrude:	Here's to your success, my son!
Claudius:	*(to Gertrude)* No! Don't drink from that cup!
Narrator 1:	It is too late. The queen is already drinking poison.
Narrator 2:	The fencing continues. Laertes wounds Hamlet. In the angry scuffle that follows, the two of them change blades. Moments later, Hamlet wounds Laertes. Over at the sidelines, the queen suddenly slumps onto the floor.
Hamlet:	The queen! What's wrong?
Claudius:	She swooned when she saw you both bleeding.
Gertrude:	*(gasping)* No! The drink! Oh, my dear Hamlet! I am poisoned!
Hamlet:	My mother is poisoned! There's a villain in this room!
Narrator 3:	The room erupts in chaos. Hamlet turns and stares with blazing eyes at the king.
Hamlet:	*(in a commanding voice)* Somebody lock the doors! I'm going to finish this now!
Narrator 1:	Just then, Laertes collapses, gasping.
Laertes:	*(in a faint voice)* It's too late, Hamlet. You only have a half-hour left to live. The blade you hold has a poisoned tip! Its wounds are fatal.
Hamlet:	Poison on the blade, as well as in the cup? Then let it do its work.
Narrator 2:	Hamlet stabs the king.
Hamlet:	And drink this!
Narrator 3:	Hamlet grabs the goblet full of poisoned wine. He holds it to the king's mouth and forces him to drink. Horatio leaps up, grabbing at the poisoned wine goblet.
Horatio:	Give me some of that poison! If my best friend is going to die, so am I!
Hamlet:	No!
Narrator 1:	In order to prevent Horatio from drinking, Hamlet downs the rest of the wine himself. Then he collapses onto the floor. Horatio kneels beside him.
Hamlet:	*(faintly)* Horatio, you must stay here and tell my sad story to this harsh world.
Narrator 2:	Tears stream from Horatio's eyes as he watches Hamlet's breathing slow, then stop.
Horatio:	*(tenderly)* A noble heart has cracked. Good night, sweet prince.

Narrator 3: Just then, a trumpet announces an arrival at the castle. An ambassador from England enters the room.

Ambassador: What a horrifying sight! I guess I have come too late to deliver my news to his lordship. I wanted to tell him that his command has been carried out. Rosencrantz and Guildenstern are dead.

Horatio: You seek thanks from one who never gave that command. *(to the others in the room)* Come, let us bear away these bodies. We will bury Lord Hamlet like a soldier, for I think that is fitting, given the struggles he faced. Had he lived, I believe he would have been a great king.

Simply Shakespeare: Readers Theatre for Young People is from *Read* magazine, a Weekly Reader publication, in collaboration with Teacher Ideas Press. Edited by Jennifer Kroll. www.weeklyreader.com. www.lu.com/tips. 1–800–541–2086.

CHAPTER 3

Julius Caesar

By William Shakespeare

Adapted by Kate Davis

Summary

In 44 B.C., Rome is a republic, governed by a senate rather than a king. However, that situation seems likely to change. The people of Rome are eager to crown the war hero Julius Caesar as their king. To save the republic, a group of senators and noblemen, including Cassius and the noble Brutus, plot to kill Caesar. They escort him to the senate chamber, where he is to be crowned. There, they stab him. Brutus, a talented orator, tries to calm the public and convince the crowds that Caesar's death is for the best. His words do their work until Mark Antony, Caesar's right-hand man, exposes Caesar's body and gives a stirring speech that turns public opinion against the conspirators. Cassius and Brutus gather armies and leave Rome for Asia Minor. Later, they do battle against the armies of Mark Antony and Caesar's nephew Octavius, with tragic results.

 Presentation Suggestions

The conspirators—Casca, Brutus, Cassius, Decius, Metellus, and Trebonius—as well as Titinius, Pindarus, Flavius, Marullus, Portia, Servants 1 and 2, and Lucius, can be placed in one grouping. Brutus and Cassius should be seated near one another and in front of this group. Julius Caesar, as well as Citizens 1 and 2, Calpurnia, Mark Antony, and Octavius, can be placed in a separate grouping. Narrators can stand to the back of or between the two groups. The Ghost of Caesar and Soothsayer can remain seated among the audience members and rise to speak their lines. An empty podium can be placed off to one side, and Mark Antony and Brutus can move behind this podium when delivering their speeches to Rome in Scene 8. The audience should be encouraged to make appropriate noises and responses during scenes in the play where a crowd is present.

Props

All male characters can wear togas made from bedsheets or the like. Calpurnia and Portia can wear either gowns or togas. The ghost of Caesar can wear a sheet or scary mask. Soothsayer can wear ragged clothing.

Cast of Characters

(main parts in boldface)
Narrators 1, 2, 3
Flavius \} *officials, tribunes*
Marullus
Citizens 1, 2
Julius Caesar, *would-be ruler of Rome*
Casca, *a nobleman and conspirator*
Calpurnia, *wife of Caesar*
Mark Antony, *Caesar's adviser; one of his successors*
Soothsayer, *a seer*
Brutus \} *noblemen and conspirators*
Cassius
Lucius, *Brutus's servant*

Decius
Trebonius } *conspirators*
Portia, *wife of Brutus*
Metellus, *conspirator*
Servants 1, 2
Ghost of Caesar
Octavius, *Caesar's grandnephew*
Titinius, *friend of Cassius*
Pindarus, *servant of Cassius*

Julius Caesar

By William Shakespeare
Adapted by Kate Davis

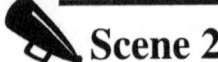 Scene 1

Narrator 1: In March 44 B.C., Rome is still officially a republic, a country without a king, governed by a senate. However, that seems likely to soon change.

Narrator 2: The city of Rome is swarming with citizens celebrating the homecoming of Julius Caesar, a popular war hero. Two officials try to manage the unruly crowd.

Flavius: Get home, you idle creatures! Why aren't you at work?

Marullus: You, there, what is your trade?

Citizen 1: I am a cobbler. I mend bad soles!

Flavius: Why do you lead these men about?

Citizen 1: To wear out their shoes! No, really, we're taking a holiday to see Caesar and rejoice in his triumph over Pompey.

Marullus: Triumph? Caesar brought home no conquests, no payments of tribute for Rome.
(to crowd) You blocks, you stones, you worse than senseless things! How many times have you waited all day just to catch a glimpse of great Pompey? You cheered at the sight of his chariot. You shouted so loud, the Tiber River trembled. Now would you strew flowers in the path of *Caesar,* who triumphs over Pompey's death? Be gone, you ingrates!

Flavius: *(to Marullus)* Caesar's power must be checked if our republic is to survive. Head to the capitol; we'll remove the decorations from his statues. We must pluck the feathers from Caesar's wings, or he will soar over us like a tyrant and keep all men as servants.

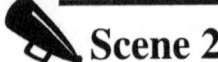 Scene 2

Narrator 3: Julius Caesar is parading through the streets with his wife and some senators and nobles. They are heading to the races. Men at arms bear tall banners. Trumpeters play fanfares.

Caesar:	*(to his wife)* Calpurnia—
Casca:	Silence all! Caesar speaks!
Calpurnia:	What is it, my lord?
Caesar:	When Antony runs in the race, stand where he can touch you. The elders say that a woman touched in a holy race will no longer be barren. Antony, be sure to touch her.
Antony:	I shall, my lord. For whenever Caesar says, "Do this," it will be performed.
Brutus:	Shhh! Listen. Someone is calling.
Soothsayer:	Caesar! Beware the Ides of March!
Caesar:	Who calls me? Let me see his face!
Cassius:	Come forward, fellow.
Soothsayer:	Beware the Ides of March!
Caesar:	He's a dreamer. Pass him by!
Narrator 1:	The procession carries on, but the two noblemen hang back.
Cassius:	Brutus, why the long face? Lately you have not smiled at me or anyone else.
Brutus:	Do not be deceived, Cassius. It is not *you* who troubles me. I am at war in *myself*.
Cassius:	What is bothering you? Many respected men are talking about you.
Brutus:	What are you suggesting, Cassius?
Narrator 2:	A great roar rises from a distance.
Brutus:	What does that shouting mean? I fear the people choose Caesar for their king.
Cassius:	Do you fear it? You do not wish it?
Brutus:	I would not have it so—even though I love Caesar. But what do you want of me? If it concerns the general good, tell me, for I love the name of honor more than I fear death.
Cassius:	I know honor is your best virtue. And honor is the point of my story. Listen: I was born as free as Caesar, and so were you. We are both as strong as he—why, stronger! I once carried him on my own shoulders when he nearly drowned. And I've heard him cry out like a sick girl when he had a fever. Now *he* has become a god and *I* am but a wretched creature who must bend to his every nod. Ye gods! How can a man of such feeble temper rule the majestic world?
Narrator 3:	The far-off crowd shouts again.

Brutus: Do they heap new honors on Caesar?

Cassius: Don't you see? He strides the world like a Colossus—a giant. We petty men walk under his legs and peep about, searching for our graves. There is no honor in that. But the fault, dear Brutus, is not in our stars, but in *ourselves*, that we are underlings. We are as good as Caesar. Our names are as fair.

Brutus: I confess I have thought these things.

Cassius: You can ignite a fire in people as well as he can. Upon what meat does Caesar feed that he should be grown so great, so arrogant? O what a shameful age! Rome has lost its noble breed.

Brutus: It's not safe for us to talk about this here. Let's meet somewhere else. Until then, I will consider what you say. But know this: I would rather be a mere villager than a son of Rome in these conditions.

Narrator 1: Soon the races are over, and Brutus and Cassius see Caesar return through the streets.

Brutus: Anger glows on Caesar's brow.

Cassius: Let's ask Casca to tell us what happened.

Narrator 2: Caesar sees Cassius whispering to Brutus. He turns to Antony.

Caesar: Antony, yonder Cassius has a lean and hungry look. Such men are dangerous.

Antony: Fear him not. He is a noble Roman.

Caesar: I don't *fear* him, for always I am Caesar! Yet if I were *inclined* to fear at all, Cassius is the kind of man I would avoid. He reads too much. He thinks too much. He looks *through* men. He seldom smiles, and when he does, it's as if he mocks himself for doing so. Such men are never at ease in their hearts when they behold one greater than themselves. Envy makes them dangerous. Antony, tell me what you think of him.

Narrator 3: As Antony walks away with Caesar, Brutus turns to Casca.

Brutus: Casca, what has upset Caesar?

Casca: Weren't you there? Why, a crown was offered to him, but he slapped it away with the back of his hand. So the people began to shout.

Cassius: I heard them shout three times.

Casca: He was offered the crown thrice by Mark Antony. Every time, he refused it, but to my thinking, he hated to take his fingers off it. Once he thought some in the crowd were happy he had refused, so he offered them his throat to cut. Then they clapped and hooted. Their breath was so bad, Caesar fell down.

Cassius: What? He fainted?

Casca: He fell, foaming at the mouth.

Brutus: He has the falling sickness.

Cassius: It is we who are falling (*with disgust*)... Did the senators say anything?

Casca: Yes. Cicero spoke, though I can't tell you what he said, for it was Greek to me. But listen, I have other news. Flavius and Marullus were executed for pulling banners off Caesar's statues.

Cassius: We must meet to talk about this further. Brutus, will you join us?

Brutus: Yes, I'll wait for you at my home.

Cassius: Good. Till then, think of the world.

Narrator 1: All three men go their separate ways.

Cassius: (*to himself*) Brutus may be honorable, but he can be swayed. We must use him in our plan, for Caesar loves and trusts him. It is fitting that noble minds should keep together. For if we do not shake Caesar's power, we shall endure worse days.

Scene 3

Narrator 2: On March 14, a terrible thunder and lightning storm shakes Rome.

Narrator 3: Casca is on his way to meet Cassius. He walks through the streets with his sword drawn, for he has seen strange signs.

Casca: Ho, Cassius, what a menacing night! The gods wish to destroy the evil world.

Cassius: This night is pleasing to honest men.

Casca: Pleasing? I've seen awful omens—a lion prowling near the capitol, women dazed with fear, swearing they saw men in flames.

Cassius: I bare my breast to the tempest and the fiery flash of lightning.

Casca: Why do you tempt the heavens so?

Cassius: Because heaven has changed natural things into instruments of fear only to warn us about a man as dreadful as this night. But he is no mightier than you or I.

Casca: You mean Caesar, don't you?

Cassius: Yes. Woe on us for tolerating him.

Casca: The senators intend to make him a king tomorrow. He will wear his crown everywhere, flaunting it on land and sea.

Cassius: I know where I will wear my dagger! Ye gods, make the weak strong and defeat the tyrants! No stony tower, dungeon, or iron chains will hold the strength of my spirit. I will shake off this tyranny!

Casca: And so will I! Take my hand. I am willing to set my foot as far as any man's to right these wrongs.

Cassius: Then we have a bargain. I have already convinced other noblemen to take up this cause. They are waiting for me now. But first we must win Brutus to our plan. Come, Casca, let's go to his house. This stormy night is fitting for such terrible work.

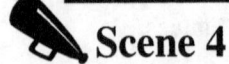 Scene 4

Narrator 1: In the small dark hours of the night, Brutus is pacing alone in his orchard.

Brutus: I have no personal cause for wanting Caesar to die. But if they crown him, he is bound to abuse his greatness. How many men climb the ladder of ambition only to turn their backs on those below? We must prevent that, for the general good. Caesar is like the egg of a serpent, and we must kill him in the shell.

Narrator 2: A servant of Brutus approaches.

Lucius: Sir, I just found a letter in your chamber. I'm sure it wasn't there earlier.

Brutus: Let me see it. Wait. What day is this?

Lucius: Fourteen days of March have passed.

Brutus: Then tomorrow is the Ides of March.

Narrator 3: Lucius leaves. Brutus reads the letter.

Brutus: (*reading*) Brutus, you are sleeping. Awake and see yourself. Shall Rome fall under one man's awe? Speak, strike, and redress!
(*to himself*) If striking will remedy the wrong, then, Rome, I promise my hand in this!

Narrator 1: Someone knocks at the gate.

Brutus: I have not slept since Cassius spoke to me about Caesar. Between the acting of a dreadful thing and the first motion, everything is like a hideous dream.

Lucius: Sir, Cassius is here to see you. There are others with him, men who hide their faces.

Brutus: (*to himself*) Let them enter.

Cassius: Good morrow, Brutus. Every man here honors you. These are all one with our cause—Trebonius, Decius, Casca, Cinna, and Metellus Cimber.

Brutus: You are all welcome. Give me your hands, one by one.

Cassius: Let us swear an oath—

Brutus: No, not an oath. Feeble men swear oaths over bad causes. Our cause is noble. We have fire and valor enough to spur us on. Countrymen, we need nothing more than honesty and the virtue of our enterprise.

Decius: Should no one but Caesar die?

Cassius: Antony should fall as well.

Brutus: No, let Antony live. We are not butchers. Caesar must be sacrificed, but we must not cut off his right arm. Our aim is not to hack him like a carcass. We must be seen as purging Rome, not murdering it.

Narrator 2: The clock strikes three a.m.

Trebonius: It is time to part.

Cassius: I doubt that Caesar will come to the capitol today; he is superstitious, and tonight's storm will frighten him.

Decius: Don't worry, I can persuade him.

Cassius: Then we will all go fetch him.

Brutus: At eight o'clock. Be merry then, so your looks don't betray you.

Cassius: Disperse, friends, and show yourselves to be true Romans.

Scene 5

Narrator 3: After the conspirators leave, Brutus's wife, Portia, comes into the orchard.

Brutus: Portia, you're sick and shouldn't be out in this raw morning.

Portia: Nor should you. Why are you out of bed? Last night you were ambling about, musing and sighing. What is bothering you? Tell me the cause of your grief.

Brutus: I don't feel well, that's all.

Portia: If that were true, a wise man like you would seek remedy. Walking half-dressed in the dank air is not healthy. You'll catch the vile contagion of night.

Brutus: I'll be fine. Now go to bed.

Portia: No, Brutus, I am your wife, and I have a right to know what's troubling your mind. *(kneeling)* By all your vows of love, tell me why you are so heavy. Who were those men hiding their faces from the darkness?

Brutus: Gentle Portia, get up.

Portia: I will if you explain what's going on. I will not tell anyone. You can share your secrets with your wife, for I am a strong, reputable woman.

	Look, I have given myself a wound in the leg as proof of my constancy. If I can bear this, then I can bear your secrets.
Brutus:	O ye gods, make me worthy of this wife! Portia, go into our chamber. I'll be there shortly and will tell you everything.

Scene 6

Narrator 1:	Others are spending sleepless nights, too. Near morning in Caesar's palace, his wife, Calpurnia, calls out in her dreams.
Calpurnia:	Help, ho! They murder Caesar!!
Narrator 2:	Caesar rises and goes into the hall.
Caesar:	Nothing is at peace tonight.
Calpurnia:	*(joining him)* Are you up? Surely you are not thinking of going out today.
Caesar:	I will go forth.
Calpurnia:	But the watchman tells me he's seen horrible sights tonight—graves opening, fiery warriors fighting in the clouds, blood drizzling down on the capital. . . . Caesar, I fear the heavens blaze forth the death of princes!
Caesar:	These signs are not meant for me but for the whole world. I am not afraid. Cowards die many times before their deaths, but the valiant never taste of death but once. Death is a necessary end and will come when it will.
Narrator 3:	Caesar's advisers warn him not to stir.
Caesar:	I *shall* go forth! Caesar is more dangerous than danger itself.
Calpurnia:	My lord, your wisdom is clouded by your confidence. Please don't go to the capitol today. Blame it on my fear, if you like.
Caesar:	All right . . . . For your sake, I'll send Mark Antony to say I am not well.
Decius:	*(arriving)* Hail, Caesar! I have come to escort you to the senate.
Caesar:	Tell them I will not come. Not that I *can* not or *dare* not, but that I *will* not.
Decius:	What reason can I give them?
Caesar:	They need none other than my will. But I'll tell *you* privately: My wife dreamed that my statue was spouting blood and that many Romans were bathing their hands in it. She believes this was a warning of evil.
Decius:	You've interpreted the dream wrong! It is a vision of *good* fortune. Rome's great men will be healed by your blood.

Caesar: Why yes, of course! You're right.

Decius: The senate intends to crown you today. If you wait till your wife has better dreams, the men may change their minds.

Caesar: I am ashamed to have listened to Calpurnia's foolish fears. Bring me my robe!

Narrator 1: The other conspirators arrive to escort Caesar and Antony to the senate.

Caesar: Be near me today, noblemen, so I may remember you in my hour of honor.

Trebonius: We will . . . . *(aside)* So near, that your friends will wish we had been farther.

Scene 7

Narrator 2: With a flourish of trumpets, Caesar and the other nobles proceed to the capitol.

Narrator 3: Caesar sees the soothsayer again.

Caesar: Ah, old man, your prediction was wrong. For the Ides of March are come.

Soothsayer: Ay, but they are not *gone!*

Narrator 1: Caesar dismisses him and walks on.

Narrator 2: A citizen tries to warn Caesar of danger, but the nobles block the man's way.

Cassius: I fear our plan will be discovered.

Brutus: It won't. Caesar suspects nothing.

Casca: *(secretively)* Are we all ready?

Decius: Yes, look: Trebonius has taken Antony away. Metellus Cimber is about to present a false case to Caesar.

Narrator 3: Caesar takes his commanding chair.

Metellus: *(kneeling)* Most high and mighty Caesar, I humbly ask you to pardon my banished brother.

Caesar: Do not fawn to me, or I'll kick you out of the way like a dog. Caesar has acted well. Your brother was banished. That is that.

Narrator 1: Brutus and Cassius second the appeal for pardon. But Caesar's mind is made up.

Caesar: I am as constant as the northern star. The skies are painted with many sparks, yet I know only one that will not be moved, and I am he!

Decius: *(kneeling)* Great Caesar—

Cassius: *(kneeling)* O Caesar—

Caesar: Brutus, will you not kneel also?

Narrator 2: Before Brutus can reply, Casca circles behind Caesar and stabs him.

Casca: My hands will speak for me!

Narrator 3: Caesar gasps and looks desperately to the others. As he reaches out, each conspirator stabs him, one by one. Brutus, the last to act, stabs Caesar in the chest.

Caesar: Et tu, Brute? Then fall Caesar!

Narrator 1: Chaos breaks out in the capitol. Senators flee. Citizens run about in confusion.

Cassius: *(yelling, triumphantly)* Liberty! Tyranny is dead! Shout it from the pulpits! Proclaim it in the streets!

Narrator 2: Brutus tries to reassure the people.

Brutus: Do not be frightened. Ambition's debt has been paid! Senators, there is no harm intended to you. Do not run away!

Trebonius: *(returning)* Antony has fled to his home. People are crying out as if doomsday has come.

Brutus: Fate, now do what you will. Come, conspirators. Let us bathe our hands in Caesar's blood. Stoop, Romans and smear your swords! Then let us all go to the square with our weapons over our heads and cry, "Peace, freedom, liberty!"

Narrator 3: The men kneel to dip their hands and daggers in the blood of Caesar's wounds.

Cassius: How many ages hence will this scene be acted over again in states that have not yet been born? Let them all call us the men that gave their country liberty!

Narrator 1: Antony's servant approaches humbly.

Servant 1: My master has a message for you. But he will only come if you guarantee his safety. He says, "Brutus is wise, valiant, and honest." He says he loved and honored Caesar. But if you let him to come here safely and tell him why Caesar deserved to die, he will love Brutus more than Caesar.

Brutus: Tell Antony he won't be harmed.

Cassius: You should not trust Antony.

Narrator 2: But Antony has already arrived. He goes straight to his friend's body.

Antony: O mighty Caesar! Do you lie so low? Are all your conquests and glories reduced to this? *(weeping)* Farewell then . . .

Narrator 3: He addresses the assassins.

Antony: If you plan to kill me, do it now. While your purple hands reek of blood, take your pleasure, for I have never been more ready to die!

Brutus: Antony, I know we must appear cruel, but if you could see our hearts, you'd know that we have pity for the wrong done to *Rome*. We have no malice toward *you*.

Antony: *(hiding feelings)* I don't doubt the wisdom in your actions. Give me your hands, men. I am with you. . . . If you can explain why he was dangerous. *(in grief)* But I did love him. Forgive me, Julius. . . .

Brutus: We'll give you our good reasons.

Antony: Then I will be satisfied. But first, allow me to bear Caesar's body to the marketplace and speak at his funeral.

Brutus. You may do so, but only if you do not blame us so. I will speak first and tell why Caesar had to die.

Antony: *(holding his tongue)* So be it.

Narrator 1: After the men leave, Antony pours out his sorrow and hidden anger.

Antony: *(to Caesar's body)* Pardon me, my bleeding piece of earth, for being gentle with these butchers. You are the ruins of the noblest man that ever lived. Woe to the hands that shed this blood! A curse upon the limbs of men, for this foul deed smells above the earth! Let Caesar's spirit seek revenge! Cry "Havoc!" and unleash your dogs of war. May fury and strife so bind Italy that rotting men will groan for burial!

Scene 8

Narrator 2: At the Roman Forum, citizens press in to hear Brutus and Antony speak.

Brutus: My countrymen, hear me. Let me tell you why I rose against Caesar—not that I loved Caesar less, but that I love Rome more. Would you rather have Caesar alive and you die as slaves? Or would you rather have him dead so that you might all live as free men?

Citizens: Give us freedom!

Brutus: As Caesar loved me, I weep for him. As he was valiant, I honor him. But as he was ambitious, I slew him. We have offended no one who loves Rome.

Citizen 2: Caesar was a tyrant! We are blessed to be rid of him! All praise Brutus!

Narrator 3: Antony carries in Julius Caesar's body. He climbs to the public chair to speak.

Antony: Friends, Romans, countrymen, lend me your ears. I come to bury Caesar, not to praise him. The evil that men do lives after them. The good is often buried with their bones. So let it be with Caesar. He was my friend, faithful and just. But Brutus says he was ambitious. And Brutus is an honorable man. Not long ago I offered Caesar a crown, and thrice he refused it. Was that ambition?

Citizen 1: It's true, he refused the crown.

Antony: Citizens, listen. I have found Caesar's will. It will make you mad to hear how he loved you.

Citizen 2: Read us the will!

Narrator 1: The crowd circles around Caesar's body. Antony points to holes in his robe.

Antony: Here is where the daggers struck. Mark how Caesar's blood flowed. And here is the wound where Brutus stabbed him. Then Caesar fell—and oh, what a fall was there!

Narrator 2: Antony flings off Caesar's robe.

Antony: And here . . . is his marred body.

Citizen 1: O pitiful spectacle!

Citizen 2: Villains! Slay the murderers!

Antony: Wait. You've not yet heard the will.

Citizen 1: Read us Caesar's will!

Antony: To every Roman, he gives 75 drachmas—and all his orchards and walks.

Citizen 2: Royal Caesar, we will avenge you! Light torches! Burn the traitors' houses!

Narrator 3: The crowd's anger is out of control.

Antony: *(to himself)* Now mischief, begin. Take what course you will. Let chaos reign!

Scene 9

Narrator 1: Brutus and Cassius flee Rome, each taking an army to Asia Minor.

Narrator 2: Before he died, Caesar named his nephew Octavius to be his heir. Octavius, 19, joins Antony and another consul as threefold rulers of Rome. They want revenge.

Narrator 3: They kill senators that they suspect as enemies and plan to fight Brutus and Cassius.

Narrator 1: Months later, far to the south in Asia Minor, Brutus is camped with his army at Sardis. Cassius and his army march to meet him. Both men are in foul moods.

Cassius: Brutus, you have done me wrong.

Brutus: What? I do not wrong my enemies, let alone my brother.

Cassius: You have condemned one of my men for taking bribes, and you have ignored my letters written on his behalf.

Brutus: Yes, because you have an itchy palm too. I hear you are selling offices for gold to those that don't deserve them. Is that the justice Julius died for? I had rather be a dog than that kind of Roman!

Cassius: Must I endure this? If you were not Brutus, this speech would be your last.

Brutus: Your threats don't frighten me. I am armed in honesty. I thought you were a better soldier than this. You were taking money on the side while denying me the gold I needed it to pay my army!

Cassius: I did not deny you gold! If I did, I will give you my heart. Here, take my dagger and strike me as you did Caesar!

Brutus: Put your weapon away. We are speaking with too ill a temper.

Cassius: So we are. Give me your hand.

Brutus: O Cassius, I am sick with grief.

Cassius: What is the matter?

Brutus: Portia has died.

Cassius: Your wife? Was she ill?

Brutus: She was sick of my absence. And she could not bear seeing Antony and Octavius become so strong in Rome. She lost her mind, and . . . swallowed burning coals.

Cassius: O ye gods! Such a bitter death!

Brutus: It is too painful to think about. Please speak no more of it . . . *(changing subject)* Antony and Octavius are heading toward Phillipi to challenge us. We should march to meet them on the battlefield.

Cassius: Let them waste their time and resources coming *here* to us.

Brutus: No. They'll gather more soldiers on their way and attack harder. We must strike now, while our armies are fired up. There is a tide in the affairs of men, which, taken at the flood, leads on to fortune. But if the moment is missed, we shall be lost in the shallows, in misery. We are now afloat on a full sea. We must ride this current or lose our venture.

Cassius: Then we shall confront them at Phillipi.

Narrator 2: After Cassius leaves, Brutus cannot sleep. He asks his servant to play music, but the sleepy boy dozes at his instrument.

Brutus: I will not wake thee, gentle knave. Why is the candle flickering so?

Narrator 3: Suddenly Caesar's ghost appears.

Brutus: Who comes here? What are you? A god? An angel? A devil? Speak!

Ghost: I am thy evil spirit, Brutus.

Brutus: Why have you come here?

Ghost: To say you shall see me at Philippi.

Brutus: I shall see you again?

Ghost: *(as it vanishes)* Aye . . . at Phillipi . . .

Scene 10

Narrator 1: Soon, the armies are ready for battle at Phillipi. Antony and Octavius spot their enemies on the hilltops.

Octavius: Brutus and Cassius have come to meet us before we advanced on them.

Antony: They might appear courageous, but I know them. Theirs is fearful bravery.

Octavius: Their battle flags are flying.

Antony: Then lead on!

Narrator 2: Cassius and Brutus see them coming.

Brutus: They want to speak to us first.

Cassius: *(to troops)* Stand fast!

Narrator 3: The four generals ride out to meet.

Brutus: Words before blows, is it?

Octavius: Better than your bad strokes—like the hole you made in Caesar's heart!

Cassius: Your words cheat the people.

Antony: And your words fooled Caesar before you hacked him in the sides. You kissed his feet only to strike him down!

Octavius: I draw my sword against you, traitors! Caesar's wounds will be avenged!

Brutus: *You* are traitors—to the republic!

Octavius: Then let's begin. . . . If you have the stomachs for it.

Narrator 1: The generals return to their armies. Cassius is worried. He speaks to a friend.

Cassius:	This morning I saw ravens and crows flying overhead, looking on us as if we were sickly prey. It does not bode well....
Titinius:	Do not believe such signs.
Cassius:	Be my witness then that against my will, I had to wager all our liberties on one battle. Now I go to meet what comes.
Brutus:	*(joining him)* And I also.
Cassius:	Brutus, this may be our last chance to speak. If we lose today, what will you do?
Brutus:	I will never be led captive through the streets of Rome. If this is our last meeting, then farewell. Now we must end what we began on the Ides of March!
Cassius:	Farewell, Brutus! Ho, men, away!

Scene 11

Narrator 2:	Amid drumbeats and alarms, the war for Rome's liberty is waged. In the first clash, Brutus overpowers Octavius, but Antony's troops burn Cassius's camp.
Narrator 3:	Cassius sees troops nearing and sends his friend and officer, Titinius, to see if it's the enemy. His servant Pindarus watches.
Pindarus:	Titinius is surrounded and taken down. Men are shouting for joy!
Narrator 1:	They think the enemy has killed him.
Cassius:	O coward that I am, to have my best friend taken. Come, Pindarus, take the hilt of my sword and run me through.
Pindarus:	No, master, I cannot.
Narrator 2:	Cassius throws himself on his blade.
Cassius:	*(dying)* Now, Caesar, you are revenged with the sword that killed you!
Narrator 3:	Pindarus flees. Soon Titinius returns. The men who had cheered were not enemies, but Brutus's army!
Titinius:	*(seeing Cassius)* Cassius is no more? Didn't you see your friends give me this wreath of victory for you? O hateful error. You've mistaken everything. Our day is gone. Our deeds are done. Come, Cassius's sword, and find my own heart!
Narrator 1:	In despair, Titinius kills himself.
Narrator 2:	When Brutus finds them he is shocked to see the two men dead on the ground.
Brutus:	Julius Caesar, you are still mighty! Your ghost walks here, turning our own swords in our guts. *(to the dead men, sadly)* Farewell, last of all the true Romans!

Narrator 3:	The fight now turns in Octavius's and Antony's favor. On Brutus's side, soon only a few soldiers and servants are left.
Narrator 1:	Brutus refuses to be taken prisoner alive. He pleads with his men to kill him.
Brutus:	Our enemies have beaten us to the pit. It is more worthy to jump in ourselves than to wait until they push us.
Narrator 2:	The men beg him to flee.
Servant 2:	Do not stay here. Fly, my lord!
Brutus:	Good fellow, if your life has honor, hold my sword so I can run upon it.
Servant 2:	First give me your hand. Farewell!
Brutus:	Farewell, good servant. Caesar, now be still. I killed you with half as much will.
Narrator 3:	He runs on his own sword—and dies.
Narrator 1:	Later that day, Octavius and Antony discover Brutus dead on the field. Although they rejoice in victory, they revere Brutus.
Antony:	This was the noblest Roman of them all. He acted not with envy but purely for the common good. Here was such a gentle, honest being, that one might say to all the world, "This was a man!"

Simply Shakespeare: Readers Theatre for Young People is from *Read* magazine, a Weekly Reader publication, in collaboration with Teacher Ideas Press. Edited by Jennifer Kroll. www.weeklyreader.com. www.lu.com/tips. 1–800–541–2086.

CHAPTER 4

King Lear

By William Shakespeare

Adapted by Jennifer Kroll

Summary

The aging King Lear decides to retire. He plans to divide his kingdom into three sections and to give a section to each of his three daughters: Goneril, Regan, and Cordelia. Before receiving her portion, each daughter is required to flatter Lear, telling him how much she loves him. Goneril and Regan, Lear's older daughters, don't like or care about their father but readily flatter him, as required. Lear's loyal and loving youngest daughter, Cordelia, refuses to lie and flatter as her sisters have done. As a result, she is disowned and banished. After she leaves for France with her husband, the King of France, King Lear's folly quickly becomes obvious. With nothing more to gain from Lear, Goneril and Regan behave in an increasingly disrespectful and finally downright cruel manner toward their father. The proud, abused old man eventually ends up wandering homeless, wet, and mad in the wilderness. Meanwhile, Goneril and Regan secretly plot to overthrow each other and seize total power. When Cordelia returns home with a French peacekeeping force, can she restore the peace and save her father, or is it too late?

Presentation Suggestions

Lear should be seated front and center. He can be seated on a platform or high stool or in a large, comfortable "throne" chair, representing his stature as king. Kent and Fool should be seated below him, on lower chairs or pillows. Goneril, Regan, and Cordelia should be clustered around Lear, with Cordelia on his right side and Goneril and Regan on his left. Oswald, Edmund, Cornwall, Albany, and Servant should be seated to the side of Goneril and Regan. Edgar, Gloucester, Knight, Doctor, and Gentleman should be seated to the side of Cordelia. The narrators may be seated or may stand at music stands in back of the other characters or in another portion of the room.

Lear's decline can be represented visually. If Lear sits on a high stool or on some other kind of "throne" during the first two scenes of the play, he can move to lower or less "thronelike" seats as the play progresses. Provide a lower or simpler chair for him to move to during Scenes 3 through 7. Finally, have him move to a pillow or cushion on the floor at the beginning of Scene 8. Cordelia can join him on a floor cushion during Scenes 10 to 12.

Props

Lear should have a crown and possibly a kingly robe that he can remove during the storm scene. He might have a rubber mouse or small stuffed animal of some kind to hold up in Scene 10 and a feather to hold up in the final scene. Goneril and Regan should wear ostentatious, dressy clothes. They can wear crowns or tiaras and showy jewelry. Cordelia can wear a skirt or dress also but should wear something of a more muted color and less showy style. The doctor can carry a stethoscope or wear a white jacket. Fool can wear a jester's cap or other funny hat or another symbol, such as a red plastic nose, indicating that he is a clown. Edgar might sport a sword of some kind. Kent and Edgar can put on a flannel shirt or other symbolic clothing item when they disguise themselves as lower- and middle-class people. Gloucester and Lear might wear gray beards to signify their age.

Cast of Characters

(main parts in boldface)
Narrators 1, 2, 3
King Lear, *king of Britain*

Goneril
Regan } *daughters of King Lear*
Cordelia
Earl of Kent, *loyal follower of Lear*
King of France, *suitor to Cordelia*
Edmund, *younger son of the Earl of Gloucester*
Earl of Gloucester
Edgar, *older son of the Earl of Gloucester*
Oswald, Goneril's steward
Knight, *in King Lear's train*
Fool, *court jester to Lear*
Duke of Cornwall, *husband of Regan*
Servant
Doctor
Duke of Albany, *husband of Goneril*
Gentleman

King Lear

By William Shakespeare
Adapted by Jennifer Kroll

Scene 1

Narrator 1: In his throne room, King Lear sits holding a map. Clustered around him are his daughters and other nobles.

King Lear: I want to be able to enjoy the final years of my life without having to worry about ruling the state. Therefore, I am passing the responsibility on to my daughters.

Narrator 2: Lear looks up from the map at his three daughters.

Lear: Each one of you shall be given a third of the kingdom to govern. But first, I want each one of you to tell me how much you love me. *(to Goneril)* As the oldest, you may speak first.

Goneril: Sir, you are dearer to me than my very freedom. I love you more than anything on this earth. More than any child ever loved a father before—that's how much I love you.

Lear: *(to Goneril)* Daughter, you've spoken well. In exchange, here's what I'm giving you.

Narrator 3: Lear holds up his map.

Lear: All this is yours, from this line to this one, to govern with your husband, the Duke of Albany. *(to Regan)* Now, my middle daughter, what do you have to say to me?

Regan: Nothing else in the world makes me even the tiniest bit happy except Your Highness's precious love.

Cordelia: *(to herself)* What am I going to say after all this?

Lear: *(to Regan)* To you and your husband, the Duke of Cornwall, this generous third of our fair kingdom now belongs.

Narrator 1: Lear turns to Cordelia.

Lear: Now, last but not least, my youngest daughter and my joy. What do you have to say?

Cordelia: *(quietly)* Nothing, my lord.

Lear:	*(with surprise)* Nothing will come of nothing. Speak again.
Cordelia:	I'm sorry, sir, but I just can't force my heart into my mouth. I love you as I should, no more and no less.
Lear:	Improve your speech a little, or you might destroy your fortune.
Cordelia:	Good lord, you have raised me and loved me. I am grateful, as I should be. I love and honor you as I should. My sisters say they love you more than anything. Why do they have husbands, then? When I marry, I plan to give my husband half my love.
Lear:	*(sounding hurt and angry)* What are you saying to me?
Cordelia:	I'm just telling the truth.
Lear:	*(raging)* Then let truth be your dowry! I disown you!
Earl of Kent:	*(with alarm)* Your Majesty—
Lear:	Silence, Kent! Don't come between the dragon and his wrath! I loved this one the most and hoped to rely on her to care for me in my old age. *(to Cordelia)* You are my child no more. I'll divide your part of the kingdom between your two sisters.
Narrator 2:	He hastily redraws the lines on the map.
Lear:	There. *(to Regan and Goneril)* You two now rule over England. I give up my power, though I keep the name and trappings of a king. Each month, one hundred of my knights and I shall journey to stay with one or the other of you, my daughters.
Kent:	*(with alarm)* Your highness, I have always loved you as a father. I beg you to listen to me. Don't divide the country or disown your daughter.
Lear:	Kent, if you value your life, shut your mouth!
Kent:	I don't care about my life so long as I can keep yours safe!
Lear:	Out of my sight, Kent!
Kent:	I can only hope that in the future your sight will be better.
Lear:	How dare you say such a thing? I give you five days to get out of my kingdom. On the sixth day, if you're still here, you will face death.
Narrator 3:	Kent leaves, looking stricken, and Lear turns to Cordelia's suitor, the King of France.
Lear:	*(to France)* Great King, I respect you far too much to ask you to marry someone I hate. This girl is no longer suitable for your hand. She has no family and no dowry.
King of France:	I still wish to marry her. She is herself a dowry.
Lear:	Take her then and be gone. I don't want to ever see her face again.
Narrator 1:	Lear stomps out of the room.

Cordelia: *(to Goneril and Regan)* I know what you are, though, as your sister, I am reluctant to name your faults. Please take care of Father. He is in your hands. I only wish he were in a better place. Farewell.

Scene 2

Narrator 2: A little later, Goneril and Regan talk privately.

Goneril: Father intends to come to stay with Albany and me tonight.

Regan: Yes. And next month he will come to stay with us in Cornwall.

Goneril: You see how he's getting in his old age. He changes his mind every five minutes and makes bad decisions.

Regan: Even when he was younger, he never had any self-awareness.

Goneril: He shouldn't have stomped out on the King of France. No good can come of that.

Narrator 3: Meanwhile, in the Earl of Gloucester's castle, Edmund, Gloucester's illegitimate younger son, is plotting a way to acquire his father's fortune. He holds a letter he's just written.

Edmund: *(to himself)* Why should I be punished because of some stupid custom that says only legitimate and oldest sons inherit the estate? I am smarter and stronger than my brother Edgar and I'm going to get his land! I have a plan. . . .

Narrator 1: Edmund's father, the Earl of Gloucester, enters the room.

Earl of Gloucester: What's been going on here while I was gone?

Narrator 2: Edmund quickly shoves the letter into his pocket, making sure his father has seen him do so.

Edmund: Oh, nothing. Nothing at all.

Gloucester: What's that?

Edmund: It's nothing.

Gloucester: Then let me see it.

Edmund: It's a letter from my brother. But I don't think it's fit for your eyes.

Gloucester: Whatever do you mean? Give me that letter, son!

Narrator 3: Edmund hands over the letter.

Gloucester: *(reading)* Why should we bow down to old men our whole lives and wait until we are old ourselves before we receive our inheritance? If our father were suddenly out of the picture, you would receive half of his income forever. *(with alarm)* Can this possibly mean what I think it means? *(to Edmund)* Are you sure the handwriting is your brother's?

Edmund: Looks like it to me.

Narrator 1: Gloucester studies the letter.

Gloucester: *(grimly)* It *is* his writing. Where is Edgar now?

Edmund: I don't know. Don't jump to conclusions until you've had a chance to talk to him.

Narrator 2: Gloucester wanders off looking devastated. A moment later, Edgar enters the room.

Edgar: What's up, Edmund? You look so serious.

Edmund: I have serious things on my mind. Tell me, Edgar, when did you last see our father?

Edgar: The night before last.

Edmund: Did you quarrel then?

Edgar: No.

Edmund: You must have done something that offended him. Think about it. I just saw him a few minutes ago, and he was furious. I would stay out of his way, if I were you. I think your life may be in danger.

Edgar: In danger? Is he *that* angry?

Edmund: Yes. Go and lay low in my quarters for awhile. I'll find Father and calm him. In the meantime, if you have to come out, wear a sword.

Narrator 3: Edgar nods and leaves.

Edmund: *(to himself)* Both my father and brother have proved remarkably easy to deceive. Honest people are always like that.

Scene 3

Narrator 1: A few days later, in the Duke of Albany's house, Goneril speaks with her steward, Oswald.

Goneril: Day and night, my father's behavior grates on my nerves. I can't stand it anymore! When he comes back from hunting, tell him I'm sick and can't speak with him.

Oswald: Here he comes now, madam.

Goneril: Give him any excuse. I'm going to go and write to my sister about how he's been acting.

Narrator 2: Goneril hurries out of the room, as the king and his attendants enter through another door. Kent also enters, disguised as a peasant.

Kent: *(to himself)* I intend to stick around and help the king, whether he wants me or not.

Lear: *(to his attendants)* Bring me my dinner and fetch my fool.

Narrator 3:	The attendants rush off.
Lear:	*(to Kent)* Who are you?
Kent:	I'm Caius, an honest fellow who wishes to be of service to you.
Lear:	OK—I can probably find some work for you to do. *(to Oswald)* Where's my daughter?
Oswald:	Milady is not well, sir. She isn't coming down.
Knight:	*(to Lear)* I'm sorry to say it, Your Highness, but lately your daughter and the duke have not been giving you your proper respect.
Lear:	Haven't they?
Knight:	No, I don't think so.
Lear:	*(sternly, to Oswald)* Go and tell my daughter that I wish to see her!
Oswald:	I already told you—she does not want to come down.
Lear:	*(furiously)* Do you know to whom you're speaking, sir?
Oswald:	Yes. You're my lady's father.
Lear:	I'm the *king*, you cur!
Narrator 1:	Lear slaps Oswald's face.
Oswald:	I'll not stand being hit.
Kent:	Perhaps you would prefer to be tripped.
Narrator 2:	Kent trips Oswald.
Kent:	The king has spoken. Now go!
Narrator 3:	Oswald stomps off angrily.
Lear:	*(to Kent)* Thanks for that! I shall be glad to have you serving me. Ah! Here comes my fool now. He'll put me in a better mood.
Narrator 1:	The fool dances into the room. As he does, he takes off his jester's cap and puts it on Lear's head.
Fool:	Sir, I wish I had two fools' caps and two daughters.
Lear:	*(with good humor)* Why is that?
Fool:	So I could give my daughters everything and keep my fools' caps for myself.
Narrator 2:	Lear realizes that the fool is making fun of him. His face darkens.
Lear:	You may be fooling around, but you had better be careful what you say.
Fool:	Let me teach you a little rhyme.
Lear:	*(more cheerfully)* Please do.

Fool:	Have more than you show. Speak less than you know. Lend less than you owe. Believe less than you hear and you've nothing to fear.
Kent:	What you just said means absolutely nothing, fool.
Fool:	Then it's like advice from an unpaid lawyer—you gave me nothing for it. *(to Lear)* Can you make no use of nothing, uncle?
Lear:	Why, no, boy. Nothing can be made out of nothing.
Fool:	*(to Kent)* Please tell him how much the rent from his land comes to. He won't believe a fool.
Narrator 3:	Goneril appears at the door of the room, looking very perturbed.
Lear:	There you are, daughter. Why are you wearing that frown?
Goneril:	Sir, you are old and should act wise and dignified. Instead, you keep this horrible fool and a hundred disorderly knights and squires carousing in my house. They abuse my servants, say shameful things, and cause me trouble. I insist that you dismiss half of your train immediately.
Lear:	*(with disbelief)* The knights of my train do not carouse! They are noble gentlemen! I'll not dismiss half of them! How dare you make such a demand? And I won't stick around here to take such abuse! I have another daughter who knows how to treat her father. How sharper than a serpent's tooth it is to have a thankless child!
Narrator 1:	Lear storms out. A little later, he is packed and ready to go.
Lear:	*(to Kent)* Take these letters to the Earl of Gloucester. My daughter Regan is to be staying at his place tonight. Let her know that I will meet her there shortly. *(to himself)* I feel as if I might be going crazy.

Scene 4

Narrator 2:	In the hallway of Gloucester's castle, Edmund spots his brother Edgar approaching. Edgar wears a sword, as he has been instructed to do.
Edmund:	*(to himself)* Ah, good. Here comes Edgar. *(pretending to be concerned)* Dear brother, you must flee! Our father is coming for you. Is it true that you've spoken out against the Dukes of Cornwall and Albany?
Edgar:	*(in puzzlement)* No! I said nothing!
Edmund:	Here comes father now! I must draw my sword on you. You should draw, too, and pretend to defend yourself. Now, run!
Narrator 3:	Edgar looks confused, but draws his sword and then runs away.
Edmund:	*(shouting)* Yield, villain!

Narrator 1: Edmund cuts himself in the arm just before Gloucester and the servants come rushing up.

Gloucester: You're bleeding! What's going on?

Edmund: It's just a scratch, sir. Edgar attacked me when he realized that he couldn't persuade me to murder your lordship.

Gloucester: The villain! *(to servants)* Go after him! Put out a warrant for his arrest! *(to Edmund)* Thank goodness that I have one loyal son. You are my only child now, Edmund.

Narrator 2: Just then, trumpets sound, announcing that Cornwall and Regan have arrived. Gloucester and Edmund go down to greet them.

Duke of Cornwall: *(to Gloucester)* We've just heard some disturbing news.

Regan: Is it true that your son, Edgar, sought to take your life?

Gloucester: Thank goodness my loyal son Edmund defended me.

Duke of Cornwall: *(to Edmund)* It is good to know that you are so loyal and trustworthy. My wife and I will count on you to be a help to us in the future.

Edmund: I will be honored to serve you in any way I can.

Regan: *(to Gloucester and Edmund)* We could use your advice now, actually. I've just received a letter from my sister. She is having some trouble with our father. . . .

Scene 5

Narrator 3: The next morning, Kent arrives at Gloucester's castle with messages. Oswald is also arriving to announce that Goneril will be there by nightfall. Oswald meets Kent in the road but doesn't recognize him.

Oswald: *(to Kent)* Good day. Can you tell me where I should put my horse?

Kent: How about in the swamp over there?

Oswald: How rude! Do you know who I am?

Kent: I know that you are not loyal to the king.

Narrator 1: Oswald and Kent get into a scuffle in the street, and Kent eventually socks Oswald in the jaw.

Oswald: *(shouting)* Help! Murder!

Narrator 2: Edmund, Cornwall, and Regan come running.

Regan: *(to Cornwall)* Look—it's my sister's steward.

Oswald: This ruffian insulted and attacked me for absolutely no reason!

Cornwall: Let's put him into the stocks until he learns to behave better.

Kent: Sir, I'm too old to learn. And, besides, I'm the king's messenger and I'm here with news from him.

Narrator 3: Kent is forced into the stocks. Later that day, Lear arrives. . . .

Lear: What's this? My messenger in the stocks? This is an outrage!

Narrator 1: Lear stomps off to find Regan and Cornwall.

Scene 6

Gloucester: *(to Lear)* I'm sorry, but they won't see you right now. They had a long journey and are tired. . . .

Lear: *(angrily)* Tired? This is nothing but an excuse! I want to see my daughter and her husband.

Gloucester: Yes, I've informed them that that's the case.

Lear: *(raging) Informed them?!* Don't you understand me? I want to see my daughter, and I want my messenger out of the stocks—right NOW!

Narrator 2: Gloucester sends a guard to free Kent and brings Cornwall and Regan into the room.

Regan: *(coolly)* I am glad to see Your Highness.

Lear: Beloved Regan, your sister's been very unkind to me. You will not believe what she's trying to do to me. She's ordered me to cut my train down to fifty men!

Narrator 3: Just then, Goneril bursts in. Regan rushes to greet her.

Lear: *(with alarm)* Regan, why are you taking that viper by the hand?

Goneril: Why shouldn't she take my hand? I've not done anything wrong.

Regan: Father, you are old and weak, and you need to learn to act that way. If my sister asks you to dismiss half of your train, you had better do so. Then go back home with her for the rest of the month and behave yourself.

Lear: No. My hundred knights and I will stay here with you, Regan.

Regan: I can't entertain you and one hundred of your followers here. Besides, I agree with my sister. I don't see why you need a train of one hundred knights. I don't even see why you need fifty.

Goneril: After all, our servants can look after all of your needs.

Regan: Yes. When you come to my place next month, I insist that you bring no more than twenty-five men with you.

Goneril: Sir, why do you even need twenty-five knights or ten or five?

Regan: Or even one?

Lear:	Don't talk about needs! The poorest beggar has more than he really needs. If you take away all the things a person has that he doesn't need, he becomes no different than an animal. Look at yourself, daughters. You don't need your beautiful clothes. They certainly don't keep you warm. . . .
Narrator 1:	Lear looks as if he is about to cry, but he holds back his tears.
Lear:	No, I'll not cry. And don't you worry—I will have my revenge! I will do terrible things. . . . *(quieter)* What those things are, I don't know yet. But you can bet they'll be terrible. . . . *(very quietly)* My heart is breaking. I think I'm losing my mind.
Narrator 2:	Lear turns and slumps out of the castle. The fool follows him. Through the open door, thunder can be heard in the distance.
Cornwall:	Sounds like there's going to be a storm.
Gloucester:	Yes, it's already starting to rain. We need to go after the king and bring him back. There's no shelter for miles around.
Cornwall:	No—let's let him go.
Goneril:	His folly can be his teacher.
Regan:	*(to Gloucester)* I forbid you to go after him. And let's lock the doors so that his followers can't break in.
Cornwall:	Let's shut the windows, too. It's a wild night.

Scene 7

Narrator 3:	Lightning flashes across the sky. Rain pours down. Out in an open field, Kent, still disguised as Caius, comes upon one of the knights from Lear's train.
Kent:	Sir, where's the king?
Knight:	I'm looking for him.
Kent:	I know you to be trustworthy, and so I'm going to share some important information with you. It's likely there will be a war between the two sisters. Both have set their sights on taking over all of England. Cordelia and her husband have heard this news, and have stationed a French peacekeeping force at Dover.
Knight:	That's big news!
Kent:	I need you to do me a favor. Go to Dover, find Cordelia, and tell her what's happened to her father. Show her my ring and she'll know who sent you. I am not who I appear to be.
Narrator 1:	Kent gives the knight his ring, and the knight rides off. Meanwhile, back at the house, Gloucester speaks with Edmund. He is upset about what has just happened.

Gloucester: They forbid me to go after the king! On a night like this! How heartless! I think they will soon get their due, though. Tonight, I received a letter informing me that there is a division between Albany and Cornwall and other serious business going on. I've locked the letter in my chamber. If there is an armed conflict, of course we'll take the king's side. I'm going out into the storm to find him now. You go distract the others so that they don't notice I've gone.

Narrator 2: Gloucester leaves.

Edmund: *(to himself)* I must go at once and report my father's actions to the duke. This is a great chance to win the Duke of Cornwall's favor. And once my father's out of the way, I'll be Duke of Gloucester!

Scene 8

Narrator 3: Kent has managed to find King Lear and the fool. The three struggle against the wind and rain.

Lear: *(raving)* Regan, Goneril—how could you throw your father out on such a night?

Kent: Here's an abandoned shack. Let's go in, sir, out of this storm.

Narrator 1: Lear, the fool, and Kent enter the dilapidated shack.

Lear: How do the poor and homeless survive on such a night? Alas—I have paid far too little attention to this.

Fool: Look! Somebody's here with us!

Narrator 2: The three suddenly realize that they are sharing their shelter with a poor vagrant dressed in rags. This vagrant is actually Edgar, who has disguised himself and is pretending to be a crazy beggar. He waves his hands wildly, as if to shoo away monsters or devils that are lurking around him.

Edgar: Away, away—you foul fiends!

Lear: *(to Kent)* Nothing but the unkindness of daughters could have brought this fellow to such a low point.

Edgar: *(in a singsong voice)* Tom's a'cold. Do de do de do.

Fool: This cold night will turn us all to fools and madmen.

Narrator 3: Lear stares at Edgar.

Lear: Is man no more than this? Take all the clothes and titles off of a person and what have you got? An animal without even fur or feathers for warmth and protection. Very well. If that's all I really am, off with these borrowed coverings!

Narrator 1: Half delirious, Lear removes his crown and begins to strip off his soaked clothing.

Scene 9

Narrator 2: Gloucester looks for the king in the stormy night. By the time he returns home, Regan and Cornwall are convinced he is their enemy.

Regan: Ah! The traitor has returned!

Cornwall: Bind his arms!

Narrator 3: Gloucester is grabbed by guards and roughly tied to a chair.

Gloucester: Your graces, what do you mean by this? You are my guests!

Regan: *(to guards)* Make the knots tighter! *(to Gloucester)* Traitor! Your son told us that you are in league with the King of France and you've been helping Lear.

Gloucester: The King of France is a neutral party. He wishes for peace.

Regan: Why did you try to help the old man?

Gloucester: Because I didn't want to see your cruel nails pluck out his poor old eyes. I didn't want to see your sister sink her fangs into his flesh.

Cornwall: Let me make sure you never have to see such things! *(to guards)* Fellows, hold him!

Narrator 1: While servants hold Gloucester down, Cornwall crushes his out eye with the heel of his boot.

Gloucester: Help! Help!

Cornwall: Now, I'll do the other eye and make both sides even.

Servant: *(to Cornwall)* Don't, my lord! Please don't hurt him any more!

Cornwall: *(to the servant)* How dare you speak to me in such a way!

Narrator 2: Cornwall draws his sword and rushes to kill the servant, who draws his own sword and fights back. The servant wounds Cornwall badly before Regan grabs a knife and kills the servant by stabbing him in the back.

Cornwall: Now . . . where was I?

Narrator 3: Cornwall rips Gloucester's one remaining eye out with his hand.

Cornwall: Out, vile jelly! Where is thy luster now?

Regan: Let's throw the blind old fool out into the night.

Scene 10

Narrator 1: Edgar finds Gloucester stumbling through the countryside, his clothing ripped and his face bloody. He helps his father as best as he can, preventing him from committing suicide by jumping off of a cliff.

Narrator 2: Meanwhile, Kent, the fool, and Lear make their way to Dover. Lear, raving mad by now, has covered himself with weeds.

Lear: *(raving)* They told me I was everything. It was a lie. I'm not even immune to the cold. *(distractedly)* Why, look—here's a little mousie.

Narrator 3: Lear holds up a mouse.

Lear: See how this subject quakes in fear at my majesty!

Narrator 1: Eventually, a search party sent out by Cordelia discovers the ailing Lear and his companions. Lear is rushed to Dover, where a French doctor tends him.

Cordelia: *(to the doctor)* How's my father?

Doctor: His mind has been deeply affected by the strain of these past few days. He's sleeping now. Perhaps he will be better when he wakes.

Cordelia: Was this a face to send out against a storm? Couldn't these gray hairs inspire any pity in my sisters?

Narrator 2: Lear's eyes flutter open.

Cordelia: My lord—how are you?

Lear: I must be dead because you are surely an angel.

Cordelia: Don't you know who I am?

Lear: I think you might be—is it possible that you are—my child, Cordelia?

Cordelia: *(tearfully)* I am! I am!

Lear: Oh, Cordelia, I have treated you terribly. Give me some poison to drink, for I know you cannot love me. Your sisters did me wrong when they had no cause. You have cause.

Cordelia: No cause, no cause.

Narrator 3: She leans over and hugs him, tears running down her face.

Scene 11

Narrator 1: Goneril's husband, Albany, is shocked when he learns what's been done to Lear and Gloucester. However, he agrees to participate with Regan and Cornwall in a united military action against the French.

Narrator 2: What Albany doesn't know is that while Goneril was visiting Gloucester's castle, she secretly began a romance with Edmund.

Goneril: *(to Edmund)* My husband disapproves of how we've handled Gloucester and my father. What an annoyance he is! But we'll get rid of him as soon as the opportunity presents itself, and then you can be my husband, Edmund.

Edmund:	That will be wonderful, my darling. Let's make a plan.
Narrator 3:	Meanwhile, Regan's husband, Cornwall, has died from his wound. Regan decides that she wants to marry Edmund, also.
Regan:	Edmund, I ask you to take command my armies. I hope that soon you will also take command of my heart.
Edmund:	I can't wait for the day.

Scene 12

Narrator 1:	The battle between the French and English forces rages for days, but in the end, Cordelia's army loses. Soldiers under Edmund's command take Lear and Cordelia captive.
Cordelia:	Are they taking us to see our sisters and daughters now?
Lear:	Let's not go see them. Let's go to prison, instead. We'll be happy there together, you and I. When you ask me to bless you, I'll kneel down and ask you for forgiveness. And we can pray and sing and tell old tales and laugh at what goes on in court and live the rest of our lives out that way.
Narrator 2:	Edmund reports the capture of Lear and Cordelia to the Duke of Albany.
Edmund:	*(to Albany)* They are safely under lock and key now, brother.
Duke of Albany:	Pardon me, but I see you as my subordinate, sir, not my brother.
Regan:	He'll soon be your brother, when he marries me.
Goneril:	*(to Regan)* You think he'll marry you? You've got another thing coming!
Regan:	Oh dear—all of a sudden I'm not feeling very well.
Narrator 3:	Regan rushes off to her tent, clutching her stomach, just as Edgar rides into camp. He is no longer disguised as a beggar, but now wears a mask over his face.
Edgar:	If anyone here goes by the name of Edmund, Earl of Gloucester, I wish to challenge him to a duel.
Edmund:	I am the Earl of Gloucester.
Edgar:	Traitor—you are not the rightful Earl. You conspired against the life of your innocent brother and father. You've also conspired against the Duke of Albany. Now prepare to receive your just deserts.
Narrator 1:	Edmund and Edgar fight, and Edgar deals Edmund a deadly blow. Seeing Edmund lying in a pool of blood, Goneril screams and runs from the scene.
Edmund:	*(to Edgar, faintly)* What you have charged me with, I have done—all that and more. Reveal yourself.

Narrator 2:	Edgar removes his mask.
Edmund:	*(faintly)* My brother!
Albany:	*(to Edgar)* Sir—we thought you had fled to the Continent. Where have you hidden yourself?
Narrator 3:	Edgar tells the story of how he has spent the last few weeks. He describes trying to help Gloucester, and watching him finally die.
Edgar:	Father is at peace now, but he died a thousand deaths before the final one.
Edmund:	*(faintly)* Hearing your story, I am filled with remorse.
Narrator 1:	Just then, a servant comes running up, carrying a bloody knife.
Gentleman:	Help! Help!
Albany:	What's this?
Gentleman:	*(to Albany)* This knife came from the heart of Goneril, sir. She confessed to poisoning her sister. Then she stabbed herself.
Edmund:	I had promised myself to both of them. Soon all three of us will be married in death.
Narrator 2:	In the midst of this confusion, Kent rides up.
Kent:	I am looking for my master, the king. Isn't he here? Where is he?
Edmund:	*(in a panic)* Before I die, I wish to do one good deed, despite my own nature. Edgar—run to the prison. Take my sword. Show it to the guards. Save Lear and Cordelia, for they are about to be executed. Goneril and I signed their death warrant. *(faintly)* Hurry now.... Run....
Narrator 3:	Edgar sprints toward the castle as Edmund collapses back, gasping his last breath. A little later, Edgar reappears, leading King Lear, who carries the dead body of Cordelia. Lear holds a feather up to her lips.
Lear:	I think the feather just moved! She's breathing! Oh let her be alive! That would make up for everything.
Kent:	O my good master!
Narrator 1:	Lear looks up and sees Kent.
Lear:	Kent? Is that you? Or Caius?
Kent:	We are one and the same. I have been with you all along.
Lear:	I see, I see. Dear Kent. Look—my darling girl has been hanged!
Narrator 2:	Lear holds up the feather to Cordelia's mouth again. It does not move. He sobs in despair.
Lear:	There's no life in her! Why should a dog, a horse, a rat, have life, while she has none at all? She'll never live again. Never, never, never, never!

Narrator 3:	All of a sudden, he imagines he sees the feather stirring.
Lear:	Look on her lips! Look there, look there!
Narrator 1:	Lear collapses to the ground.
Edgar:	Get a doctor!
Kent:	Oh, let him go! Don't make him endure the torture of this world any longer.
Narrator 2:	Edgar checks Lear for a pulse.
Edgar:	He is gone, indeed.
Kent:	It's a wonder that he even endured so long.
Albany:	*(to servants)* Bear all the bodies out of here. *(to all)* This is a time of mourning. *(to Kent and Edgar)* Friends, you two shall rule the realm and try to hold our bloodied state together.
Kent:	I have a journey on which I must go. My master calls me to join him, and I cannot say no.
Edgar:	The weight of this sad time we must obey—saying what we feel, not what we ought to say. The oldest have endured the most. We that are young shall never see so much or live so long.

Simply Shakespeare: Readers Theatre for Young People is from *Read* magazine, a Weekly Reader publication, in collaboration with Teacher Ideas Press. Edited by Jennifer Kroll. www.weeklyreader.com. www.lu.com/tips. 1–800–541–2086.

CHAPTER 5

Macbeth

By William Shakespeare

Adapted by Kate Davis

Summary

In A.D. 1040 Macbeth, a Scottish thane, or regional leader, is returning from battle when he has a mysterious encounter with three supernatural beings, the "Weird Sisters." The Sisters hail Macbeth as not only the Thane of Glamis (his current title) but also as Thane of Cawdor and King of Scotland. Macbeth is confused by this but later learns that he has, in fact, recently been given the title Thane of Cawdor. Amazed that the Sisters spoke the truth, Macbeth becomes captivated by the idea that he may someday become king. Macbeth's wife, Lady Macbeth, encourages her husband to take bold action to make this prophesied event come to pass, and together the two plot the murder of the current king, King Duncan. Because the king's murder can only be hidden—and the way to the throne smoothed—with additional bloodshed, Macbeth and Lady Macbeth are soon plunged into a deep pit of murder and madness.

Presentation Suggestions

Position Macbeth and Lady Macbeth front and center. Seat the narrators, Maid, Doctor, Criminal, and Servant behind the Macbeths. Place the supernatural beings—the Weird Sisters, Hecate, and Phantoms—in a grouping to one side of the Macbeths. Place Malcolm, Duncan, Captain, General, Ross, Banquo, Macduff, Lennox, and Messenger in a grouping on the other side of the Macbeths.

Props

The Scottish lords can wear plaid. They can wear kilts, if available, or blankets fashioned as kilts. The Weird Sisters and Hecate can wear black or dark colors and witches' hats. A bucket or drum of some kind can be placed in front of them to serve as their cauldron, and they may hold spoons or ladles with which to stir their brew. The phantoms can wear white sheets or scary masks. The doctor can wear a white lab smock or a stethoscope. The maid can wear an apron. Audience members can be given branches with which to play the part of the hidden army advancing on Dunsinane. They can be enlisted to make marching sounds in the background to create tension during Scene 16.

Cast of Characters

(main parts in boldface)
Narrators 1, 2, 3
Hecate, *queen of the witches*
Weird Sisters, 1, 2, 3
Malcolm, *King Duncan's son*
Duncan, *king of Scotland*
Captain, *in Duncan's army*
Ross, *a Scottish nobleman*
Macbeth, *thane of Glamis; later thane of Cawdor and king of Scotland*
Banquo, *a general in the king's army*
Lady Macbeth
Messenger
Macduff, *Thane of Fife*

Lennox, *a Scottish nobleman*
Criminal
Phantoms 1, 2, 3
Maid, *to Lady Macbeth*
Doctor
General, *in Scottish army*
Servant

Macbeth

By William Shakespeare

Adapted by Kate Davis

Scene 1

Narrator 1: The setting is Scotland, the year A.D. 1040 At the edge of a foggy bog, four craggy-faced witches appear. The three Weird Sisters and their queen, Hecate, are plotting chaos for Macbeth as a storm is brewing.

Hecate: (*in a scratchy voice*) Where have you three been since nine?

Weird Sister 1: Singing spells and killing swine.

Weird Sister 2: (*stirring cauldron*) Conjuring tempests on a thane to make some future trouble reign.

Weird Sister 3: Here is a soldier's torn-off thumb to make the curse quickly come!

Hecate: When shall we all meet again—in thunder, lightening, or in rain?

Sister 1: When the storm and uproar's done, when the battle's lost and won.

Sister 2: We'll gather on the barren heath.

Sister 3: There to meet with Thane Macbeth.

Hecate: When the fog is thick and thin, we will hover over him. He'll not know we're here or there, when fair is foul, and foul is fair!

Scene 2

Narrator 2: A war has broken out against Scotland. At a battle camp, King Duncan waits for the results.

Narrator 3: Malcolm, the king's son, and Ross, a nobleman, help a wounded man into Duncan's tent.

Malcolm: The war is over. This courageous captain saved my life.

Duncan: Poor, bleeding man—give me an account of the battle.

Captain: (*weakly*) The Irish ran at us with axes in hand. Then brave Macbeth brandished his sword till it smoked with blooded execution! Swiftly, he carved a path through the army, faced the rebel leader, and cut him from navel to chin.

Duncan:	Worthy Thane Macbeth!
Captain:	No sooner had the Irishman died than the Norwegians attacked.
Malcolm:	The Thane of Cawdor turned and sided with Norway.
Duncan:	Traitor!
Captain:	Macbeth and Banquo redoubled their strokes. But whether they won or not, I cannot say, for I grew faint from wounds.
Duncan:	(*to servant*) Give this man aid!
Ross:	(*to king*) Thanks to Macbeth, the victory fell to us.
Duncan:	Great happiness! But Cawdor has betrayed us. I sentence him to death. Strip him of his title and give it to our hero, Macbeth.

Scene 3

Narrator 1:	Returning from battle, Macbeth and Banquo slog across the heath. Odd shapes seem to appear and disappear in the fog.
Macbeth:	Victory shines, yet the air hangs dismally. So foul and fair a day I have never seen.
Narrator 2:	Suddenly, three withered witches appear out of the mist.
Banquo:	What are these, that look like no inhabitants of earth? (*to sisters*) Are you mortal? I might think you to be women, yet your beards forbid me to believe that.
Macbeth:	Speak, if you can.
Sister 1:	All hail, Macbeth, Thane of Glamis.
Sister 2:	All hail, Macbeth, Thane of Cawdor.
Sister 3:	All hail, Macbeth, that shall be *king* hereafter!
Macbeth:	(*dazedly*) Thane of Glamis I may be, but how can I become Cawdor? The present Cawdor is still alive. And how can I be *king*? That is unbelievable!
Banquo:	Strange sisters, if you can look into the seeds of time, tell me what will grow for *me*.
Sister 1:	Lesser than Macbeth, but greater.
Sister 2:	You shall bring forth kings, yet you shall be none.
Banquo:	Riddles without meaning!
Macbeth:	Why do you stop us on this blasted heath to give us strange prophecies? Tell us more!
Sisters:	All hail, Banquo and Macbeth!
Narrator 3:	Without saying anything more, the Weird Sisters fade into the fog.

Macbeth:	They've vanished, as breath into the wind!
Banquo:	Did you hear what I heard? Or are we hallucinating?
Macbeth:	They said your children shall be kings.
Banquo:	And you—Thane of Cawdor and king!
Narrator 1:	Out of the fog a weary nobleman approaches.
Ross:	Ah, Macbeth, I've found you! I come from the king. He had heard of your victory in battle. He names you the new Thane of Cawdor!
Narrator 2:	Macbeth and Banquo exchange looks of amazement.
Macbeth:	(*as if stunned*) Can this be so? (*to Ross*) Rest from your journey while we consider this.
Ross:	I will. And then the king bids me bring you to him.
Narrator 3:	As Ross sits a way off, Macbeth and Banquo speak softly.
Macbeth:	If those hags know the truth and call me Cawdor, perhaps your children really will be kings!
Banquo:	And you might be king. But beware: There may be great harm in believing the instruments of darkness. They may win us over with small truths, then betray us with more harmful deceptions.
Narrator 1:	Banquo goes over to speak with Ross, leaving Macbeth alone.
Macbeth:	(*to himself*) Harm us how? These supernatural events seem more good than ill, for truly I am now Thane of Cawdor. But king? I hate to think what I would have to do to replace good King Duncan. The image is so horrible, it makes my heart knock at my ribs.
Banquo:	(*calling*) Macbeth, are you ready to go?
Macbeth:	(*to himself*) If chance would make me king, then chance will have to crown me. (*aloud*) Come, friends, let us go to the king.

Scene 4

Narrator 2:	Macbeth and Banquo join Duncan at his royal palace.
Duncan:	Worthy Macbeth! For your loyalty and valor, I owe you more thanks than I can pay.
Macbeth:	Serving you with love and honor is payment in itself.
Duncan:	Banquo, I also hold you near my heart.
Banquo:	My duty is to you alone.
Duncan:	I have planted both of you and will see you grow. Signs of nobleness, like stars, shall shine on all who are deserving. I hereby place the two of you at the right side of my son, Malcolm.

Narrator 3:	Banquo and Macbeth bow.
Duncan:	I also invest Malcolm as Prince of Cumberland. When I am gone, your loyalty shall go to the prince. Now, let us go to your castle in Inverness, Macbeth, and celebrate your new title.
Macbeth:	With pleasure, my king. I will go on ahead and give this joyful news to my wife, so that we might prepare for your visit.
Duncan:	Go, valiant kinsman. We will follow shortly.
Narrator 1:	As he leaves the palace, Macbeth reflects on the changes.
Macbeth:	*(to himself)* Malcolm is now Prince of Cumberland? A great step for him, yet one that lies in my way if I were to seek the throne. I would trip over it . . . unless I leapt over it. . . .
Narrator 2:	Macbeth feels suddenly ashamed of his thoughts.
Macbeth:	Stars, hide your fires. Let not light see my black and deep desires.

Scene 5

Narrator 3:	Macbeth sends a note on ahead to his wife telling her about the witches and his new fortune. At the castle, Lady Macbeth reads her husband's letter.
Macbeth:	*(reading)* So, dear partner in greatness, I am to be the new Thane of Cawdor . . . and maybe more: These women also said I shall be king! Think on how this could take place, but tell no one.
Lady Macbeth:	*(to herself)* My lord dreams of becoming great, but he is too kind to ever make it happen. He has ambition, but he's not sick enough to do what it takes to rise to the position. Yet, if he would *have*, he must *do*.
Narrator 1:	A messenger enters, interrupting Lady Macbeth's thoughts.
Messenger:	My lord sends word that the king is coming.
Lady Macbeth:	The king? Go make ready for his arrival!
Narrator 2:	The messenger obeys.
Lady Macbeth:	*(to herself)* This is a timely stroke of luck. Now I will chase away all that keeps Macbeth from the golden crown. I will see he has what prophecy has promised. Duncan's visit will be . . . a fatal one. Come, spirits, take the softness of my heart away and fill me with cruelty. Let nothing shake my purpose—not remorse or any other weak emotion. Come, thick night, and wrap me in the smoke of hell, so that I cannot see the wounds I make. And let not heaven reach through the blanket of darkness to stop me!
Narrator 3:	Shortly, Macbeth arrives. Lady Macbeth rushes to embrace him.
Lady Macbeth:	Great Thane of Glamis and now of Cawdor! Greater even than both of these—your letter has uplifted me!

Macbeth:	Greetings, my lady. King Duncan and the prince arrive tonight.
Lady Macbeth:	So I have heard. Leave tonight's business to me.
Macbeth:	Have you made plans?
Lady Macbeth:	Aye. Indeed I have. The king shall not see tomorrow's sun.
Narrator 1:	Macbeth looks worried.
Macbeth:	I meant the feast....
Lady Macbeth:	Husband, your face can be read like a book. Listen! If we are to do this deed, you must show welcome in your eye, hand, and speech. You must look like the innocent flower but be the serpent under it.
Macbeth:	But I'm not so sure—
Narrator 2:	Blaring trumpets announce the arrival of the king.
Macbeth:	Go greet him while I wash. (*quietly*) We will speak about his later.
Narrator 3:	Macbeth goes to his chamber, while Lady Macbeth greets the king.
Lady Macbeth:	Welcome, Noble King! Your Majesty honors our house.
Duncan:	Fair hostess, we are your guests tonight. Where is the Thane of Cawdor? We love him highly.
Lady Macbeth:	First, rest from your journey. Then I'll bring him to you.

Scene 6

Narrator 1:	Alone in his room, Macbeth reflects on his wife's words.
Macbeth:	(*to himself*) Would my lady have me assassinate the king? Could I? If it is to be done, it is best done quickly.... Still, there is judgment to be dealt with. If this act were the be-all and end-all—that would be one thing. But the bloody deeds we do return to plague us.
Narrator 2:	Macbeth talks himself out of killing Duncan.
Macbeth:	I am Duncan's kinsman and subject. As his host, I should block the door to those who would harm him, not bear the knife myself! What's more, he is well loved. His death will evoke the pity of all, and their tears will drown the wind. No. I have nothing but ambition to spur me on. And that is not enough.
Narrator 3:	Lady Macbeth comes looking for her husband.
Lady Macbeth:	The king asks for you.
Macbeth:	You and I must go no further with plans to remove him. He has just honored me with a new title. People think well of me now.
Lady Macbeth:	(*angrily*) Has your hope of being king gone pale? Or are you afraid to be the same in action as in desire? What are you, a man or a coward?

Macbeth:	(*bristling*) Peace, woman! You question my manhood? I dare do everything a man would do!
Lady Macbeth:	What beast made you change your mind? When it was a vague idea, you dared to do it; *then* you were a man. Now that you have a real opportunity, you shrink from it. If I had sworn to do something, I would kill my own child before I would break my vow!
Macbeth:	What if we fail?
Lady Macbeth:	Fail? Set the arrow of your courage right! We will not fail. When Duncan is asleep, I will ply his men with wine till they lose all reason and memory. When they sleep like pigs and the king is unguarded, you and I can do anything. We'll use his attendants' daggers so they will bear the guilt.
Macbeth:	You have more mettle than ten men. But I ask you, will others believe that Duncan's own servants have done the deed?
Lady Macbeth:	They will when they hear how loudly we roar with grief.
Macbeth:	Then I'm settled. I summon my strength to the feat. Let's go to the king's feast. False face must hide what the false heart does know.

Scene 7

Narrator 1:	The banquet ends very late that night. Finally, the king retires. Macbeth paces the halls, thinking of the crime he may commit. In the dark, he comes upon Banquo.
Banquo:	Who goes there?
Macbeth:	A friend—I, Macbeth. Why are you wandering here?
Banquo:	I cannot get to sleep. Cursed thoughts and visions keep appearing to me. Why aren't *you* at rest?
Macbeth:	Thoughts of the king have kept me awake—whether he was pleased with the feast, that is.
Banquo:	I'm sure he was. Tonight I dreamed of the Weird Sisters. They told you some truth, didn't they?
Macbeth:	(*lying*) I haven't thought about them in a while. *(yawning)* Milady is fixing me a tonic and will ring a bell when it is ready. Try to sleep, now.
Banquo:	Thanks, sir. And you, too.
Narrator 2:	When Macbeth is alone, be begins to hallucinate. A knife appears.
Macbeth:	(*unbelieving*) Is this a dagger I see before me, the handle toward my hand? *(to knife)* Come, let me clutch you.
Narrator 3:	He swipes at the hovering dagger but cannot grasp it.
Macbeth:	I see you but cannot grasp you. Are you a dagger of the mind?
Narrator 1:	The dagger beings to drip.

Macbeth:	(*with horror*) Now your blade is smeared with blood! Lack of sleep and wicked nightmares are playing tricks on my mind.
Narrator 2:	The phantom dagger floats toward the king's chamber. As if hypnotized, Macbeth follows.
Macbeth:	You lead the way I was going. So my horror follows your horror. Let me move like a ghost, so that my steps are not heard.
Narrator 3:	A bell tolls. It is Lady Macbeth's signal that all is clear.
Macbeth:	I go to do what I must. Duncan, hear not this sorry bell, for it is your death knell.

Scene 8

Narrator 1:	Lady Macbeth is sneaking through the castle halls. She see that Duncan's door is open.
Lady Macbeth:	Macbeth is about it. The drugged attendants are snoring.
Macbeth:	(*from within*) What ho!
Lady Macbeth:	(*fretfully*) Suppose they've woken and the business is not done? I laid their daggers out so he couldn't miss them!
Narrator 2:	Macbeth stumbles out into the hallway.
Macbeth:	(*nervously*) I have done the deed. Did you hear a noise?
Lady Macbeth:	When?
Macbeth:	Just now.
Lady Macbeth:	I heard you speak.
Macbeth:	I didn't speak. One of the servants laughed in his sleep; the other cried, "Murder!"
Narrator 3:	Macbeth stares at his bloody hands.
Macbeth:	This is a sorry sight.
Lady Macbeth:	Do not regret your action.
Narrator 1:	All of a sudden, Macbeth jumps, frightened.
Macbeth:	Did you hear that? I swear just now I heard a voice saying, "Sleep no more. Macbeth murders sleep."
Lady Macbeth:	Think not on these deeds, or they will make us mad.
Macbeth:	(*in despair*) Macbeth shall never sleep again.
Lady Macbeth:	Snap out of it! A sick mind will bend your noble strength. Get some water and wash this filthy witness from your hand. And why did you bring these daggers with you? They must lie next to his attendants! Take them back and smear *their* hands with blood.

Macbeth:	I cannot. I dare not look again on what I have done.
Lady Macbeth:	Do you forget your purpose! Here, I'll do it myself!
Narrator 2:	She enters Duncan's bedchamber, replaces the knives, and smears blood on the servants to make it look as if they killed the king. Then she hurries back to her husband, who stands brooding in the hallway.
Lady Macbeth:	Don't be so lost in thought. A little water clears us of this deed.
Macbeth:	All Neptune's ocean will not wash this blood from my hand.

Scene 9

Narrator 3:	At the crack of dawn, Lennox and McDuff, two noblemen, arrive at Inverness looking for the king. Macbeth, who has not slept, hurries to open the door when he hears the knocking.
Macduff:	(*to Macbeth*) The king has asked us to call for him early.
Macbeth:	Yes, I heard he has to leave today. Come, here is his room.
Narrator 1:	As McDuff enters to wake the king, Lennox and Macbeth wait in the hall.
Lennox:	(*to Macbeth*) Last night, during the storm, strange screams of death were heard. Some say the earth itself did shake.
Macbeth:	It was a rough night.
Macduff:	O horror!
Narrator 2:	Macduff rushes back out of the room.
Macbeth & Lennox:	What is it?
Macduff:	Unholy murder! His majesty has been murdered!
Macbeth & Lennox:	Murdered?
Macduff:	The king is dead! Go see for yourselves. Murder! Treason!
Narrator 3:	Lennox and Macbeth rush into the king's chamber.
Macduff:	(*shouting*) Ring the alarm! Banquo! Malcolm! Awake! Rise up and witness this horror!
Narrator 1:	A bell is rung throughout the castle. Lady Macbeth, Banquo, and Malcolm run into the hall.
Lady Macbeth:	What awfulness calls us?
Macduff:	Our royal master (*to Malcolm*) and father is murdered.
Lady Macbeth:	Woe, alas! In our house?
Banquo:	Dear Duff, say it isn't so!
Malcolm:	Who has done this?

Narrator 2: Lennox and Macbeth stumble back out of the bedchamber.

Lennox: His servants' hands and daggers are smeared with blood.

Macbeth: I could not hold back my fury. I killed those murderers.

Macduff: Why did you do that?

Macbeth: Who can be wise when they see their king dead and next to him, his slayers. My love outran my reason.

Lady Macbeth: (*fainting*) Oh, help us!

Narrator 3: As everyone tends to her, Malcolm slumps against the wall.

Malcolm: (*to himself, suspiciously*) Hold off, sorrow. To show sadness is easy for a false man.

Banquo: Let us investigate this bloody piece of work.

Macbeth: Get dressed and ready yourselves to fight this treason, then meet me in the hall.

Narrator 1: All leave but the prince.

Malcolm: (*hiding*) Not I. It is not safe here. My father's servants would never have killed their lord! *I* ride for England. Who murdered a king would also remove a prince.

Scene 10

Narrator 2: In the coming days, King Duncan is buried.

Narrator 3: When Macbeth learns that the king's son has disappeared, he blames Duncan's murder on Malcolm.

Narrator 1: Prince Malcolm cannot rule Scotland from England, so the crown goes to the next in line—Macbeth. He is made king and moves into the palace. Banquo and his son, Fleance, visit.

Banquo: (*to himself*) The witches were right: Macbeth now has it all—Glamis, Cawdor, and King. But I fear he played foully for it.

Narrator 2: The new king and queen welcome Banquo to court.

Macbeth: (*to lords and ladies*) Our chief guest has arrived! Tonight we shall have a solemn supper. You will attend, won't you, Banquo?

Banquo: (*guardedly*) My duty is to do what Your Highness commands.

Macbeth: I hear that Malcolm is making up tales. He denies killing his father. What do you think of that?

Banquo: Counsel me on what I should think.

Narrator 3: When Macbeth is alone again, he paces nervously.

Macbeth: (*to himself*) Banquo bears himself royally and has clear sight and wisdom. I fear no one else the way I fear him.

Narrator 1: Macbeth calls for a servant, who enters, bowing.

Macbeth: Find me two men who need work.

Narrator 2: The servant bows and leaves, and Macbeth returns to his dark thoughts.

Macbeth: The sisters said Banquo would father a line of kings. Have I murdered Duncan only to see Banquo's sons take my crown?

Narrator 3: A little later, the servant returns with two rough peasants. He leaves them with Macbeth.

Criminal: Why does the king call upon men of misfortune like us?

Macbeth: Your low fortune is the fault of Lord Banquo. He is an enemy of the common folk and me.

Criminal: For a fee or a favor, we will do away with him for you, Sire.

Macbeth: Strike him down for good. And see that his son, Fleance, embraces the same fate. Be my assistants in this and I will see that you have new positions in life. But keep this business quiet.

Criminals: It is done, Sire.

Scene 11

Narrator 1: That evening, the king proceeds to supper with the queen.

Lady Macbeth: You seem so preoccupied, my lord. Have we gained what we desired only to lose our joy?

Macbeth: I am afflicted by terrible nightmares. I'd be better off with the dead, whom we've sent to peace.

Lady Macbeth: What's done is done.

Macbeth: While Banquo lives, my mind is full of scorpions.

Lady Macbeth: Forget him. Be bright with your guests tonight, or they will guess our secret.

Narrator 2: Macbeth and Lady Macbeth enter the banquet hall.

Macbeth: Hearty welcome! Sit and partake!

Narrator 3: But before the king sits, he is called aside by one of the criminals.

Macbeth: Is Banquo dispatched?

Criminal: His throat is well cut.

Macbeth: And his son the same?

Criminal: Fleance has escaped.

Macbeth: Fool! Go look for him!

Narrator 1: Macbeth stumbles back.

Macbeth:	(*to himself*) The walls bind me. I feel a fit coming on. . . .
Lady Macbeth:	(*quietly*) My lord, you must appear more cheerful!
Macbeth:	(*trying*) A toast to all—good health in body . . . and in mind.
Narrator 2:	Macbeth approaches his chair on the platform, but it is occupied—by Banquo's ghost!
Macbeth:	(*angrily*) Who is this?
Lennox:	Why don't you sit, Sire?
Macbeth:	The table is full.
Lennox:	No, here's a seat for you.
Narrator 3:	No one else but Macbeth can see that Banquo—pale, bloody, accusing—sits in the royal chair.
Macbeth:	(*questioning*) Banquo?
Ross:	He has not come. His absence breaks his promise.
Macbeth:	(*to chair, seemingly crazed*) Do not shake your gory locks at me! You cannot say I did this deed!
Narrator 1:	Lady Macbeth quickly rises and tries to cover for the king.
Lady Macbeth:	Pay no attention to my husband. He often has strange fits—a condition from childhood.
Macbeth:	(*to Lady Macbeth*) Strange indeed! (*to Banquo's ghost*) Your face appalls the devil. Get back to the grave!
Ross:	Gentlemen, let us leave. His Highness is not well.
Lady Macbeth:	No, stay! Sit and eat. You will offend him if you notice his infirmity. Pay no attention to him, and his fit will pass more quickly.
Narrator 2:	She grabs Macbeth and speaks to him in an angry whisper.
Lady Macbeth:	Fie, for shame! You're looking at an empty chair!
Macbeth:	There was a time, when the brains were out, a man would die. But now dead men rise again and push us from our stools.
Lady Macbeth:	Stop this! Your guests are watching!
Macbeth:	(*in embarrassment*) Worthy friends, do not wonder at me. Fill my glass. Health to all!
Lady Macbeth:	You've ruined the mood.
Macbeth:	How can you look on such a sight and not go pale?
Ross:	What sight, my lord?
Lady Macbeth:	Questions will enrage him. It might be best if you all go.
Lennox:	(*leaving*) Good night, then. Better health, Your Majesty.

Lady Macbeth:	(*to Macbeth*) What is all this?
Macbeth:	I have had Banquo killed. Yet he haunts me here. Say, why isn't Macduff here?
Lady Macbeth:	You worry too much. It is unmanly. Go get some sleep.
Macbeth:	Yes. Sleep. Fear abuses me. I have stepped so far in blood that I should wade no more.

Scene 12

Narrator 3:	The next day, Macbeth seeks the witches to foretell his fate. He finds them in a cave.
Narrator 1:	Hecate and the Weird Sisters are stirring a black kettle.
Sister 1:	Round about the cauldron go; in the poisoned entrails throw. Toad with sweating venom got, boil first in the charmed pot.
All:	Double, double, toil and trouble; fire burn, and cauldron bubble.
Sister 2:	Fillet of snake, boil and bake; eye of newt and toe of frog, wool of bat and tongue of dog.
Sister 3:	Lizard's leg and owlet's wing, make the potion's magic sting.
All:	Double, double, toil and trouble; fire burn, and cauldron bubble.
Hecate:	By the pricking of my thumbs, something wicked this way comes!
Narrator 2:	Macbeth enters the cave.
Macbeth:	How now, my midnight hags! What does my future hold?
Hecate:	Our spell will show you.
Narrator 3:	Thunder resounds as an armored head rises from the pot.
Phantom 1:	Beware Macduff! Beware the Thane of Fife!
Macbeth:	(*to the head*) Why should I? What will happen?
Narrator 1:	The phantom does not answer and disappears. Another phantom appears.
Phantom 2:	Be bloody and bold. None of woman born shall harm Macbeth.
Macbeth:	*All* are born of women. Thus I have no need to fear *anyone*—not even Macduff!
Narrator 2:	A third phantom appears—a crowned child with a tree in his hand.
Phantom 3:	Be courageous and proud, for Macbeth shall never be vanquished until Great Birnam Wood shall come to Dunsinane.
Macbeth:	Ha! A forest cannot unfix its roots and move. I shall live long! But tell me—will Banquo's children be kings?

Narrator 3: A vision appears, showing eight kings standing in line. The last one holds a mirror reflecting an endless line of heirs. Banquo's ghost follows, laughing in scorn.

Macbeth: (*in horror*) NOOOO!

All sisters: (*cackling*) Ha ha ha!

Macbeth: Curses on you all!

Narrator 1: Shaken, Macbeth rides back to the palace and steals inside. Around a corner, he overhears Macduff's wife telling a nobleman that she doesn't know where her husband has gone.

Narrator 2: Macbeth grows furious.

Macbeth: (*to himself*) If Macduff has turned against me and fled, then he too shall taste my wrath!

Scene 13

Narrator 3: Macduff, Thane of Fife, had gone to England to find Scotland's true heir, Prince Malcolm.

Macduff: (*to prince*) Scotland is in chaos. Banquo is murdered, and Macbeth blames Fleance, his son.

Malcolm: Just as he blamed *me* for *my* father's death when I fled. That is too much coincidence. Macduff, you thought Macbeth was honest, yet he is treacherous!

Macduff: I've lost all hope for him.

Malcolm: Our country sinks beneath his yoke. It weeps, it bleeds, and each day a new gash is added to its wounds. Macbeth is deceitful, malicious, smacking of every sin that has a name.

Macduff: Then raise an army and return to claim your throne!

Malcolm: I have none of the graces that make a good king—not justice, mercy, or patience. I am too quarrelsome, too greedy. With power in my hands, peace and unity would never reign.

Macduff: (*in despair*) O Scotland! When will your wholesome days return? Your king was a saint, but your prince feels unfit to rule. My hope is gone. I banish myself from Scotland!

Malcolm: No, good Macduff! Your passion moves me to put off these weak thoughts. I am young and inexperienced, but I pledge myself to your honor and to my country.

Narrator 1: As he speaks, a nobleman from Scotland bursts in.

Macduff: Lord Ross! What news from Scotland?

Ross: (*breathlessly*) I have ridden all night to find you. At home, more men have grown distrustful of Macbeth. They have left the court and are ready to fight with us against him.

Macduff: Then I will rally the thanes. How fares my wife?

Ross: (*hesitantly*) If only I could howl the words where none could hear . . .

Macduff: (*worriedly*) What words? (*shaking him*) Let me hear it!

Ross: Your wife . . . has been savagely slaughtered.

Malcolm: Merciful heaven!

Macduff: And my children?

Ross: Wife, babies, servants—everyone was murdered that could be found. Your castle was surprised.

Macduff: (*in shock*) All my pretty ones? All that was precious to me? At one fell swoop? Who did this?

Ross: The same as killed Duncan.

Narrator 2: Macduff collapses to the ground in anguish.

Macduff: God rest my family.

Malcolm: Let grief convert to anger and be your sword! The King of England has offered me an army 10,000 strong and a general to lead them. Let us march on Dunsinane and rout out the bloody tyrant!

Macduff: (*seething*) Heaven bring me face to face with this fiend of Scotland—and he shall not escape!

Malcolm & Ross: Vengeance!

Scene 14

Narrator 3: In Macbeth's castle, the queen's maid talks with a doctor.

Maid: Every night I see her rise from her bed and sleepwalk.

Doctor: Has she uttered anything?

Maid: I dare not say. Shh—she's here.

Narrator 1: As they peer down the hall, Lady Macbeth walks as if in a trance, carrying a candle. She sets it down.

Doctor: Look how she rubs her hands together.

Maid: She does that over and over again, as if washing her hands.

Lady Macbeth: (*raving*) Out, damned spot! Out, I say! Fie, my lord! What need we fear who knows it? No one has power over us. Yet, who would have thought the old man to have had so much blood in him?

Doctor: Did you hear that?

Lady Macbeth:	(*madly*) The Thane of Fife had a wife. Where is she now? (*rubbing again*) Will these hands never be clean? No more killing, please, my lord! You'll ruin everything!
Maid:	What has she known?
Lady Macbeth:	Here's the smell of blood still. All the perfumes of Arabia will not sweeten this little hand.
Doctor:	This disease is beyond me. She needs a priest, not a doctor.
Lady Macbeth:	Banquo is buried, I tell you; he can't come out of his grave!
Doctor:	Foul whisperings!
Lady Macbeth:	To bed, to bed. What's done cannot be undone.
Doctor:	Unnatural deeds do breed unnatural troubles. (*to maid*) Look after her and listen to what she might confess. Infected minds discharge secrets to their pillows.

Scene 15

Narrator 2:	On heath and plains, the Scottish army marches towards Dunsinane to gather with Malcolm, Macduff, and the English forces.
Lennox:	We will join the English troops near Birnam Wood. What news do we have of the tyrant?
Messenger:	He is fortified in his castle. Some say he is mad.
Lennox:	Now he feels his secret murders sticking on his hands.
General:	Scotland is in revolt.
Lennox:	Now his title hangs loose about him, like a giant's robe upon a dwarfish thief.
Narrator 3:	Meanwhile, back in the castle at Dunsinane, Macbeth prattles about overconfidently, with blind pride.
Macbeth:	(*to servant*) Bring me no more reports of rebellion. Nothing can touch me "till Great Birnam Wood shall come to Dunsinane," or so the Sisters said. And what is Malcolm? Born from woman like everyone—he has no power over me. My mind and heart shall never sag with doubt or shake with fear!
Servant:	(*in terror*) Soldiers are coming—there are ten thousand of them!
Macbeth:	I'll fight till the flesh is hacked from my bones. My armor!
Narrator 1:	As the servant runs to get it, the queen's doctor enters.
Macbeth:	What news of my lady?
Doctor:	Her mind is very troubled.
Macbeth:	Can't you cure a diseased mind? Pluck sorrow from a memory? Cleanse the stuff that weighs a heart?

Doctor: For that, a patient must minister to herself.

Macbeth: I will have none of that. (*shouting down the hall*) Bring me my armor! I will not be afraid of death and bane, till Birnam Forest shall come to Dunsinane!

Scene 16

Narrator 2: Back on the battlefront, Malcolm addresses the armies.

Malcolm: Here at Birnam Wood we join to fight the tyrant! Soldiers, cut down a branch or bow, then bear it before you to hide our numbers.

General: Macbeth keeps in his castle. Those few he commands do only what they're told; they have no heart in it.

Malcolm: Then let us advance!

Narrator 3: Nearly alone, Macbeth in armor clatters around the castle like a chain against cold stone.

Macbeth: Hang out our banners! Our castle's strength will laugh them to scorn. (*cackling insanely*) Let them lie outside the walls till famine and fever eat them alive!

Narrator 1: A scream pierces the air.

Maids: Eeeeeeeee!

Macbeth: What is that noise?

Servant: The cry of a woman.

Narrator 2: The servant runs towards the sound, but Macbeth is unfazed.

Macbeth: Have I forgotten the taste of fear? I have supped so full with horrors that terrifying sounds no longer frighten me.

Narrator 3: The servant returns, looking upset.

Servant: My lord—the queen is dead!

Narrator 1: Despite his previous calm, the king sinks onto his throne aghast.

Macbeth: (*gloomily*) Tomorrow, and tomorrow, and tomorrow creeps in this petty place from day to day, to the last syllable of recorded time; and all our yesterdays have lighted fools the way to dusty death. Out, out, brief candle! Life's but a walking shadow, a poor player that struts and frets his hour upon the stage and then is heard no more. It is a tale told by an idiot, full of sound and fury, signifying nothing.

Narrator 2: A messenger dashes in.

Messenger: I don't know how to report what I just saw. As I stood on the ramparts, Birnam Wood began to move!

Macbeth: (*in terror*) LIAR!

Messenger:	Go see for yourself.
Macbeth:	The phantom said, "Fear not, till Birnam Wood shall come to Dunsinane"—and now . . . Birnam Wood is moving toward Dunsinane! Ring the alarm!
Narrator 3:	Meanwhile, in the distance . . .
Macduff:	Sound the trumpets!
Malcolm:	Throw down your leafy screens, men. We're near enough!
Narrator 1:	Macbeth peers out a window and sees the army advancing.
Macbeth:	Blow, wind, as you may. I will laugh their swords to score, for all men are "of woman born."
Narrator 2:	Macduff storms the castle.
Macduff:	(*calling*) Tyrant, show your face! Fortune, let me find him, for I will avenge my family's death!
Narrator 3:	Sword drawn, Macduff rounds a corner and spies Macbeth.
Macduff:	Turn, hellhound, turn!
Macbeth:	Get back. My soul is charged to draw your blood.
Macduff:	I will not waste words on a villain. My voice is in my sword!
Macbeth:	Let fall your sword! I bear a charmed life, which will not yield to one "of woman born."
Macduff:	Despair that charm, for I was ripped from my mother's womb before her time was due!
Macbeth:	(*in shock*) Curses on your tongue! I will not fight with you.
Macduff:	Yield then. We'll strap you to a pole and display you as a monster, with a sign reading, "Here hangs the tyrant."
Macbeth:	I will not yield! Even though Birnam Wood has come to Dunsinane and you are of no woman born, still I will fight to the last. Lay on, Macduff, and damned be he who cries "enough!"
Narrator 1:	Filled with passion for his country and family, Macduff brandishes his sword with skill.
Narrator 2:	Sparks spit as metal strikes metal. Two passionate beasts fight to the death, like armored dragons.
Narrator 3:	Through the halls, the sound of soldiers' boots echo like thunder.
Soldiers all:	Die, murderous villain! For Scotland!
Narrator 1:	Malcolm enters the hall. As he does so, Macduff strikes one last triumphal blow. He grasps the bloody head of Macbeth.
Macduff:	(*to Malcolm*) Hail, the new king! For so you are. Behold the usurper's cursed head.

All: Hail, King of Scotland!

Malcolm: My thanes and kinsmen: Call home our exiled friends who fled the tyranny of this dead butcher and his fiendish queen, who died by her own violent hand. You shall be Scotland's honored earls. By the grace of Grace, our thanks to all. And now each one we invite to see us crowned.

Simply Shakespeare: Readers Theatre for Young People is from *Read* magazine, a Weekly Reader publication, in collaboration with Teacher Ideas Press. Edited by Jennifer Kroll. www.weeklyreader.com. www.lu.com/tips. 1–800–541–2086.

CHAPTER 6

A Midsummer Night's Dream

By William Shakespeare

Adapted by Kate Davis

 Summary

Hermia, a young Athenian woman, is in love with Lysander. Her father, however, insists that she marry Demetrius, another of her suitors. Rather than marry Demetrius, Hermia decides to run off with Lysander. She tells her friend Helena of her plan. Hoping to gain the love and thanks of Demetrius, Helena exposes Hermia's plan to him. When Lysander and Hermia run off, Demetrius follows close behind, with Helena following him. The four lovers end up in an enchanted forest filled with interfering sprites and fairies. Oberon, the king of the spirits, takes pity on Helena when he sees how much she loves Demetrius and how badly Demetrius treats her. Oberon decides to cast a spell on Demetrius so that he will return Helena's love. However, identities become confused, the spell is bungled, and much merriment results.

Presentation Suggestions

You may wish to designate part of the room "Athens" and part "the Enchanted Forest." Seat or stand Puck, Titania, Oberon, Quince, Bottom, and Spirits 1 and 2 in the Enchanted Forest. Seat Egeus, the duke, Demetrius, Lysander, Hermia, and Helena in Athens. Leave open chairs or floor cushions in the "Enchanted Forest" area, and move the lovers, Duke, and Egeus to the forest at appropriate moments in the play. Place the narrators behind the other cast members or off to the side.

 Props

If you use the presentation strategy above, you may wish to add scenery touches to help establish the two separate sections of the room. Plants can be placed or green cloths draped in the forest area. Statues or pillars could help establish the other section of the room as Athens. Oberon, Puck, Titania, and the spirits can be dressed in earth tones and may go barefoot. Titania and the spirits may wear skirts and flowers in their hair. The Athenians should wear bolder tones. Bottom and Quince can wear flannel shirts and Bottom can put on and take off paper donkey ears. Puck can hold a real or plastic flower blossom with which to charm the lovers.

Cast of Characters

(main parts in boldface)
Narrators 1, 2, 3
Hermia, *in love with Lysander*
Egeus, *father of Hermia*
Duke of Athens
Demetrius, *promised by Egeus to Hermia*
Lysander, *in love with Hermia*
Helena, *Hermia's friend*
Oberon, *king of the spirits*
Puck, *impish trickster and Oberon's messenger; also called Robin Goodfellow*
Spirits 1, 2
Titania, *queen of the spirits*
Quince, *a carpenter*
Bottom, *a weaver*

A Midsummer Night's Dream

By William Shakespeare

Adapted by Kate Davis

Scene 1

Narrator 1: Just outside the palace of the Duke of Athens, a love dispute disrupts the peace. Shouting is heard in the courtyard. The duke steps outside.

Narrator 2: Egeus has entered the palace grounds, dragging his daughter, Hermia, behind him. With them are two young men.

Narrator 3: Hermia is trying to pull free of her father's hold.

Hermia: *(shouting)* You cannot make me!

Egeus: *(shouting)* I am your father. I can do with you as I wish!

Narrator 1: When they see the duke, both father and daughter stop shouting and smile politely at him.

Egeus: Our noble duke! How are you?

Duke of Athens: What's going on here?

Egeus: I have come to complain about my daughter, Hermia.

Narrator 2: Egeus gestures to Demetrius.

Egeus: I have given this good man, Demetrius, consent to marry Hermia.

Narrator 3: Egeus points his finger angrily at Lysander.

Egeus: But this man has bewitched my daughter's heart. He has given her flowers and sweets and sung her songs by moonlight. He has turned her obedience as a daughter to stubbornness. And now Hermia refuses to marry the man I have chosen.

Duke: What say you, Hermia? Demetrius is a worthy gentleman.

Hermia: So is Lysander.

Duke: Yes, he is. But your father sees Demetrius as the mate for you.

Hermia: *(boldly)* I wish my father looked with my eyes.

Duke: *(scolding her)* Hear me well, fair maid. To you, your father should be as a god. You must yield to him.

Hermia: And what if I refuse?

Duke: Then the law is that you must either die or take the vow of a nun. I cannot change the laws of Athens. Therefore, Hermia, question your desires carefully.

Narrator 1: Hermia does not hesitate.

Hermia: I would rather die than give myself to a man I do not love! Besides, my good friend Helena loves Demetrius. Let him marry *her*.

Demetrius: Helena? *(laughing)* I do not want Helena. I want you.

Lysander: I've got an idea, Demetrius. Egeus loves you. Why don't you marry *him*?

Duke: Enough!

Narrator 2: Changing his tone, Lysander appeals to the duke.

Lysander: Hear me, my lord. I am every bit as good as Demetrius. My background and fortune match his. But my love for Hermia far exceeds his. Why should I not deserve her?

Duke: The law is the law. *(to Hermia)* By tomorrow, you must make up your mind. Do as your father wishes or, by the law, you shall die or be sent away forever to live as a nun.

Scene 2

Narrator 3: After the others leave, Hermia and Lysander linger in the palace courtyard. Hermia begins to cry.

Hermia: Oh why must I choose love by another's eyes?

Lysander: *(comfortingly)* Why is your cheek so pale? The course of true love never did run smooth. Hear me, gentle Hermia: I have a plan.

Narrator 1: Hermia stops crying. Lysander looks over his shoulder to be sure no one can hear.

Lysander: I have a widow aunt. She has no child and thinks of me as her only son. She lives far from Athens. The law cannot pursue us there.

Hermia: *(sounding encouraged)* Go on.

Lysander: If you love me, then sneak out of your father's house tonight. I'll wait for you in the woods out of town. We'll go to my aunt and be married. Will you do it?

Hermia: *(very happily)* Oh, Lysander, yes! By all the vows that ever men have broke or ever women spoke, I will be there. I swear it!

Narrator 2: As they embrace, Helena enters the courtyard, surprising the two lovers.

Hermia:	Fair Helena!
Helena:	You call *me* fair? Demetrius thinks of your eyes as bright stars and your voice a sweet melody. He loves *you*, not me. How do you sway his heart?
Hermia:	I frown upon him, yet he loves me still.
Helena:	I smile upon him, yet he hates me still.
Hermia:	The more I hate him, the more he follows me.
Helena:	The more I love him, the more he hates me.
Lysander:	Tomorrow that may all change.
Helena:	*(suspiciously)* Why? What then?
Narrator 3:	Hermia knows she should keep their plans a secret, but she cannot contain her excitement.
Hermia:	Lysander and I are running away. Once I am gone, Demetrius will surely return to you.
Narrator 1:	Hermia hugs her friend.
Hermia:	Lysander and I shall meet in the wood where you and I often traded secrets. Then we shall flee Athens. Farewell, Helena.
Narrator 2:	Lysander and Hermia hurry away.
Helena:	*(sadly)* I am as fair as Hermia—fairer—yet Demetrius does not see it. I guess love looks not with the eyes but with the mind.
Narrator 3:	Helena suddenly has an idea.
Helena:	Maybe I can win Demetrius's heart by telling him of Hermia's flight. Yes! He'll be so grateful, he'll fall for me.

Scene 3

Narrator 1:	That night, the enchanted forest in which Hermia will meet Lysander is speckled with fireflies. But sparks of a different sort also fill the air. A quarrel between the king and queen of the woodland spirits has been brewing.
Oberon:	*(pacing)* I must have that changeling boy that Titania found! She has taken him into her train of fairies and is keeping him with her, but I want him to serve me and run with me through the forest!
Narrator 2:	A short way off, pixies and spirits weave their charms over flowers and brambles. Robin Goodfellow, or "Puck," the spirit king's impish messenger, flies in.
Puck:	What are you up to, spirits?
Spirit 1:	Over hill and dale, from bush to briar, flood and fire . . .

Spirit 2:	. . . we wander seeking dewdrops here and place them in a blossom's ear.
Spirits 1, 2:	Soon our spirit queen comes.
Puck:	You'd do well to keep your queen away from here. Good King Oberon is in these parts, and he's in a foul mood.
Spirit 1:	Here she comes now.
Spirit 2:	And he as well!
Narrator 3:	When they see Oberon, the spirits immediately scatter.
Oberon:	*(annoyed)* Ill met by moonlight, Titania.
Titania:	Ill met yourself!
Oberon:	Wait—don't walk away from me! Am I not your lord?
Titania:	Not when you act so jealously. Your brawling so disturbs my pixies' work. They can no longer keep fog from the land or frost from off the rose. Instead they run to hide in acorn cups. Nature itself is so confused, the world no longer knows which season is which.
Oberon:	A simple remedy will mend all that, Titania: Give me the child!
Titania:	Cease your pleading, Oberon. He's mine. Leave us to our work. My elves and I fly off—away!
Narrator 1:	Titania departs.
Oberon:	*(muttering after her)* Go if you like. I'll torment you for this stubbornness!
Narrator 2:	Oberon has a devious idea and summons his assistant.
Oberon:	Come here, Puck. Remember that exotic purple flower I showed you once? A single drop of its juice will make a person fall madly in love with the next creature she sees. Go quickly. Fetch me that herb!
Puck:	I'll circle the earth in a flash and bring it to you!
Oberon:	When Titania sleeps, I'll drop this juice onto her eyes. When she awakes, she'll pursue with the soul of love whatever next she looks upon—be it bear or monkey or bull! I'll not remove the charm until she yields the boy to me.

Scene 4

Narrator 3:	Having heard of Hermia's escape, Demetrius searches through the woods for her. Helena shadows him. They enter Oberon's domain.
Oberon:	What mortals are these? I'll make myself invisible and eavesdrop.
Narrator 1:	Demetrius stops. Helena, right on his heels, bumps smack into him.

Demetrius:	Stop following me! You said Lysander and Hermia would be here; now where are they?
Narrator 2:	Helena looks longingly into Demetrius's face.
Demetrius:	For the last time, I say: I do *not* love you.
Helena:	Even though you tell me that, I love you all the more. You draw me like a magnet, and my heart is true as steel. Use me, neglect me—anything. Just let me follow you.
Demetrius:	*(disgustedly)* I am sick when I look on you.
Helena:	And I am sick when I look *not* on you.
Demetrius:	*(in exasperation)* Listen. A girl like you shouldn't be roaming about in a place like this at night.
Helena:	It is not night when I see your face.
Demetrius:	*(threateningly)* Go back to Athens before I do you some mischief!
Narrator 3:	He reaches menacingly toward his sword in an attempt to scare her off.
Helena:	You've already done my heart mischief. You've broken it. And I would make a heaven of hell, were I to die upon the hand I love so well.
Narrator 1:	Demetrius runs off, with Helena trailing him. Oberon, still watching unnoticed, feels sorry for Helena and decides to help her.
Oberon:	I promise that before that young man leaves this grove, it will be *he* who follows *you* seeking love.
Narrator 2:	Puck suddenly appears.
Puck:	My King, here is the purple flower you requested.
Oberon:	Ah, give it to me. I know a bank where wild thyme blows. There Titania takes her sleep at night. I shall with this juice cause her to fantasize.
Narrator 3:	Oberon draws Puck closer.
Oberon:	Listen carefully, Puck. I want you to search the forest for a sweet young woman and an arrogant man who scorns her. Drop this juice into his eyes so that the next thing he spies is this lady. You will know him by his Athenian clothes.
Puck:	I am your devoted servant and will do as you wish. Fear not.

Scene 5

Narrator 1:	In another part of the forest, Titania prepares to rest.
Titania:	Come now, pixies, spirits, urchins, elves. Sing me to sleep.

Spirit 1: Spotted snakes with double tongue, thorny hedgehogs, be not seen. Newts and blind worms, do no wrong. Come not near our pixie queen.

Spirit 2: Away now, all is well.

Narrator 2: When Titania is sleeping, Oberon tiptoes to her and squeezes the juice on her eyes.

Oberon: *(whispering in her ear)* What you see when you awake, do for thy own true love take. Be it beast or boar with bristled hair, wake when some vile thing is near.

Narrator 3: King Oberon disappears.

Scene 6

Narrator 1: Meanwhile, nearby, Lysander and Hermia stumble exhausted through the forest.

Lysander: We've lost our way from so much wandering. You look faint, love. Let's take a little rest.

Hermia: That's a good idea. But since we're not married yet, move off a bit and find another bed. On this bank, I'll rest my head.

Lysander: *(pleadingly)* My heart is already yours. Our two hearts are one.

Hermia: Still, for virtue's sake, lie over there.

Narrator 2: She points to a spot not far away. Lysander obediently goes to lie down a little way away from Hermia.

Hermia: Good night, my love.

Narrator 3: No sooner are the two asleep, than Puck wanders past Lysander.

Puck: Through the forest I have gone, but no Athenian have I found to drop this flower magic on. But wait—who is this here? He wears the clothes of Athens; it must be he who scorns the maid, as Oberon described.

Narrator 1: Puck spots Hermia.

Puck: And here is the pretty rejected soul lying off a bit.

Narrator 2: Puck drops the potent juice onto Lysander's eyelids.

Puck: All the power of this charm I throw. When you awake, new love you'll know.

Narrator 3: Puck quickly disappears. Soon after, Demetrius enters the area where the lovers lie sleeping. Helena is still tagging along behind him.

Helena: Demetrius, wait for me!

Demetrius: *(calling back)* Get away! Stop haunting me!

Helena:	*(panting)* Oh, I'm out of breath.
Narrator 1:	All of a sudden, she trips over the sleeping body of Lysander.
Helena:	What's this? Lysander! Wake up, good sir, if you are alive!
Narrator 2:	Lysander sits up and rubs his eyes. Spying Helena, he smiles broadly, then reaches out to pull her passionately to him. The flower juice has clearly worked its magic.
Lysander:	May my gaze never stray from your eyes! I would run through fire for your sake!
Helena:	*(in surprise and alarm)* What are you doing? Lysander, how can you say that? What about *Hermia*?
Lysander:	I regret the wasted time I've spent with her. It is not Hermia but *you* I love. Who would not change a raven for a dove?
Helena:	*(angrily)* Do you mock me? Isn't it enough I can't win one sweet look from Demetrius? And yet you tease me? Farewell, Lysander, for I must confess, I thought you lord of more true gentleness.
Narrator 3:	Hurt, Helena runs off. Lysander, entranced, runs after her. Meanwhile, Hermia wakes up from a nightmare to find herself alone.
Hermia:	Help! Lysander? Slay the snake that eats away my heart! Oh, was that a dream? Lysander? Where are you? I nearly faint with fear.
Narrator 1:	She gets up and heads off to search for Lysander.
Hermia:	Either you or death I'll soon find near.

Scene 7

Narrator 2:	Having completed his mission for Oberon, Puck spies a few common working men traveling through the woods.
Puck:	What homespun bumpkins have we here, so near to where the pixie queen sleeps? I think I'll have some fun with them.
Narrator 3:	Rough-cut and unwashed, the simpletons stumble along the dark path.
Quince:	I thought you knew the way.
Narrator 1:	Bottom scratches his unkempt beard.
Bottom:	In faith, nothing quite looks the same at night.
Narrator 2:	An owl hoots. Bottom's courage does not match his brawn. He dives for cover behind a log.
Quince:	What's that? Some beast?
Bottom:	I'll stay here; you check it out.
Quince:	You're the largest—you go.
Narrator 3:	Bottom is pushed off alone.

Narrator 1: Puck watches the cowardly bumpkins with amusement. He can't control his urge to play a joke on them. In a flash, he magically changes Bottom's head into that of a donkey.

Bottom: *(braying)* Eee-aw! All clear!

Narrator 2: Although Bottom is unaware of the change, his new appearance terrifies his friends.

Quince: *(in horror)* Oh, monstrous strange! We're haunted! Help!

Narrator 3: The workmen run in circles, hollering. Puck, watching the scene, has to cover his mouth so as not to laugh out loud.

Bottom: *(to himself)* Why do they run from me? Ther're trying to scare me!

Quince: Bless thee, Bottom; you are transformed.

Narrator 1: Bottom's companions run off, leaving him alone.

Bottom: What? They want to make an ass of me. Well, I'll show them. I'll sing so loud they'll hear I'm not afraid. *(singing loudly)* The blackbird with his tawny bill . . .

Narrator 2: In her nearby bower, Titania wakes, stretching. She spies Bottom and hears his singing.

Titania: What angel wakes me from my flower bed? Sing again, gentle mortal.

Bottom: *(singing)* The plain-song cuckoo dares not trill. . . .

Narrator 3: Titania gazes with lovestruck eyes at Bottom. She advances toward him and whispers sweet nothings in his long furry ears.

Titania: My eye is taken with thy shape. Thy beauty moves me at first sight to swear I love thee!

Bottom: *(shyly)* Methinks, mistress, you have little reason for that. Though in truth, reason and love do keep little company together nowadays. *(braying)* Eee-aw!

Titania: Oh, thou art as wise as thou art beautiful!

Bottom: In truth, if I had any wisdom, I'd get out of these woods.

Titania: Do not leave! I'll have pixies wait on thee, bring thee jewels and sing thee to sleep on a bed of flowers. Spirits, come!

Spirits 1, 2: What wilt thou, Queen?

Titania: Be kind to this gentleman. Feed him with apricots and dewberries. Fan the moonbeams from his eyes with painted wings of butterflies. Lead him to my bower, sprites.

Spirits 1, 2: *(to Bottom)* Hail, mortal!

 **Scene 8**

Oberon: How now, mad spirit Puck? Tell me, has Titania wakened yet? What creature has she fallen for?

Puck: My mistress is in love with a monster. Near her resting place I happened upon a troupe of unlikely fools. The thickest one of all—I fixed upon him the head of a donkey. He frightened the others so much they ran off and left him. Whereupon Titania waked and straightaway loved an ass!

Oberon: This is working out better than I could have planned. Now as to the Athenian: Did you do as I said?

Puck: I found him sleeping, and the woman nearby. His eyes I touched with purple drops so that as soon as he awoke he would see her.

Narrator 1: Suddenly, from different directions, Demetrius and Hermia wander into Oberon's lair.

Oberon: *(to Puck)* These are the Athenians. Make yourself unseen.

Narrator 2: Oberon and Puck turn invisible.

Puck: This is the woman but not the same man.

Demetrius: *(to Hermia)* My love!

Hermia: You! What have you done with Lysander?

Demetrius: I haven't done anything with him. Your harsh tone pierces my heart, for I would still marry you.

Hermia: Never!

Narrator 3: Hermia sprints off.

Demetrius: I can't talk to her when she's so fierce. Oh well. Let her go for now. I'm weary. I'll take a short nap.

Narrator 1: He lies down and stretches out for a nap.

Oberon: This is the man but not the same woman. Puck, have you made a mistake? He was to love another woman, not this one.

Puck: Fate must have meddled with my hand. For these wear Athenian clothes, as you said. Can we mend what has been mixed up?

Oberon: Go find the other woman and, by some magic, bring her here. I'll charm his eyes till she appears.

Puck: I go swifter than an arrow.

Narrator 2: Puck vanishes. Oberon leans over Demetrius.

Oberon: Flower with the purple dye, sink into the apple of his eye. When thou wakest, she will be by, and then though shalt love her eye to eye.

 **Scene 9**

Narrator 3: Puck manages to find Helena and Lysander and uses magic to lure them to the place where Demetrius lies sleeping.

Puck: *(to Oberon)* Here she is, my king, with the youth I'd mistaken. Shall we watch them for a bit for our amusement? Lord, what fools these mortals be.

Lysander: *(to Helena, in desperation)* Would I be crying tears of love if I were trying to mock you?

Helena: You are so cunning. Have you thrown away your vows to Hermia?

Lysander: I was not in my right mind when I swore to her.

Helena: Nor do I think you're in your right mind now to give her up.

Lysander: Let her go to Demetrius. He loves her, and he doesn't love you.

Narrator 1: All of a sudden, Demetrius wakens and sees Helena.

Demetrius: Helena, goddess divine! What shall I compare thee to? Let me kiss this, princess!

Helena: *(angrily)* What? Are both of you bent on making fun of me? First you rival each other to love Hermia, now you rival to mock me.

Lysander: Demetrius, I yield my part of Hermia to you. Bequeath me Helena, for I love her to death.

Demetrius: You can keep Hermia. My feelings for her have vanished. Now my heart is sworn wholly to Helena. Look, here comes Hermia.

Hermia: There you are, Lysander! Why did you leave me?

Lysander: Why should I stay when love for Helena has called me away?

Hermia: What? Say it is not so!

Helena: Now even *she* joins them to trick me! Hermia, why are you doing this to me, your friend?

Hermia: Who is doing what to whom? It seems that now both of them love you. It is *you* who wrongs *me*!

Helena: Have you put them up to this?

Hermia: What are you talking about?

Helena: I suppose you laugh at me behind my back. Well, I'm tired of being made a fool of. I'm leaving!

Lysander: Stay, my love, my soul!

Demetrius: She will not stay for *you*. But *I* can compel her. I would lose my life for her love.

Lysander: Then prove it with your sword!

Demetrius:	Gladly! Let's go!
Narrator 2:	Both men draw their swords.
Hermia:	But sweet Lysander . . .
Narrator 3:	Desperate, Hermia throws herself at Lysander's legs. He drags her, trying to shake her loose.
Lysander:	*(to Hermia)* Get off, thou cat, thou vile thing. I desire never to see thee more. It is Helena I love.
Hermia:	*(to Helena)* You thief! You have come by night and stolen my love's heart!
Narrator 1:	Hermia lunges at Helena, ripping at her hair.
Helena:	Have you no shame? How low would you go that you would tear at me? You little puppet!
Hermia:	Are you insulting my height? I see their high esteem has made you grow even more immense than you already are. Think me not so short that my nails cannot reach your eyes!
Helena:	Gentlemen, do not let her hurt me! She may be little, but when she's angry, she's a fierce vixen.
Narrator 2:	The men try to block Helena from Hermia's slaps and punches.
Hermia:	Insults! Let me at her!
Helena:	I swear I've never wronged you, Hermia. I just told Demetrius you'd fled to these woods. I thought he'd thank me with his devotion. But all he's done is leave me to the wild beasts. I'm going back to Athens.
Hermia:	Good. Who's stopping you?
Narrator 3:	Lysander and Demetrius make it clear that they are. They look at each other fiercely and draw swords again.
Lysander:	Come now, Demetrius, if you dare. We'll see who has the right to Helena!
Narrator 1:	Oberon and Puck watch as the group of mortals moves off into another part of the forest.
Oberon:	Puck, this has gone too far. Here's what you do: While these rivals seek a place to fight, lead them astray one from another and put them to sleep. Then crush this other herb in Lysander's eye. It will remove the error from his sight.
Puck:	We'll have to work in haste. Night is nearly over.
Oberon:	I will fly quickly to my queen and win the boy from her. Then I'll release her from the spell, and peace will be restored.

Scene 10

Narrator 2:	Puck finds Demetrius and Lysander dueling in a grove. He causes them to lose each other. Then he makes them drowsy.
Narrator 3:	Helena stumbles into the same grove and sinks down to rest.
Helena:	Oh, weary night.
Puck:	What, only three? One more makes them four. Here she comes.
Narrator 1:	Hermia enters the grove.
Hermia:	I can no farther crawl. My legs cannot keep pace with my desires. I'll rest until break of day.
Narrator 2:	Hermia lies down and falls asleep. When all four Athenians are asleep, Puck doses Lysander with the herb.
Puck:	On the ground, all sleep sound. I'll apply to you, gentle lover, remedy. When you awake, you shall take true delight in the sight of your former lady's eye. Jack shall have Jill, nothing will go ill, and all shall be well.

Scene 11

Narrator 3:	In Titania's grove, Oberon watches the queen doting on Bottom.
Titania:	*(to mule-headed Bottom)* Come, sit with me, and let me pet your furriness. My pixies will wrap flowers around your neck while I kiss your great large ears.
Bottom:	Scratch my head, pixies. I must get to the barber, for methinks I am marvelous hairy about the face.
Titania:	Would you like some music? Perhaps a bite to eat?
Bottom:	Truly, I crave a bag of oats. Or maybe a good bale of hay. But no bother. I feel a sleep coming on.
Titania:	Sleep, and I will wind thee in my arms. Spirits, away. *(to Bottom)* Oh, I do love thee so!
Narrator 1:	Puck suddenly appears beside Oberon.
Oberon:	Welcome, Robin Goodfellow. Isn't this a sweet sight? But I must say, in truth, I'm beginning to pity Titania. While she was charmed, I teased her till she begged what favor she could do for me. I asked her to give me the changeling boy, and she did so straightaway. Now I'll undo this spell.
Narrator 2:	He touches the herb to her eyes.
Oberon:	Wake now, my sweet queen.
Titania:	Oberon, what visions I've seen! I dreamed I loved a donkey.

Oberon:	There lies your love.
Titania:	*(screaming)* How did this happen? Oh, how I loathe the sight of him now!
Oberon:	Puck, take the donkey's head from this fool. Come, Titania. Take hands with me, and we will soon dance with all these sleeping lovers at their weddings.
Puck:	My King, I hear the morning lark.
Titania:	Then let us go, and tell me how it came to pass . . . that I was sleeping with an ass.

Scene 12

Narrator 3:	Egeus and the duke are out hunting. They stumble upon the four sleeping lovers.
Duke:	What wood nymphs are these?
Egeus:	*(in surprise)* No nymphs, but my daughter . . . and Lysander near! And here is Demetrius . . . and Helena.
Duke:	This is the day Hermia is to make her choice, is it not? We'll wake them with our hunting horns.
Narrator 1:	Horns are sounded, and the couples wake up.
Duke:	*(to the couples)* Stand up and tell what you are doing here.
Lysander:	In truth, Hermia and I were stealing from Athens to be wed.
Egeus:	*(to the duke)* My lord, I must invoke the law! *(to Demetrius)* They nearly defeated us—and deprived you of your wife.
Demetrius:	But I love Helena now, and she loves me. My desire for Hermia has melted as the snow does. Please, sir, allow your daughter to marry the man she loves.
Egeus:	I will do that.
Duke:	Then, lovers, you meet with good fortune. We'll hear the whole story later. Egeus, these couples shall be wed at my palace. We'll hold a great feast. Come away, all.
Narrator 2:	The duke, Egeus, and the others depart. Hermia, still sleepy, rubs her eyes.
Hermia:	I seem to see everything double.
Lysander:	*(sounding sleepy and puzzled)* Was the duke here?
Demetrius:	And did he bid us follow him back to Athens?
Helena:	It seems as if we are all still asleep. Yet I have found Demetrius, like a jewel, at last.

Narrator 3: Demetrius takes Helena's hand and smiles into her eyes. Lysander and Hermia also join hands.

Demetrius: Then let's return home and, on the way, recount our dreams.

Narrator 1: As the four lovers leave the enchanted forest, Bottom awakes.

Bottom: Heigh-ho! Where is everyone? Stolen away and left me sleeping here? I have had a most rare dream. Methought I was an . . .

Narrator 2: Bottom reaches up to feel for his long donkey ears, which have vanished.

Bottom: Methought I was an . . . *(suddenly braying)* AAAH!

Simply Shakespeare: Readers Theatre for Young People is from *Read* magazine, a Weekly Reader publication, in collaboration with Teacher Ideas Press. Edited by Jennifer Kroll. www.weeklyreader.com. www.lu.com/tips. 1–800–541–2086.

CHAPTER 7

The Merchant of Venice

By William Shakespeare

Adapted by Jennifer Kroll

Summary

A Venetian man named Bassanio asks his friend Antonio for a loan. Bassanio explains that he needs the money to court a rich heiress named Portia. Antonio is happy to give Bassanio what he needs, but because his own money is currently tied up in shipping and trade ventures, he must ask for a loan to do so. Antonio pays a visit to Shylock, a moneylender whom he dislikes. Shylock is well aware of Antonio's negative attitude toward him and prejudice against him for being Jewish. Shylock grants Antonio the loan but makes him sign a contract in which he promises to forfeit a pound of his own flesh in case of failure to pay back the loan in time. Unfortunately, while Bassanio is off courting Portia, a series of disasters leaves Antonio unable to pay back his loan. When Shylock demands the promised pound of flesh, Bassanio's shrewd new wife, Portia, saves the day by dressing up as a judge and outwitting Shylock in the courtroom.

 Presentation Strategies

Seat or stand the characters as follows. Front row: Narrators 1 and 2, Nerissa, Portia, Bassanio, Antonio, and Shylock. Back row: Messenger, Balthasar, Morocco, Arragon, Duke of Venice, Gratiano, Solanio, and Salerio. You may wish to have a podium situated facing the readers and to have Portia move to this podium when she takes on her role as judge in Scene 10.

Props

Portia and Nerissa should wear feminine clothes, possibly skirts or dresses. They might throw on baseball caps and masculine shirts for Scene 10, when they are disguised as men. Alternatively, they might wear choral robes or some other sort of cloaks when they are pretending to be legal professionals in Scene 10. The other characters should dress nicely. Duke can wear a crown. Three music or jewelry boxes might be placed on a little table in front of Portia to represent the caskets from which the suitors must choose.

Cast of Characters

(main characters in boldface)
Narrators 1 and 2
Bassanio, *a young nobleman of Venice*
Antonio, *a merchant of Venice, Bassanio's friend*
Portia, *a rich heiress*
Nerissa, *Portia's lady-in-waiting*
Balthasar, *Portia's serving man*
Shylock, *a moneylender*
Messenger
Morocco
Arragon } *suitors seeking Portia's hand in marriage*
Salerio
Solanio } *friends of Antonio and Bassanio*
Gratiano
Duke of Venice

The Merchant of Venice

By William Shakespeare

Adapted by Jennifer Kroll

🔊 Scene 1

Narrator 1: On a Venice street, a merchant named Antonio speaks to his friend Bassanio.

Bassanio: Antonio, I have a great favor to ask.

Antonio: My dear friend—ask away.

Bassanio: You know how much money I've lost over the past few years. I've lived beyond my means, and now I'm broke. I owe money to everybody, and, of course, I owe the most to you.

Antonio: I have faith in your character, Bassanio. I know you'll pay me back when you can.

Bassanio: That's just it. I know this is going to sound strange. But I feel confident that I will be able to pay back my whole debt within a few weeks or months, if only you will lend me a little more.

Antonio: My money and I are at your service. What is your plan?

Bassanio: The woman I'm in love with is very rich—an heiress. Her name is Portia, and she lives in Belmont. She is amazingly beautiful, but, even better than that, she is wise and of good character.

Antonio: I've heard of her.

Bassanio: Yes, she's quite famous. Men come from all over the world to court her. However, I have reason to think that she favors me. I notice the way she looks at me. As broke as I am, though, I really can't compete for her hand. I need some money so that I can go to Belmont and court her.

Antonio: You know that all my money is tied up in my ships right now. I don't have any cash on hand. However, I can use my good name to get a loan from one of the moneylenders in town. Then I'll give the money to you.

Bassanio: Thank you, Antonio. You're such a good friend to me.

Scene 2

Narrator 2: Meanwhile, in Belmont, the rich heiress, Portia, and her lady-in-waiting, Nerissa, discuss Portia's recent string of suitors.

Portia: All these suitors! I feel exhausted, Nerissa.

Nerissa: Too much of a good thing can be just as bad as not enough.

Portia: I think it would all be less exhausting if I had the ability to choose my husband for myself. Unfortunately, I don't have that luxury! In his will, my father set up the way in which my husband would be selected. Three caskets are to be set before an interested suitor—one of gold, one of silver, and one of lead. If the suitor chooses the casket containing my picture, he wins my hand in marriage.

Nerissa: I know it doesn't seem like the best way to get a husband, but cheer up! Your good, kind father devised this system on his deathbed. Such holy men always have good inspirations when they are about to die. I'm sure that only someone you can truly love will choose the correct casket.

Portia: I hope you are right, Nerissa.

Nerissa: What have you thought of your recent suitors? Did you like the Neapolitan prince?

Portia: Ugh. All he ever talks about is his horse. He bragged on and on about how he could shoe the beast himself! I couldn't stand him.

Nerissa: Did you like Count Palatine any better?

Portia: He does nothing but frown. If he's this serious as a young man, I can only imagine what he'll be like by the time he's old!

Nerissa: What about Falconbridge, the young English baron?

Portia: He doesn't speak any language I understand. I don't want to marry someone I can't even talk to!

Nerissa: How did you like the young German, the Duke of Saxony's nephew?

Portia: I didn't like him at all in the morning, when he was sober, and I liked him even less in the afternoon, when he was drunk. I sure hope I don't have to marry him.

Nerissa: But if he chooses the right casket, you'll *have* to marry him, won't you?

Portia: I'll do anything, rather than marry that sponge! *(laughing)* Maybe you could just put a glass of wine in front of one of the wrong caskets for me, Nerissa. He'd be sure to pick it.

Nerissa: I don't think you'll have to worry about marrying him or any of the others. They all seem ready to return home. I think that unless they

Portia:	can win your heart and hand by some method other than the caskets, they're not interested.
Portia:	The sooner these suitors leave, the better! And, yet, I fear I'll be doomed to die an old maid.
Nerissa:	Do you remember, lady, how, when your father was still alive, a Venetian scholar and soldier came here for a visit, accompanied by the Marquess of Montferrat?
Portia:	*(smiling)* Yes, of course I do. His name was Bassanio.
Nerissa:	He, of all the men I've ever met, seems best deserving of a lady like you.
Portia:	I remember him well, and I remember him as worthy of your praise.
Narrator 1:	A serving man enters the room.
Balthasar:	Madam, your four suitors wish to bid you farewell. And two messengers have arrived, announcing that two new suitors will be here before nightfall.
Portia:	Thanks for the news. Come, Nerissa, let's bid our farewells and prepare to welcome the new guests.

Scene 3

Narrator 2:	Antonio and Bassanio visit the office of Shylock, the Jewish moneylender, in order to ask for a loan.
Shylock:	Three thousand ducats—well . . .
Bassanio:	Yes. Lent for three months, sir. Antonio, here, will sign the promissory note. You know he's good for the money.
Narrator 1:	Shylock steps into the back room, rubbing his chin and muttering to himself.
Shylock:	I know this Antonio fellow, and I can't stand him. To start with, he's always rude and abusive to me. He's a Christian, and he looks down his nose at all Jews. Secondly, I hate him because he's always lending money to people who would have to come to me for loans. And he makes his loans without asking for any interest! I lose lots of money on account of this Antonio fellow.
Narrator 2:	Shylock steps back out to the counter, still rubbing his chin.
Shylock:	Three thousand ducats, huh? I wonder if I can manage it. How long was it for, again?
Antonio:	Three months, Shylock. You know that I don't normally lend or borrow money on interest, but I'm making an exception here in order to help my friend.
Narrator 1:	Shylock continues puttering about and stalling. A mischievous look is in his eye.

Antonio: *(impatiently)* Well, Shylock—am I beholden to you or not?

Shylock: Frankly, Antonio, I'm amazed that you would come to me for a loan. I've heard the things you say about me. Often, you have condemned me for the way I lend money in order to collect the interest. You've cursed me, spit at me, and called me a dog. And now I'm supposed to be your friend and lend you money?

Antonio: *(angrily)* I'm likely to call you names again, if you continue stalling like this! You know I'm good for the money, Shylock. I don't ask you to be my friend, just to make the loan.

Shylock: Well, look at you—all upset! I would like to be friends with you and conduct business in a friendly fashion. . . .

Antonio: That's a laugh!

Shylock: *(getting angry, too)* Very well, then. If you don't believe me capable of friendship, this is the sort of kindness I will show you. Come with me to the notary, and there we'll sign a contract that reads as follows: If Antonio does not repay Shylock on such a day, in such a place, such an amount, let him forfeit a pound of his own flesh. The flesh will be cut off and taken from whatever part of his body Shylock pleases.

Antonio: *(indignantly)* All right, then! I'll sign your ridiculous contract! *(sarcastically)* Then I'll tell everybody in town about the fabulous kindness of Shylock!

Bassanio: No, Antonio! You cannot sign such a contract for my sake! I won't allow it!

Antonio: Don't worry. I won't have to forfeit any of my flesh to greedy old Shylock. My trading ships will return to port between now and then, and I expect to have three times the amount I've signed for by the time the loan comes due.

Shylock: Then off to the notary we go!

Scene 4

Narrator 2: The same evening, at Portia's home in Belmont, one of her new suitors decides to try his luck with the gold, silver, and lead caskets.

Morocco: I have sworn the oath, as required. I have promised that if I choose the wrong casket I will never tell anyone which I chose. Furthermore, I will never court another woman and seek her hand in marriage. Finally, I will leave your house immediately.

Portia: That is the oath that must be sworn by every man who tries the caskets. *(to her servant)* Draw the curtains aside, please, and let the noble prince see his choices.

Narrator 1: The servant parts the curtains, and the Prince of Morocco begins reading the inscriptions on each of the caskets.

Morocco:	The first casket, made all of gold, says this: "Whoever chooses me will gain what many men desire." The second silver casket says: "Whoever chooses me will get as much as he deserves." The third, made of dull lead, bears this warning: "Whoever chooses me must give and risk all he has." How do I know which one to choose?
Portia:	Only one of them contains my picture, Prince. If you choose that one, I'm yours.
Narrator 2:	The prince continues studying the caskets.
Morocco:	Let me see. The lead one says, "Whoever chooses me must give and risk all he has." Now why would anybody give and risk everything for lead? Doesn't make sense. I'll not pick that one.
Narrator 1:	He paces back and forth between the silver and gold caskets.
Morocco:	What does the silver one say? "Whoever chooses me will get as much as he deserves." And the gold says, "Whoever chooses me will gain what many men desire." Surely that one speaks of the lady! Many men desire her! That's the one, then. Give me the key, and I'll unlock the gold casket!
Portia:	Very well, sir.
Narrator 2:	The servant hands the Prince of Morocco a key. Fumbling with the key, he unlocks the casket.
Morocco:	Oh, no! What's this?
Narrator 1:	He picks up a small skull that's been locked in the casket. Inside the skull, a note is tucked.
Morocco:	*(reading)* All that glitters is not gold. Fare you well. Your suit is cold. (*to her servant*) Well, that's that then. The lady will not be my wife. I will prepare to depart immediately.

Scene 5

Narrator 2:	The next day, a second prince tries to win Portia by guessing amongst the caskets.
Portia:	Behold the caskets. Choose the one that contains my picture, and we shall be married straight away.
Arragon:	Hmm. Let's see. The lead says, "Whoever chooses me must give and risk all he has." I'd have to be crazy to give and risk everything for lead.
Narrator 1:	The prince moves over and stands before the gold casket.
Arragon:	The gold says, "Whoever chooses me will gain what many men desire." I think I understand the message here. This inscription speaks of the worldly things that most people wrongly chase after. I won't be fooled into choosing this casket.
Narrator 2:	He moves over and stands before the silver casket.

Arragon:	*(reading)* Whoever chooses me will get as much as he deserves. *(aloud)* Do I deserve the lady? Do I have the courage, honor, the gentlemanly breeding that would make me worthy of her? Yes, I think I have all these things. Therefore, I select the silver. Give me the key for this casket.
Narrator 1:	A servant hands the Prince of Arragon the key. A silence falls over the room as he turns it and looks inside the box.
Arragon:	What's this? A portrait of a blinking idiot? Do I deserve nothing better? Very well, then. I have been chastised for my pride. I'll be gone.

📢 Scene 6

Narrator 2:	Meanwhile, Solanio and Salerio, two friends of Bassanio and Antonio, stand talking in a Venice street.
Salerio:	I've heard some bad news. One of Antonio's ships has been wrecked at sea.
Solanio:	Oh no! Poor Antonio! Where did the ship go down?
Salerio:	At the Goodwin Sands, a dangerous spot off the coast of Kent.
Narrator 1:	The two friends suddenly recognize Shylock, who is hurrying by them on the street.
Solanio:	Hello, Shylock. What's new with you? Is it true that Antonio has suffered a loss at sea?
Shylock:	I lent money to that man, and he turns out to be bankrupt, a beggar! He better just make sure he can pay that loan back!

📢 Scene 7

Narrator 2:	Bassanio and his friend Gratiano arrive at Portia's house in Belmont. While Gratiano and Nerissa become acquainted, Bassanio speaks with Portia. After some time, he announces his desire to try his hand with the caskets.
Portia:	Please, I beg you—wait a day or two before you make your guess. If you choose wrongly, I immediately lose your company. I would like to keep you at my side as long as I can. Perhaps more time with me will help you to choose the correct casket.
Bassanio:	Dear lady, let me choose now. Waiting would only be torture.
Portia:	Away then we go to the caskets.
Narrator 1:	Bassanio spends a long time pondering the caskets and trying to make the correct decision.
Bassanio:	*(to himself)* Gold and silver—these are beautiful substances, but they are also substances that divide people and cause strife. Lead is

	common and unpretty. But life has taught me that external appearances often do not match what's on the inside. The paleness of this leaden casket moves my heart more than the ornate beauty of these others. *(to the others in the room)* I will choose the lead.
Narrator 2:	He takes the key from the servant and turns it in the lock.
Bassanio:	What's this I find inside? It's fair Portia's picture!
Portia:	*(to Nerissa)* My heart is overflowing with joy!
Narrator 2:	Bassanio eagerly unfurls a small scroll.
Bassanio:	*(reading)* You who choose not by the view, choose most fair and choose most true. Turn to where your lady is and claim her with a loving kiss." *(turning to Portia)* May I, dear lady?
Narrator 2:	She smiles and nods. They kiss.
Portia:	Lord Bassanio, I am yours.
Bassanio:	My heart feels as if it is about to burst!
Nerissa:	My lord and lady—I feel so much joy for you!
Gratiano:	I, too, wish you all the joy in the world. Now, wish the same to me, for I intend to be married also.
Bassanio:	Of course you will be married—just as soon as you find a wife.
Gratiano:	I've found one, Your Lordship.
Narrator 1:	Gratiano gestures toward Nerissa, who comes to stand beside him, smiling.
Gratiano:	This dear lady has agreed to do me that honor.
Portia:	Is this true, Nerissa?
Nerissa:	Madam, I do wish to marry this man, but only with your blessing.
Portia:	You have it, of course, my dear.
Narrator 2:	The two new couples talk and laugh, until they are interrupted by a messenger's entrance.
Messenger:	Lord Bassanio—I am sorry to interrupt you, but I come bearing some very bad news. Your friend Antonio has been arrested and will be tried tomorrow.
Bassanio:	Arrested? Oh, no! What has happened?
Messenger:	He was unable to pay back money he owed to Shylock.
Bassanio:	How is that possible? Has there been a disaster at sea?
Messenger:	Many disasters, sir. He lost three merchant ships bearing valuable goods in the past week. You can read the rest of the news in this letter.
Narrator 1:	The messenger hands a letter from Antonio to Bassanio. Bassanio reads, frowning.

Portia:	*(to Bassanio)* Is this man who is in trouble your dear friend?
Bassanio:	The dearest friend to me in the entire world. He took out that loan so that I could have money. He signed a contract promising to either pay on time or forfeit a pound of his own flesh.
Portia:	He must indeed be a good friend! What sum does he owe?
Bassanio:	Three thousand ducats.
Portia:	That's all? That's nothing. Pay this Shylock six thousand ducats and have him nullify the contract. If that's not enough, triple the amount.
Narrator:	Bassanio studies his letter from Antonio.
Bassanio:	Antonio believes that no amount of money from any source is going to be acceptable to Shylock. He says the man is out for his blood.
Portia:	You must go to Venice and try to sort this problem out. But first, let us go to the chapel immediately and become husband and wife. After that, you and Gratiano can leave. When you have freed your friend and paid his debt, bring Antonio back here with you. In the meantime, my maid Nerissa and I will go to stay in the convent. There we will live a life of prayer and contemplation until you return.
Bassanio:	Dear lady, that seems to be a good plan. We will go off to the chapel to celebrate our marriage. Then Gratiano and I will leave for Venice.

Scene 8

Narrator 2:	Shylock and Solanio accompany Antonio as he is led to a jail cell.
Shylock:	Jailer, look at this fool. He lent out all his money without asking for interest.
Antonio:	Shylock, I beg you! Have mercy!
Shylock:	I'll have what's been promised to me in our contract—a pound of your flesh. Nothing else will do. You called me a dog when you didn't even have any cause to do so. All right, then. If I'm a dog, beware of my fangs!
Antonio:	Please—just listen to me.
Shylock:	I will not listen to a word you say. I'll have what's mine by law—a pound of your flesh.
Narrator 1:	Shylock stomps off.
Solanio:	I'm sure the duke will never allow you to be put to death.
Antonio:	The duke can't stop it from happening, I'm afraid. The contract that I signed with Shylock was legally binding.

Scene 9

Narrator 2: Meanwhile, in Belmont, Portia hatches a secret plot to help Antonio.

Portia: Balthasar, you have always been a faithful servant. Be so again now. I'm giving you a letter to deliver to my cousin in Padua, Doctor Bellario. When you deliver it, take care of the notes and garments that he gives you. Bring them to me as quickly as possible. Go now!

Balthasar: I'll be back in no time.

Portia: Come on, Nerissa. We've got work to do. We're going to see our husbands again sooner than they think.

Nerissa: Will they see us?

Portia: They will, Nerissa, but we'll be dressed up in such a way that they won't recognize us. *(joking)* I'll bet you that when we've turned into men, I'll be the more handsome of the two of us!

Nerissa: So we're dressing up as men? Why? How will that help Lord Bassanio's friend?

Portia: I'll tell you my whole plan once we're in the coach and on our way to Venice!

Scene 10

Narrator 1: On the day of Antonio's trial, Antonio, Bassanio, Solario, Solanio, Gratiano, Shylock, and the duke wait in a courtroom for the judge to arrive.

Duke of Venice: Antonio, I feel sorry for you. Your adversary seems to be a man incapable of pity, void of any small amount of mercy.

Antonio: I heard you trying to talk him into behaving mercifully. Thank you for making such an effort on my behalf.

Duke: I tried my best, but he would not listen to me. He's full of rage and out for blood. *(to Shylock)* Is there no way that your cold heart can be swayed to mercy in this case? This man, here . . .

Narrator 2: The duke gestures toward Bassanio.

Duke: . . . is ready to pay the three thousand ducats on Antonio's behalf. Won't you accept the money and let Antonio go free?

Shylock: *(smugly)* The contract was signed. Antonio failed to pay the money by the agreed date. Therefore, legally, a pound of his flesh belongs to me. I will have what is mine by law.

Bassanio: *(anxiously, to Shylock)* Antonio only owes you three thousand ducats. I'll pay you six thousand, if you agree to drop this suit and spare his life.

Shylock: *(spitefully, to Bassanio)* Even if you were able to give me a million times that much, I wouldn't accept it. I hate Antonio for the way he has always treated me.

Duke: *(to Shylock)* How can you ever expect to receive mercy from others when you are unwilling to show mercy yourself?

Shylock: Why would I ever need anyone to show me mercy, since I do nothing wrong? I stand here today representing the law, the power of justice. I simply ask for what's legally mine.

Duke: A learned doctor of law from Padua, the famed Bellario will be here shortly to try this case.

Narrator 2: While they wait for Judge Bellario, Shylock sharpens a knife. The others watch nervously. Suddenly, Nerissa bursts into the courtroom, dressed up as a lawyer's clerk. In her costume, nobody recognizes her.

Nerissa: The learned Judge Bellario is with me. He requests entry into this courtroom.

Duke: Escort him in.

Narrator 1: Nerissa escorts Portia into the room and up to the front. Portia is dressed up as a judge.

Duke: Judge Bellario, are you familiar with both sides of the case that is before you here?

Portia: I am thoroughly informed. Which of these men is Antonio?

Narrator 2: Antonio stands forward.

Portia: Which is Shylock?

Narrator 1: Shylock stands forward.

Portia: *(to Shylock)* Well, sir, it seems to me that Venetian law cannot hinder you from taking a pound of this man's flesh. Yet, I urge you to be merciful. It is what you should do.

Shylock: *(stubbornly)* Why should I be merciful? No law forces me to be so.

Portia: Mercy is something that cannot be forced. It is like the rain that falls from heaven upon the dry ground. It is twice blessed, for mercy blesses both the giver and receiver. It suits a king better than his crown. Mercy is a noble quality. It is a quality of God himself. Therefore, I urge you to be merciful.

Shylock: Mercy? Pah! I crave the law! I want what's legally mine!

Portia: *(to Shylock)* Does Antonio remain unable to pay back his debt?

Bassanio: *(interrupting)* I've got the money here—all that Antonio owes and more! But Shylock won't accept it!

Portia: We cannot force him to accept it. He acts within his legal rights.

Shylock:	Oh, wise young judge! How I honor you for your wisdom!
Portia:	Does somebody here have the contract in question? I'd like to take a look at it.
Narrator 2:	Shylock passes the contract to Portia, who reads it over, frowning.
Portia:	*(softly, to Antonio)* I'm sorry, but it looks like you're going to have to prepare yourself for Shylock's knife.
Narrator 1:	Bellario, Solario, Solanio, and Gratiano all gasp in horror. Antonio looks very pale.
Portia:	*(to Shylock)* Do you have a surgeon nearby, to stop this man's wounds so that he doesn't bleed to death?
Shylock:	Does it say in the contract that I must have such a surgeon nearby?
Portia:	No it doesn't. But it would be a charitable act on your part.
Shylock:	If it's not in the contract, then I'm not doing it.
Portia:	All right then. *(to Antonio)* You, merchant—do you have any last words to say?
Narrator 2:	Antonio appears shaky, but he manages to maintain his composure.
Antonio:	I'm ready to die. Give me your hand, Bassanio.
Narrator 1:	Bassanio clutches his friend's hands, a look of terror and despair on his face. Tears stream from his eyes.
Antonio:	Farewell! Don't be sad that this happened to me. I know you would have acted the same for my sake, had our fortunes been reversed.
Bassanio:	*(desperately)* My dearest friend! I would give up everything in the world if only I could save you!
Portia:	*(in a matter-of-fact voice)* All right, then, Shylock. A pound of this merchant's flesh is yours. You may cut it off him now. The law allows it and the court awards it.
Shylock:	Wise judge! Noble judge!
Narrator 2:	Shylock raises his knife.
Portia:	But before you strike, there's something else you need to know. The exact wording of the contract reads "a pound of flesh." Therefore, in cutting this man, you must make sure that you don't shed a drop of his blood. No blood is yours by law, only flesh. In fact, according to this city's law, if you shed a drop of any fellow citizen's blood, your lands and goods can be confiscated by the state.
Gratiano:	*(mocking Shylock)* Wise judge! Noble judge!
Portia:	The moneylender will have his justice, according to the exact letter of the law. The merchant is ready to be cut. Why do you pause, Shylock? Take what's yours.

Shylock: *(in a subdued manner)* I've changed my mind. I'd like to just take the three thousand ducats and go now, please.

Portia: But you refused the money in front of all in this court. You said the only thing that would satisfy you was justice and a pound of flesh.

Shylock: Can't I just have my three thousand ducats?

Portia: No. You won't have anything except what you wanted.

Shylock: *(angrily)* This is unfair! I'm leaving!

Portia: Stay where you are, Shylock. The law has yet another hold on you. You are guilty of plotting to kill a citizen of Venice. That is illegal. The penalty for that action is this: Half of your goods are to be seized by the state. The other half are to be given to the person against whom you plotted.

Shylock: No! My fortune! You take my very life when you take the money and goods that sustain my life!

Duke: The noble judge has spoken. Shylock, half of your estate must now be given over to Antonio—the man you wanted dead. As for the half you owe to the state, I'm willing to show you the mercy you would not show. If you pay a small fine to the state, you can keep that half of your belongings.

Portia: Clerk, draw up a deed of gift, transferring half of Shylock's estate to Antonio.

Shylock: *(weakly)* Please, just let me go home now. I'm not feeling well. Send the deed over to my house this afternoon, and I will sign it.

Simply Shakespeare: Readers Theatre for Young People is from *Read* magazine, a Weekly Reader publication, in collaboration with Teacher Ideas Press. Edited by Jennifer Kroll. www.weeklyreader.com. www.lu.com/tips. 1–800–541–2086.

CHAPTER 8

Much Ado About Nothing

By William Shakespeare

Adapted by Jennifer Kroll

Summary

Returning home from a war, Don Pedro, Don John, Benedict, and the young war hero Claudio stop off at the home of Leonato, the governor of Messina. While there, Claudio falls in love with Leonato's daughter, Hero, and the two decide to marry. At the same time, Leonato's niece, the funny and intelligent Beatrice, resumes her long-standing battle of wits with the equally clever Benedict. Spurred on by Beatrice's and Benedict's disdainful attitudes toward love, marriage, and each other, Hero, Claudio, Leonato, and Don Pedro plot to bring the two sworn singles together in marriage. Through a series of staged, overheard conversations, they convince Beatrice that Benedict is secretly in love with her and vice versa. Meanwhile, the jealous Don John plots to ruin Claudio's happiness with Hero by tricking him into believing that Hero is secretly seeing another man. The plot works. Instead of marrying Hero as planned, Claudio shames her on her wedding day, publicly accusing her of misconduct. After Hero collapses in the chapel in shock and horror, Leonato, Beatrice, Benedict, and Friar Francis must work to make wrongs right and ensure that everyone ends up happily married in this classic Shakespearean comedy.

Presentation Suggestions

Place Hero, Claudio, Beatrice, and Benedict front and center. Place the villains Don John, Borachio, and Conrade with Dogberry in a cluster to one side. Place Leonato, Messenger, Don Pedro, Margaret, Ursula, and Friar Francis in a cluster on the other side. Seat the narrators on tall stools to the back of the other cast members. Alternatively, to inject more action into the reading, seat all the cast members in one row but leave about five open chairs or reading stands in front of that row. Have readers move down to the open chairs during scenes in which they are present.

Props

Hero, Beatrice, Margaret, and Ursula can wear long dresses or skirts or flower garlands. Claudio, Benedict, Don Pedro, and Don John can wear fatigues, camouflage, military-style caps, or any article of clothing indicating their military status. Don John can wear black or a villain's mustache to indicate that he's a bad guy. Dogberry can wear a police badge or hat to indicate that he's a constable. Friar Francis can wear a sheet or blanket as a priestly robe. Borachio can hold a bottle or can to pass to Conrade in Scene 8. He might also hold coins to show Conrade. Benedict can draw a ruler or similar object as a sword in Scene 10. The women can wear masks during Scene 11. Claudio and Hero should each have a "love letter" to hold up during this scene.

Cast of Characters

(main parts in boldface)
Narrators 1, 2, 3
Leonato, *the governor of Messina*
Messenger
Beatrice, *Leonato's niece*
Hero, *Leonato's daughter*
Don Pedro, *the prince of Arragon*
Benedict, *a young lord of Padua*
Claudio, *a young lord of Florence*
Conrade, *a follower of Don John*

Don John, *half brother of Don Pedro*
Borachio, *a follower of Don John*
Margaret
Ursula } *ladies-in-waiting to Hero*
Dogberry, *a constable*
Friar Francis

Much Ado About Nothing

By William Shakespeare

Adapted by Jennifer Kroll

 **Scene 1**

Narrator 1: Leonato stands in front of his home with a messenger. He holds a letter. His daughter and niece come down the steps to join him.

Leonato: I have just learned that Don Pedro, the prince of Arragon, will be staying here tonight. He is passing through on his way home from the war.

Messenger: He was only a couple miles off when I left him.

Leonato: I read here that one soldier, a young man named Claudio, has been greatly honored by the prince for his bravery in the last skirmish.

Messenger: Claudio very much deserves his honors, sir.

Beatrice: *(to the messenger)* Please tell me, sir, has Signior Bigmouth Benedict returned from the war?

Hero: My cousin means Signior Benedict of Padua.

Messenger: Oh, Signior Benedict—a very pleasant fellow and a great friend of young Claudio. He's a good soldier, too, one without compare, lady.

Beatrice: *(pretending to misunderstand)* A good soldier compared to a lady? I don't doubt it.

Messenger: Signior Benedict seems to be stuffed with all honorable virtues.

Beatrice: A stuffed man! That sounds about right. I can only wonder of what his stuffing is made.

Leonato: *(to the messenger)* Don't pay any attention to my niece, sir. There is a merry war going on between her and Signior Benedict. The two never meet without having a skirmish of wits.

Narrator 2: Just then, Don Pedro arrives. With him are Claudio, Benedict, and Don Pedro's half brother, Don John.

Don Pedro: Good Signior Leonato, have you come out to meet your troublesome guests?

Leonato:	I could never be troubled by someone like Your Grace.
Don Pedro:	This must be your daughter.
Leonato:	Yes. This is Hero. And this is my niece, Beatrice.
Benedict:	*(to Beatrice)* What? My dear Lady Disdain! Are you still living?
Beatrice:	Could disdain ever die when it has the likes of Signior Benedict to feed it?
Benedict:	All ladies love me, except you. It's too bad that my heart's so hard and I don't love any of them back.
Beatrice:	That's actually a blessing to women everywhere. This way, they don't have to put up with an offensive suitor. I thank the heavens for my own cold heart. I personally would rather hear my dog bark at a crow than hear a man swear he loves me.
Benedict:	Let's just hope you stay in that frame of mind so that some unfortunate man can avoid having his face scratched by you.
Beatrice:	Scratching couldn't make his face worse—not if he looked like you.
Benedict:	Well, you surely would make a good parrot teacher. You say the same things over and over.
Narrator 3:	While Beatrice and Benedict are sparring, Don Pedro and Leonato have been making arrangements.
Don Pedro:	Then everything is settled.
Leonato:	Yes, indeed. I am honored to have you as guests in my home for the next several weeks. Please come inside.
Narrator 1:	They all move into the house, except Benedict and Claudio.
Claudio:	Benedict, did you see Signior Leonato's daughter just now?
Benedict:	I saw her, but I didn't really pay any special attention to her.
Claudio:	What do you think of her?
Benedict:	Are you asking me for my true judgment? Or do you want me to be as merciless as I usually am about women?
Claudio:	No, Benedict. Please—I want your honest opinion.
Benedict:	Well, she seems too little for great praise, and too tan to be called fair. So I guess the only good thing I can really say about her is that if she were other than she is, she wouldn't be nearly as attractive.
Claudio:	You think I'm joking around. But tell me the truth. Do you like her?
Benedict:	Why? Are you looking to buy her or something?
Claudio:	Could all the gold in the world buy such a jewel? I think she's about the sweetest lady I've ever met—the most beautiful, too.

Benedict: You need glasses! If her cousin Beatrice weren't possessed by some sort of demon, she would be by far the prettier of the two.

Claudio: Benedict, I'm thinking of asking for Hero's hand in marriage.

Benedict: *(joking)* Alas! Has it come to this? Will I never see a bachelor reach 30 years of age again?

Scene 2

Narrator 2: A couple of hours later, the prince's half brother, Don John, sits talking with one of his companions, Conrade, in the courtyard of Leonato's house.

Conrade: Why the blazes are you in such a bad mood today?

Don John: I don't need any special reason. It's just my nature.

Conrade: Not too long ago, you were completely out of favor with your brother, the prince. Now he has forgiven you for all your past mischief. You're back in his good graces. And if you want to stay that way, you had better put on a happy face.

Don John: I hate pretending I'm nice when, honestly, I'm a plain old villain.

Conrade: You're so unhappy all the time, Don John. Can't you make some use of all your discontent?

Don John: I *do* use my unhappiness. It's the one thing that drives me in everything I do.

Narrator 3: Borachio, another of Don John's companions, enters the courtyard.

Don John: What's up, Borachio?

Borachio: I bring you gossip about an intended marriage.

Don John: Who's the marrying fool?

Borachio: Your brother's right-hand man, Claudio.

Don John: And his intended bride?

Borachio: Lady Hero, Leonato's daughter and heir.

Don John: Claudio, that little upstart, has had far too much glory lately! My brother lavishes attention on him. Well, well. If I can cross him in any way, the pleasure will be all mine.

Scene 3

Narrator 1: By the next day, Claudio has asked for Hero's hand in marriage, and Leonato has agreed. The wedding is set to take place several days later.

Leonato: Count Claudio, take my daughter and with her my fortunes.

Narrator 2: Smiling Claudio is speechless. Hero beams back at him.

Beatrice: Speak, Count! This is your cue!

Claudio: If I were only a little bit happy, I could say how happy I am. But since I am completely happy, only silence can express my joy. *(to Hero)* Lady, I am yours.

Narrator 3: Hero takes Claudio's hand.

Beatrice: Speak, cousin! It's your cue now! Or, if you cannot speak, stop his mouth with a kiss and keep him from having to say anything more.

Narrator 1: Claudio and Hero kiss.

Don Pedro: *(to Beatrice)* Lady, you have a merry heart.

Beatrice: It's true, my lord.

Narrator 2: Hero whispers into Claudio's ear.

Beatrice: Look, she's telling him she loves him. So goes the world—everyone gets married. Only I remain single.

Don Pedro: Lady Beatrice, I will get you a husband!

Beatrice: *(joking)* Does Your Grace have a brother like yourself? It seems to me that your father created some superb husbands, if only a girl could come by one of them.

Don Pedro: *(also joking)* Did you wish to marry me, lady?

Beatrice: No, my lord, unless I could have another husband for ordinary workdays. You seem too valuable for everyday use. But please forgive me. I'm only joking, as usual.

Don Pedro: Your silence would offend me more than anything you could ever say in jest. Being merry suits you best.

Leonato: *(interrupting)* Niece, will you see after those things I told you about?

Beatrice: Yes, of course, uncle. Cousins, may you have great joy!

Narrator 3: Beatrice leaves.

Don Pedro: My word, she is a pleasant, high-spirited lady.

Leonato: She's almost never melancholy.

Don Pedro: She can't endure the thought of having a husband.

Leonato: No. She's terrible. She makes fun of all her suitors and chases them away.

Don Pedro: Seems to me she would make an excellent wife for Benedict.

Leonato: Oh, goodness! In just a week of marriage, those two would talk themselves mad!

Don Pedro: I'll wager you that between now and the wedding next week, we can get those two together. I'd love to see Beatrice and Benedict married, and I think I know how to bring it about. Are you with me?

Leonato: I'll help you even if I have to stay up ten nights in a row to do it!

Claudio: Just tell me what to do.

Hero: I'll do my part, as well.

Scene 4

Narrator 1: Don John and Borachio talk privately.

Don John: So it's all set. Count Claudio is supposed to marry Leonato's daughter.

Borachio: Yes, but I know how to stop the marriage from happening.

Don John: What have you got in mind?

Borachio: I think I told you that Margaret, one of Hero's ladies-in-waiting, fancies me.

Don John: Yes, I knew that. Go on.

Borachio: Well, I'm certain that she can get me into Hero's chamber.

Don John: How will that help us prevent the marriage?

Borachio: Here's the plan. At some arranged hour when Lady Hero is not in her chamber, you'll go to your brother. Tell him that Claudio has been dishonored and that Lady Hero has been seeing another man—me.

Don John: They won't believe it. How will I prove it?

Borachio: You'll lead them into the street below Hero's window. I will get Margaret to put on one of Hero's cloaks to fool Claudio. While you, Don Pedro, and Claudio watch, Margaret and I will stand at the window and kiss.

Don John: An excellent plan. If it works, you'll get fifty gold coins for your trouble.

Scene 5

Narrator 2: Benedict is alone, strolling through Leonato's garden.

Benedict: *(muttering to himself)* Claudio has always laughed at the follies of men in love. It amazes me to see him fall into the love trap himself. Not long ago, all he cared for was battle. Now look at him! He used to speak in plain language. Now he speaks flowery nonsense all the time!

Narrator 3: Benedict pauses and sits down.

Benedict:	Will I ever be converted and see through the eyes of love? I don't think it will ever happen to me.
Narrator 1:	Benedict spots Don Pedro, Leonato, and Claudio coming.
Benedict:	Here comes Mr. Love now, along with the prince and Leonato. I'll hide in this arbor until they pass.
Don Pedro:	*(whispering to the others)* Do you see Benedict hiding over there?
Narrator 2:	Claudio and Leonato smile and nod at Don Pedro.
Don Pedro:	*(in a loud, clear voice)* Signior Leonato, what was it that you were saying earlier about your niece, Beatrice, being in love with Benedict?
Claudio:	I thought that lady would never love any man!
Leonato:	I thought the same. It's amazing how she dotes on Benedict while pretending she can't stand him.
Benedict:	*(to himself)* Can this possibly be true?
Leonato:	Yes, she's madly in love with him.
Don Pedro:	Maybe she's faking it.
Leonato:	Faking it? If that's the case, then never was pretended passion so similar to real passion.
Benedict:	*(to himself)* I would think this was a trick if the old gentleman were not saying it!
Claudio:	*(whispering to the others)* Do you think Benedict is buying this?
Don Pedro:	*(in a loud voice)* Has Beatrice made her love known to Benedict?
Leonato:	No, and she swears she never will. She says it is her torment to bear.
Claudio:	Beatrice feels she can't say anything because she has so often treated Benedict with scorn.
Leonato:	Hero says that Beatrice gets up twenty times a night and sits writing her feelings down on paper. Then she tears the paper up and falls down weeping.
Don Pedro:	Maybe somebody ought to tell Benedict about the lady's passion.
Claudio:	What would the purpose be? He would just make fun of her.
Don Pedro:	If he did, he'd deserve to be hanged! Beatrice is such a sweet, lovely, virtuous lady.
Claudio:	And she is exceedingly wise.
Don Pedro:	In everything but in loving Benedict!
Narrator 3:	Don Pedro, Claudio, and Leonato continue like this for some time, then walk out of the garden.
Benedict:	It can't have been a trick. They all sounded so serious! They have heard the truth from Hero.

Narrator 1:	Benedict comes out onto the walkway and paces back and forth.
Benedict:	They think I am proud. Are they right? They say the lady is fair and wise. She is all that and more. Oh, dear! Perhaps I am in love with Lady Beatrice, just as she is with me.
Narrator 2:	Suddenly, he sees Beatrice approaching.
Beatrice:	Against my will, I have been sent to bring you in to dinner.
Benedict:	Fair Beatrice, I thank you for taking pains to come and get me.
Beatrice:	If it had been painful, I wouldn't have come!
Benedict:	Then you enjoyed delivering your message?
Beatrice:	About as much as I'd enjoy being held at knife point. Aren't you hungry? I am. Good-bye.
Narrator 3:	She turns and leaves him trying to interpret what he's just heard.
Benedict:	"Against my will, I have been sent to bring you in to dinner." There's a double meaning in that somewhere! There must be! If I don't take pity on the poor lady, I'm a villain!

Scene 6

Narrator 1:	The next day, in the garden with Margaret and Ursula, her ladies-in-waiting, Hero begins her part of the scheme to bring Beatrice and Benedict together.
Hero:	Margaret, find Beatrice. Tell her that Ursula and I are in the garden talking about her behind her back. I know she'll take the bait, come out, and hide where she can overhear us.
Margaret:	It's as good as done.
Narrator 2:	Margaret leaves.
Hero:	Now, Ursula—when Beatrice comes, all we do is walk up and down and talk about how Benedict is in love with her. Here comes Beatrice now!
Narrator 3:	Ursula and Hero begin to stroll near where Beatrice has concealed herself.
Ursula:	But are you sure that Benedict really is wildly in love with Beatrice?
Hero:	That's what the prince and Claudio say.
Ursula:	Did they want you to tell her?
Hero:	Yes. But I told them I wouldn't. I convinced them that they should help Benedict get his feelings under control.
Ursula:	Why did you do that? Don't you think Benedict deserves Beatrice?

Hero:	He deserves everything a man could ever have. He is truly a great man, in speech, appearance, and honor. But there's never been a prouder woman than Beatrice. She's full of disdain and scorn. She prizes her wit so much that nothing else matters to her. No—Beatrice can't love anyone. She's too in love with herself.
Ursula:	I think you're right. And therefore it's certainly not a good idea to tell her about Benedict's love. She would just make fun of him.
Narrator 1:	The conversation between Hero and Ursula continues. Beatrice is stunned by their words.
Beatrice:	*(to herself)* What's this I'm hearing? Can it be true? Does everyone condemn me so much for my pride? I guess it's time to say good-bye to scorn and contempt. Nothing good is said of a scornful person when her back is turned! Benedict—keep loving me, and I will tame my wild heart so that it loves you back. Others are saying that you deserve to be loved, and I believe it.

Scene 7

Narrator 2:	That evening, Leonato, Don Pedro, and Claudio come upon Benedict sitting alone and sighing mournfully.
Leonato:	Signior Benedict, you look so sad and thoughtful.
Claudio:	Maybe he's in love.
Don Pedro:	There's no drop of blood in this man that could ever be touched with love. If he's sad, it's because he needs money.
Benedict:	I have a toothache.
Don Pedro:	And you're sighing over it?
Claudio:	I still say he's in love. That's what all the symptoms point to. Look—he's been to the barber.
Leonato:	Yes, indeed. He looks much younger without his beard.
Don Pedro:	And what's this smell? Is our Benedict wearing cologne?
Claudio:	Yes, he is. And that gives it away completely. He is surely in love!
Don Pedro:	The greatest symptom of all is his melancholy.
Benedict:	None of this foolishness is making my toothache feel any better. *(to Leonato)* I would like to have a few words with you, sir, somewhere away from these buffoons.
Narrator 3:	Leonato and Benedict leave the room together. A moment later, Don John rushes in.
Don John:	Dear brother, good evening. If you have a moment, I would like to speak with you and Count Claudio.
Don Pedro:	What's the matter?

Don John:	*(to Claudio)* Do you still plan to get married tomorrow?
Claudio:	Why? Is there some reason I shouldn't?
Don John:	You may think that I'm not your friend, Claudio, but I'm about to spare you from making a great mistake. I've discovered that your bride-to-be isn't loyal.
Don Pedro:	Leonato's Hero?
Don John:	Leonato's Hero, Claudio's Hero, every man's Hero . . .
Claudio:	Are you saying what I think you're saying?
Don John:	Come with me tonight, and you'll see Hero in her chamber with another man—on the very eve of her wedding! If you still love her then, marry her tomorrow, but I think it would be wiser to change your mind.
Claudio:	Can he be speaking the truth?
Don Pedro:	I don't think so.
Don John:	Just come with me and then make up your mind.
Claudio:	If tonight I see any reason why I shouldn't get married tomorrow, I will shame the woman I was planning to wed right there in the church.
Don Pedro:	What a strange and terrible turn this day has taken!

Scene 8

Narrator 1:	Late that night, after the trick has been played on Claudio, a night watchman overhears a conversation between Borachio and Conrade.
Dogberry:	Who's this, now? These two look suspicious. I'll hide myself and listen to their conversation.
Borachio:	Have a drink of this, Conrade. I'll be able to buy plenty more. I've just earned fifty gold pieces from Don John!
Conrade:	What vile deed could possibly be worth that much?
Borachio:	All I had to do was kiss Margaret in the window of Lady Hero's chamber.
Conrade:	That's it?
Borachio:	Well, I also had to call her Hero in a loud voice so that the prince and Claudio would hear and mistake Margaret for Hero.
Dogberry:	*(quietly)* What's this I'm hearing? It sounds like a plot against the prince and Claudio! I must inform Signior Leonato!
Narrator 2:	The next morning, as Leonato is preparing for the wedding, Dogberry rushes in.

Leonato:	I'm in a hurry right now. I must get to the chapel. What do you want with me, sir?
Dogberry:	I've heard some villains discussing a terrible plot. I think you need to question these men.
Leonato:	Arrest them, and I'll question them later. Or else you can do the questioning. I am too busy right now to look after matters of the law.

Scene 9

Narrator 3:	Hero, Leonato, Claudio, Beatrice, Benedict, Don John, and the prince are gathered in the church for the wedding.
Leonato:	Come, Friar Francis, keep the ceremony brief.
Friar Francis:	You've come here today, Count Claudio, to marry this lady.
Claudio:	No.
Narrator 1:	Leonato thinks Claudio is making a joke.
Leonato:	Claudio comes *in order to be married to her.* You're the one doing the marrying, Friar.
Narrator 2:	Everyone laughs—except Claudio and the prince.
Friar:	Lady, you've come here today in order *to be married to* this count.
Hero:	I have.
Friar:	If anyone knows any reason why these two souls should not be joined together, let that person speak now.
Claudio:	Do you know a reason, Hero?
Hero:	None, my lord.
Friar:	Do you know a reason, Count?
Narrator 3:	There is uncomfortable silence.
Leonato:	I can speak for the count. He knows none. Let's proceed.
Claudio:	Wait just a moment, Friar. Father Leonato, do you with a clear conscience give your daughter to me?
Leonato:	Of course. She is yours.
Narrator 1:	Claudio hands Hero to Leonato.
Claudio:	Here, Leonato—take her back. She's a rotten orange. Look how she blushes, pretending to be an honest, modest maiden. I know better, though!
Leonato:	What do you mean?
Claudio:	I mean not to be married!

Don Pedro:	My friend Count Claudio has been dishonored. Your daughter, Leonato, was seen last night kissing another man in her bedchamber.
Leonato:	I can't believe my ears! Does the prince speak the truth, Hero?
Hero:	*(completely stunned)* The truth?
Claudio:	Hero! Hero! You tricked me, pretending to be what you are not. You broke my heart. Now fare thee well. I want nothing more to do with you.
Narrator 2:	Hero faints.
Beatrice:	Cousin!
Narrator 3:	Don Pedro, Don John, and Claudio storm off, while Beatrice tries to revive Hero.
Benedict:	*(to Beatrice)* How is she?
Beatrice:	She hardly seems to breathing. Hero! Hero!
Leonato:	Better she should die than live in shame. I wish I could die as well.
Friar:	I watched this lady's face as the accusations were brought against her. Her angelic face was filled with horror. There has surely been some error.
Narrator 1:	Hero's eyes flutter open.
Friar:	Lady, what man are you accused of kissing?
Hero:	Only my accusers know. I don't.
Friar:	*(to Leonato)* She's telling the truth. Until we find out what's going on, here is what I think you should do. Claudio and the prince left the girl for dead. Let everyone think that she is indeed dead. At the idea of her death, hearts will soften toward her. Meanwhile, she can remain hidden in the convent.
Benedict:	Signior Leonato, listen to the friar's good advice. Although I have a great friendship with the prince and Claudio, I promise to keep your secret.
Leonato:	I agree to this plan.
Narrator 2:	The friar and Leonato escort Hero out. Only Beatrice and Benedict are left in the chapel.
Benedict:	Lady Beatrice, surely your sweet cousin has been wronged.
Beatrice:	If any man could right this wrong, he would be my greatest friend.
Benedict:	I would like to be that friend. You might think it strange, but I find that I love nothing as well as you.
Beatrice:	It's only as strange as the fact that I love nothing as well as you.
Narrator 3:	She acts embarrassed and flustered.

Beatrice:	Don't believe me! Yet, I'm telling the truth. . . . I confess nothing and deny nothing.
Benedict:	I'd swear, Beatrice, that you do love me! And I love you, too, with all my heart. Come, ask me to do anything for you.
Beatrice:	The thing I need most I cannot ask.
Benedict:	Ask it!
Beatrice:	Kill Claudio.
Benedict:	Ha! Not for the whole world!
Beatrice:	Then there is no love in you.
Narrator 1:	As she turns to leave, he stops her.
Benedict:	Don't go yet. We must part as friends.
Beatrice:	If you were my friend, you would fight my enemy.
Benedict:	Is Claudio your enemy?
Beatrice:	That villain has slandered and dishonored my cousin! If I were a man, I would challenge him myself.
Narrator 2:	She turns again to leave.
Benedict:	Stay, Beatrice. For your sake, I will challenge Claudio and make him pay. Go comfort your cousin. I will go and make my challenge.

Scene 10

Narrator 3:	Claudio and Don Pedro stand talking in the street. They have heard the report that Hero is dead and have also just learned that Don John has fled the town. Benedict approaches them.
Don Pedro:	Here comes the man we've been looking for.
Benedict:	Good day, my lord.
Claudio:	We have been up and down looking for you. We are melancholy and need you to cheer us up. Will you use your wit?
Benedict:	My wit's in my scabbard. Should I draw it?
Claudio:	Yes, for we need it badly.
Narrator 1:	Benedict takes hold of the handle of his sword, preparing to draw.
Don Pedro:	My word! He looks so pale! Benedict, are you sick or angry?
Narrator 2:	Benedict draws his sword.
Benedict:	*(to Claudio)* You are a villain! You have killed a sweet lady, and her death shall fall heavily on you. You can answer my challenge when you dare and with whatever weapon you dare use. Good day.
Narrator 3:	Benedict walks off.

Don Pedro:	I don't think he's joking!
Claudio:	He's actually challenging me! It must be for love of Beatrice.
Narrator 1:	Dogberry and some other officers come down the street leading Conrade and Borachio, who are handcuffed. Leonato comes out of his house to meet the constables and their prisoners.
Dogberry:	Justice will tame you, sirs.
Leonato:	Which is the villain? Let me see his eyes. Then, when I note another man like him, I can avoid him.
Narrator 2:	Borachio hangs his head in shame.
Borachio:	I fooled the prince and Claudio into thinking they saw Hero kissing me. I am wholly responsible for innocent Hero's death.
Leonato:	That's not the whole story. I hear that another villain, Don John, has fled from Messina. *(scathingly to Claudio and Don Pedro)* I thank you, sirs, for my daughter's death. Record it with your other great and noble deeds.
Narrator 3:	Claudio and Don Pedro have heard the words of Borachio and are stunned.
Claudio:	*(to Leonato)* I see that I've made a terrible mistake. I don't know how to ask for your forgiveness, Signior Leonato. Whatever price you wish for me to pay, I'll pay.
Leonato:	You cannot bring my daughter back to life. That's impossible. So I ask you only to come to her tomb tonight and hang a notice of her innocence there. Then, since you cannot be my son-in-law, I ask you to become my nephew instead. My brother has a daughter who is almost a copy of my dead child. Marry her tomorrow morning, and I'll need no revenge.
Claudio:	You are too kind! I gladly accept your offer.
Leonato:	Until tomorrow then, lords, farewell.
Narrator 1:	Leonato departs with Dogberry, the other officers, and the captives, Borachio and Conrade.

Scene 11

Narrator 2:	The next morning, Leonato, Benedict, Margaret, Ursula, Beatrice, Hero, and the friar are gathered in the front room of Leonato's house.
Friar:	Didn't I tell you that Hero was innocent?
Leonato:	So are the prince and Claudio. They were victims of one of Don John's tricks. *(to Hero and the other women)* Well, ladies, time to disappear for a while. The prince and Claudio will be here soon.
Narrator 3:	The women leave the room.

Benedict:	*(to the friar)* Father, I have to ask you a favor.
Friar:	Yes, signior?
Narrator 1:	Benedict looks embarrassed. He turns from the friar to Leonato.
Benedict:	Signior Leonato, the truth is, your niece looks on me with favor . . . and I find myself feeling the same.
Leonato:	I have noticed as much. But what do you wish for?
Benedict:	I ask the honor of being married today to Beatrice.
Leonato:	I would be glad to see that!
Narrator 2:	Don Pedro and Claudio arrive.
Don Pedro:	Good morning, sirs.
Leonato:	Good morning. *(to Claudio)* Are you still determined to marry my brother's daughter?
Claudio:	I'll stick to the bargain.
Leonato:	*(calling)* Ladies!
Narrator 3:	The women enter with their faces masked.
Claudio:	Which is the one I am to marry?
Narrator 1:	Leonato escorts the masked Hero to Claudio's side.
Claudio:	Give me your hand in front of this holy friar. I am your husband, if you wish it.
Narrator 2:	Hero removes her mask.
Claudio:	Another Hero!
Hero:	One Hero died of shame, but this one lives and still loves you.
Don Pedro:	It *is* Hero! The same Hero!
Leonato:	She only died as long as her name was slandered. Let's be off to the chapel now.
Benedict:	Wait a moment. Which one of you ladies is Beatrice?
Narrator 3:	Beatrice removes her mask.
Beatrice:	I'm the one who answers to that name. What do you wish?
Benedict:	Do you not love me?
Beatrice:	Why, no—no more than is reasonable.
Benedict:	Then your uncle and the prince and Claudio have been deceived. They swore you loved me beyond reason.
Beatrice:	Do you not love me?
Benedict:	No more than is reasonable.

Beatrice:	Then my cousin, Margaret, and Ursula were very much deceived. They swore you did.
Benedict:	They swore that you were almost sick with love for me.
Beatrice:	They swore that you were as good as dead of love for me.
Benedict:	Then you don't love me?
Beatrice:	Just as a friend.
Leonato:	Oh come, niece! I am sure you love the gentleman.
Claudio:	I can prove that he loves her. Here's a love sonnet written to her in his penmanship!
Narrator 1:	Claudio shows the poem.
Hero:	And here's another, written in my cousin's handwriting and stolen from her pocket. It's to Benedict.
Narrator 2:	Hero shows the poem.
Benedict:	It's a miracle. Our own hands prove our hearts guilty as charged. Come, I will marry you. *(joking)* I'll take you out of pity.
Beatrice:	*(joking)* And I will marry you, but only to save your life, for I was told you were at death's door.
Benedict:	For once, I will silence you!
Narrator 3:	He kisses her.
Benedict:	Well, it looks as if I'm getting married, after all. In fact, nobody can stop me!
Narrator 1:	Benedict takes Beatrice's hand.
Benedict:	*(to Claudio)* I think I would have beaten you in the duel. But since we're going to be cousins now, I'll let you live on unbruised.
Claudio:	Thanks for sparing me, cousin!
Leonato:	Let's get the weddings started!
Narrator 2:	They all begin to move toward the chapel. Hero is on Claudio's arm, and Beatrice on Benedict's.
Narrator 3:	Benedict looks over at Don Pedro, who is walking all by himself.
Benedict:	*(to Don Pedro)* Poor Prince! All alone and lonely! I know the remedy for that! Get thee a wife! Get thee a wife!

Simply Shakespeare: Readers Theatre for Young People is from *Read* magazine, a Weekly Reader publication, in collaboration with Teacher Ideas Press. Edited by Jennifer Kroll. www.weeklyreader.com. www.lu.com/tips. 1–800–541–2086.

CHAPTER 9

Othello

By William Shakespeare

Adapted by Kate Davis

 Summary

Othello, a dark-skinned "Moor," is a general and war hero in Venice. He has secretly married a Venetian woman named Desdemona, with whom he is deeply in love. Othello is not liked by everyone. Roderigo had hoped to marry Desdemona and is therefore jealous of Othello. Iago is angry with Othello for having promoted a man named Cassio to a position that he himself hoped to gain. Together, Iago and Roderigo plot to destroy Othello's happiness. They expose Othello's secret marriage to Desdemona, angering her father. When Othello and his officers are called away to help defend Cyprus against Turkish invaders, Iago continues his evil plotting from Cyprus. He tries to make Cassio look incompetent and lose his position. Iago also works hard to convince Othello that Desdemona and Cassio have been having an affair. His efforts are successful. Filled with self-doubt and consumed with jealousy, Othello loses control of his actions and emotions, and tragedy results.

Presentation Suggestions

Place Othello and Desdemona front and center. Arrange Cassio, Bianca, and Emilia to the side of Desdemona. Place Iago to the side of Othello, with Roderigo and Brabantio near him. Arrange the remaining characters in a row behind the others. You may place the narrators off to the side or separate them in some other way.

 Props

Othello, Cassio, and Iago could wear fatigues or some type of military clothing to indicate that they are soldiers. (Sailor caps or marching band jackets might be used to indicate the same.) Othello can be decorated with medals to indicate that he is a general. The ladies can wear long skirts. Roderigo, Brabantio, Senator, Duke of Venice, Montano, and Lodovico can wear nice clothing or suit jackets to indicate that they are gentlemen. A handkerchief plays an important role in the plot, and you may wish to have students pass a handkerchief back and forth at appropriate moments in the play.

Cast of Characters

(main parts in boldface)

Narrators 1, 2
Iago, *Othello's standard bearer*
Roderigo, *suitor of Desdemona*
Brabantio, *Desdemona's father; a senator*
Othello, *a general, the North African Moor*
Cassio, *Othello's new lieutenant*
Senator
Duke of Venice
Desdemona, *Brabantio's daughter; Othello's wife*
Lookout
Montano, *governor of Cyprus*
Emilia, *Iago's wife*
Bianca, *Cassio's mistress*
Lodovico, *Brabantio's kinsman*

Othello

By William Shakespeare
Adapted by Kate Davis

Scene 1

Narrator 1: Iago, a soldier, and Roderigo, a nobleman, are talking on a street in Venice.

Iago: I must admit, I hate Othello. Why shouldn't I? I was supposed to be his lieutenant. Instead, he chose Cassio, who knows less about battle than a spinster does! He's never led a squad of men onto the field. I've proved my war service, yet the Moor grants me the job of flag bearer!

Roderigo: I'd rather be his hangman. Don't follow him anymore.

Iago: I follow him only to serve my own ends. Some men dote on their masters, but I'm not that kind of person. I perform my duty, but I don't wear my heart on my sleeve just so birds can peck at it. No, in following Othello, I follow myself. I may appear to be dutiful, but I am not what I am.

Roderigo: Othello has stolen the woman I love.

Iago: Does Desdemona's father know that she ran off with Othello?

Roderigo: I don't know. There's her father's house.

Iago: Wake him and tell him! Poison what he holds dear. His anger will vex Othello's joy.

Narrator 2: Roderigo pounds on the door of the house where Desdemona's father, Brabantio, lives.

Roderigo: Ho! Brabantio!

Iago: Awake! Thieves!!

Narrator 1: Brabantio comes to the window.

Brabantio: What's going on?

Roderigo: Are your doors locked?

Brabantio: Why do you ask me that?

Iago: You are robbed! A black ram is breeding with your white ewe.

Brabantio: Have you lost your wits? Who's there?

Roderigo: It is I, Roderigo.

Brabantio: I told you to stay away from my daughter. Instead you come here drunk to ruin my peace?

Roderigo: I come sober. Your daughter has fallen into the arms of a black man. Have you given permission for her to spend her beauty and wit on that stranger? Check and see if she's home.

Brabantio: *(to servants)* Bring me a candle!

Iago: *(to Roderigo)* I should leave. I can't be seen opposing Othello in public. I hate him like the pains of hell, but I must pretend to love him. Lead Brabantio to Othello. I'll be there.

Narrator 2: Desdemona's father comes outside.

Brabantio: You're right, Roderigo, she's gone. O unhappy girl! Did you say she is with the Moor? Are they married?

Roderigo: I think they are.

Brabantio: How did she get out? Blood treason! Fathers, trust not your daughters' minds! The Moor must have put a spell on her. Can you find them?

Roderigo: Call your guard and follow me.

Brabantio: *(to servants)* Fetch an officer! Bring weapons! *(to Roderigo)* Lead on!

Scene 2

Narrator 1: Iago finds Othello and warns him that Desdemona's father is looking for him.

Iago: I tried to calm him down, but he spoke with such scurvy against you. Are you married officially? Brabantio might bring the law down on you.

Othello: We're legally married. Let him say what he will. The services I've provided this city outweigh his complaints. And I love Desdemona.

Narrator 2: Othello's lieutenant, Cassio, joins them.

Othello: What news, friend?

Cassio: The duke summons you to appear before him.

Othello: On what matter?

Cassio: He has news from Cyprus and is meeting with consuls.

Othello: Let me get my things. . . .

Cassio: *(to Iago)* What is he doing here?

Iago:	Othello got married tonight.
Cassio:	What? To whom?
Narrator 1:	Before Iago can answer, Othello returns, then Brabantio's search party arrives.
Iago:	*(to Othello)* Get inside, sir!
Othello:	I will not. I have nothing to hide.
Roderigo:	Here is the Moor, sir.
Narrator 2:	Everyone draws weapons.
Brabantio:	Down with him! Thief!
Othello:	The dew will rust your swords. Sir, you command more respect with age than your weapons. What is this about?
Brabantio:	Foul thief! Where have you stowed my tender daughter? She was so opposed to marriage she shunned the wealthy, good-looking men of Venice. She would never run to the sooty bosom of such a thing as you. Have you used magic on her? Abused her with drugs? *(to officers)* Arrest him for practicing illegal arts!
Othello:	Hold your hands! Sir, where can we go to discuss this charge?
Brabantio:	To prison!
Othello:	I cannot. I must answer the duke's summons.
Cassio:	*(to Brabantio)* The duke is in council and has sent for you too, Senator.
Brabantio:	At this time of night? Then we shall go before him. He will sympathize with this wrong. If acts like this go free, all statesmen will be slaves.

Scene 3

Narrator 1:	Othello and Brabantio go to talk with the duke in the council chambers.
Senator:	A huge Turkish fleet is heading to Cyprus! Montano begs our aid.
Duke:	Othello, you must go fight this enemy.
Brabantio:	*(arriving)* Pardon, Your Grace. I have an overbearing grief.
Duke:	What is the matter?
Brabantio:	My daughter . . .
Duke:	Has she died?
Brabantio:	She has been stolen from me, abused, and corrupted by spells!
Duke:	Who has done this?

Brabantio:	Here is the man—this Moor.
Duke:	*(to Othello)* What do you have to say?
Othello:	Sir, the only magic I have done is to win his daughter's love. I have married her.
Brabantio:	It is against all laws of nature that she would fall for a man so unlike her. I swear he used potions to overtake her.
Duke:	Your swearing is not proof.
Senator:	Have you charmed or poisoned her?
Othello:	Let my lady speak for herself.
Duke:	Fetch Desdemona.
Othello:	Until she comes, I'll explain how we fell in love . . . . Her father often invited me to his house and asked me to tell stories of my life. I told of disastrous chances, accidents, floods, hair-breadth escapes. I told of being sold into slavery and released. I told of travels through deserts and hills that reached to heaven. I spoke of cannibals and strange men.
Narrator 2:	The duke and senators are entranced.
Othello:	Desdemona listened with greedy ear to the tale of my pilgrimage and often wept. When my story was over, she'd sigh that it was "passing strange." She loved me for the dangers I had passed, and I loved her that she did pity them. This is the only spell I cast on her.
Duke:	This tale would win my daughter, too.
Brabantio:	Here is Desdemona. Hear her speak. If she confesses her love, then let destruction fall on me for blaming this man.
Desdemona:	My noble father, I am bound to you for my life and education, and I respect you. But this man is my husband. I owe him as much duty as my mother showed you. I love this man.
Brabantio:	God be with you! Moor, I give you that which I would keep from you. I am done. *(to the duke)* Continue the affairs of state, your grace. . . .
Duke:	In time your grief and injury will end.
Brabantio:	I will bear my sorrow and my bruised heart. Carry on. . . .
Duke:	Agreed. *(turning to Othello)* You are the only one who knows Cyprus well. I must send you on this expedition.
Othello:	I will undertake these wars against the Ottomans. Humbly, I ask fit lodging for my wife.
Duke:	Where do you wish to stay?

Desdemona:	I loved the Moor and wanted to live with him. I pledged my soul to his valiant mind and honor. He will be gone a long time. Please let me go with him.
Othello:	If she comes, I assure you, it will not corrupt your serious business.
Duke:	You must leave immediately. Keep an officer behind to bring her after.
Othello:	Iago, my standard bearer, is trustworthy. He can convey my wife to me.
Duke:	Then let it be. Brabantio, know this: Virtue may lack beauty, but your son-in-law is far more fair than he is black.
Brabantio:	Perhaps. But beware, Moor! She deceived her father and may deceive you.
Othello:	I give my life on her faith. Come, Desdemona. We have only one hour together before I leave.
Narrator 1:	After they go, Roderigo takes Iago aside. He is miserable because he's lost the one he loves.
Roderigo:	I'm going to drown myself.
Iago:	Drown blind puppies, if you must, but be a man! A match between a barbarian and a Venetian cannot last. Desdemona will find error in her choice.
Roderigo:	Will you help me win her?
Iago:	I guarantee it. I hate the Moor. Let us be allies in revenge against him. If you steal his wife, you do yourself pleasure and me, sport. Go, and speak not of drowning.
Iago:	*(to himself)* Now I have that fool in my pocket. I hate Othello. I suspect he has played around with my wife. As for Cassio, how will I overtake his position? . . . The Moor is so honest, he can be led by the nose. I will suggest to the Moor that Cassio is too familiar with his new wife! That's my plan. May hell and night bring this monstrous birth to world's light.

Scene 4

Narrator 2:	Othello, his lieutenant Cassio, and Iago, with Desdemona, all sail to Cyprus in separate ships. Othello is the last to arrive, and all fear that he has been lost in a terrible storm.
Narrator 1:	Governor Montano learns that the same storm has destroyed the Turkish fleet and drowned the Ottomans. Cyprus is saved!
Narrator 2:	When Desdemona arrives, Cassio greets her. Iago watches carefully.

Cassio: Bend your knees, men of Cyprus. Hail to thee, lady. I extend my courtesy.

Narrator 1: Cassio takes Desdemona by the hand. Then, releasing her hand, he kisses the fingers that have touched her.

Iago: *(to himself)* Cassio smiles at her and whispers. With this little web, I will turn his courtesies to flirtations and ensnare him. Such tricks may strip him of his position as lieutenant.

Lookout: Hark! A sail! The general comes!

Othello: *(to his wife)* My soul's joy! If after every tempest come such calms, may the winds blow until they've wakened death!

Desdemona: Dearest Othello!

Othello: *(to governor)* How is my old friend?

Montano: Our wars are done; the Turks are drowned! Come, let's go to the castle.

Narrator 2: As Desdemona and Othello accompany the governor to the castle, Iago and Roderigo go to the ship.

Iago: Roderigo, I think Desdemona is in love with Lieutenant Cassio.

Roderigo: What? I don't believe it!

Iago: Didn't you see him dally with her hand? His affections are loose. I tell you, her tenderness will find little beauty in the old Moor. She will look for someone more handsome—and will find him in Cassio. He is a slippery knave.

Roderigo: I wish he were out of the way.

Iago: Then here's a plan. Tonight he stands watch. Find some way to anger him. Provoke him to strike you. I will drum up a ruckus that will unplant him from his office. Then you will have a shorter journey to your desire.

Roderigo: I will do it. Farewell. *(to himself)* I cannot endure Othello. The thought that he has been with the woman I want for my wife gnaws at my innards. I must get even with him. I will plant jealousy in him so strong that his best judgment won't cure it. And when he sees what an upstart Cassio is, he will reward me.

Scene 5

Narrator 1: That evening, Cyprus celebrates its escape from the Turks. Cassio is assigned to guard watch.

Iago: Cassio, you're not on duty until ten o'clock. Let's have some wine.

Cassio: I have poor brains for drinking.

Iago: Come on. We'll toast Othello's bride.

Cassio:	She is exquisite.
Iago:	She has an inviting eye.
Cassio:	Inviting, but modest. She's perfection.
Iago:	Then drink to their happiness.
Cassio:	No, really, I can't hold my liquor.
Iago:	Montano and his men are waiting for us.
Cassio:	I really shouldn't . . . but all right. . . .
Narrator 2:	Cassio is soon drunk. As he wanders away, Iago points out Cassio's drunken state to Governor Montano.
Iago:	See how Cassio goes tipsy to his watch. Othello trusts him, but I fear Cassio may harm this island.
Montano:	Then we must advise the general.
Narrator 1:	Suddenly, Cassio comes running back toward Iago and the governor, chasing Roderigo at sword point.
Roderigo:	Help! Help!
Cassio:	You rogue! I'll beat you!
Montano:	*(to Cassio)* Hold your hand, lieutenant!
Narrator 2:	The governor tries to restrain Cassio.
Cassio:	Let me go!
Montano:	You are drunk.
Cassio:	Drunk?! Who calls me drunk? Why, I'll punish *you*!
Narrator 1:	Cassio turns his sword on Montano.
Montano:	Ah, I am wounded! I bleed!
Narrator 2:	While Montano struggles with Cassio, Iago turns to Roderigo.
Iago:	*(secretly)* Ring the mutiny bell.
Narrator 1:	Roderigo does as Iago suggests. Soon chaos breaks out all over the isle.
Iago:	Alas! Help!
Narrator 2:	Othello comes running up.
Othello:	*(entering)* What is going on? Stop this barbarous brawl! Silence that bell! Who started this fight?
Iago:	We were all friends, then everyone was tilting swords.
Othello:	Would you men discard your reputations for the sake of a private quarrel? Iago, how did this foul rout begin?

Iago: I would rather have my tongue cut out than speak against Cassio.... But, you see ... Montano and I were talking, when Cassio came slashing his sword at a man. I chased the other fellow, but he got away. I'm sure Cassio must have been done an indignity....

Othello: Enough. Clearly, you mince words to protect him. Cassio, I love thee, but I must make an example of you. Never more be my officer!

Narrator 1: Othello takes Montano inside to doctor his wounds and asks Iago to patrol the town. Iago and Cassio are alone.

Cassio: I'm lost! My reputation is gone!

Iago: Don't fret. Reputation is often won without merit and lost without merit as well. There are ways to mend things with the Moor.

Cassio: How could I have disappointed so good a commander? Wine, I call thee devil! Oh, why do we drink? We put an enemy in our mouths to steal our brains, and it turns us into beasts!

Iago: Pull yourself together. Listen, here's what you do: Kind Desdemona has the general's ear. Beseech her to help heal this broken joint.

Cassio: I'll speak with her in the morning.

Iago: *(alone)* Ha! While this fool begs Desdemona for help, I'll whisper to the Moor that lust is what makes her take Cassio's case. Thus will I weave a net to enmesh them all.

Scene 6

Narrator 2: The next morning, Iago arranges for Cassio to speak with Desdemona. He also arranges for Othello to walk the city walls so Desdemona and Cassio can be alone.

Cassio: Madam, can you do anything to heal this rift?

Desdemona: Don't worry. I will appeal on your behalf and have you two friends again.

Cassio: I am forever your servant.

Desdemona: I know you love him. I vow to talk him out of this suit or die in the cause.

Narrator 1: Before long, Othello returns.

Cassio: I must leave. The sight of me might anger him further.

Narrator 2: Othello and Iago step into the room just as Cassio goes out another door.

Iago: *(quietly to Othello)* I like that not.

Othello: What? Was that Cassio?

Iago: It can't be. Why would he be here and steal away so guiltily?

Desdemona: My dear, I was just speaking with a man who suffers from displeasing you.

Othello: Who might that be?

Desdemona: Cassio. Please reconcile with him. He truly loves you.

Othello: Some other time.

Desdemona: When? Tonight? Tomorrow? Just name the time. Have you forgotten that you used to send him to woo me for you? This is not a trivial matter—

Othello: Oh, all right, let him come. I won't deny you. But leave me alone a bit.

Desdemona: I obey.

Narrator 1: Desdemona leaves.

Iago: Lord Othello, did Cassio know you loved Desdemona?

Othello: Of course. Why?

Iago: Nothing . . . I didn't think he knew her.

Othello: He is an honest man, isn't he?

Iago: Honest? I don't know. . . . Honest?

Othello: Don't echo me. You knit your brow, again. What are you thinking?

Iago: That men should be what they seem.

Othello: And if not, then what?

Iago: Sometimes my mind has vile, false thoughts. . . .

Othello: Do you know something?

Iago: It's only a guess. . . . I cannot divulge—

Othello: Tell me!

Iago: Beware of jealousy, my lord. It is a green-eyed monster. To dote on someone but doubt her brings misery.

Othello: I have no reason to doubt my wife. She is fair and virtuous.

Iago: Good. Because I have no proof . . . But I will say this: Observe your wife well with Cassio. Women from my country often keep things hidden from their husbands.

Othello: Is that so?

Iago: Didn't she deceive her own father? But I've said too much. . . . I hope our talk has not caused undue suspicion.

Othello: Not a jot. Desdemona is honest, I'm sure. . . .

Iago: Long live she so!

Othello: Yet nature sometimes errs.... Have your wife watch her carefully.

Iago: I will. And maybe you should keep Cassio off a bit. You might observe better whether your wife strains to see him.

Othello: I will. Now farewell. *(to himself)* This fellow understands humans well. If Desdemona has wronged me, it will tear my heartstrings. O curse of marriage, that we call these delicate creatures ours, but not their desires. I'd rather be a toad and live in a dungeon than keep what I love just to be used.

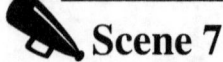

Scene 7

Narrator 2: That evening, Othello admires his wife's beauty and kindness, but doubts have begun to sicken him.

Desdemona: My lord, the islanders wish you to dine with them.

Othello: Tell them my forehead pains me.

Desdemona: Let me bind it with my handkerchief, and it will heal.

Othello: This cloth is too small to wrap. Nevermind. Let's go to dinner, my love.
(to himself) If she is false, then heaven mocks itself!

Narrator 1: Othello drops the hankie. When they leave the room, Emilia finds it while cleaning.

Emilia: This is the very cloth my husband has been after me to borrow! Milady said it is the first token the Moor gave her. But if I don't give it to Iago, he will be angry.

Narrator 2: Iago enters.

Iago: What are you doing?

Emilia: I have something for you—the handkerchief you've requested.

Iago: That's a good wench. Give it to me.

Emilia: What will you do with it?

Iago: None of your business.

Emilia: Milady will go mad missing it.

Iago: Well, I need it. Now go! *(to himself)* I will drop this in Cassio's lodging and let him find it. Such a trifle will make proof of suspicions. My poison already burns in the Moor. Here he comes. He looks as if he'll never sleep again.

Othello: You've set me on the rack.

Iago: What is it, my lord?

Othello: *(in a distraught tone)* My mind will never be at peace! I had no thoughts of my wife's stolen hours. If the whole camp had shared her, I wouldn't know. I was happier then, not knowing. Now I care for nothing!

Iago: Is it possible, lord?

Narrator 1: Othello grabs Iago by the throat.

Othello: Villain, if my wife is having an affair, bring me the proof! Or by my soul, you'll wish you'd been born a dog!

Iago: Has it come to this?

Othello: Leave me no doubts. Or if you slander her, horror will fall on your head.

Iago: Heaven defend me! Is that what I get for being honest?

Othello: I don't know what to think. Is my wife honest? Are you just? You've made her name black as my face. Bring me proof!

Iago: Sir, you are tortured with passion. I wish I had never said anything. What proof do you want? To catch them in the act?

Othello: Damnation, no! But give me some reason you think she is disloyal.

Iago: If you insist... I heard Cassio cry out in his sleep one night, "Sweet Desdemona." He said, "Let us be wary and hide our loves." He puckered and sighed, "Sweet creature!" Then: "Cursed fate, that gave thee to the Moor."

Othello: O monstrous! I'll tear her to pieces!

Iago: It was only a dream. She may be honest yet. We have seen nothing. But tell me—have you ever seen her use a little handkerchief spotted with strawberries?

Othello: I gave her that—my first gift. Why?

Iago: I saw Cassio wipe his beard with it.

Othello: What? Rise up, my black vengeance! Love's crown, yield to hate. I want blood!

Iago: Patience, you may change your mind.

Othello: No. My violent thoughts will not look back till revenge swallows them!

Narrator 2: He kneels, and Iago joins him.

Iago: I give my wit, hands, and heart to your service. Whatever you command, be it bloody work, I shall obey.

Othello: Thank you for your devotion. Within three days, let me hear that Cassio is dead.

Iago: It will be done. But let her live....

Othello: Damn her! I will find some swift means of death for that fair devil. Now, friend, you are my lieutenant.

Iago:	And I am yours forever.

🔊 Scene 8

Narrator 1:	Later that night, Othello tests his wife. Unaware of his doubts, she tries to appeal on Cassio's behalf again.
Desdemona:	My lord. How is it with you?
Othello:	*(with difficulty)* Fine. Give me your hand. Why is it so moist? Devils have sweaty hands. But it is a good hand. . . .
Desdemona:	I should say. It is the hand that gave you my heart. But no more of this. Remember your promise to speak with Cassio? I've sent for him.
Othello:	Not now. I don't feel well. Lend me your handkerchief. The one I gave you, with little strawberries embroidered.
Desdemona:	I . . . don't have it on me.
Othello:	Indeed? That handkerchief was given to me by my mother. She said it was made by an Egyptian and was magical. If it was lost or given away, it would cause the owner's husband to loathe her.
Desdemona:	I wish I had never seen it.
Othello:	Why? Is it lost?
Desdemona:	No, it's not lost.
Othello:	Then where is it? Gone?
Desdemona:	I don't know. . . . Why? Is this a trick to get me to forget my suit for Cassio?
Othello:	Fetch me the handkerchief—now!
Desdemona:	Cassio is a good man, one who has shared all your dangers—
Othello:	*(storming out)* Away with you!
Desdemona:	*(to her maid)* Emilia, I've never seen him like this.
Emilia:	Men are all alike. Look, here comes my husband and Cassio.
Iago:	*(to Cassio)* There is no other way. She *must* ask him.
Cassio:	Madam, I beseech you, do not delay in my appeal. I must know if I can honor Othello again with my service.
Desdemona:	I've done what I can. It is not a good time to ask more. He's not himself. Something has muddled his spirit.
Emilia:	I hope it's not jealousy.
Desdemona:	Keep that monster from his mind. If I can do any more on your behalf, Cassio, I will.

Cassio: Humbly, I thank you.

Narrator 2: Later, Cassio's mistress goes to his room looking for him.

Bianca: Dear Cassio, I haven't seen you for a week. Where have you been?

Cassio: I'm sorry, Bianca. I've been very busy. But here is a token of my affection.

Bianca: A hankie. Where did you get this? From another girlfriend?

Cassio: No. I found it in my room. I like it though. Will you copy the embroidery before the owner claims it? Go on. . . .

Bianca: Go? Don't you care for me anymore? When will I see you again?

Cassio: I'm not sure. . . . Now go.

Scene 9

Narrator 1: Othello is like a man possessed. He is outraged at the thought of his wife's having betrayed him.

Narrator 2: While pretending to sympathize, Iago baits Othello further.

Iago: What if I told you I heard Cassio talking about Desdemona?

Othello: Did you? Did he confess?

Iago: I don't know for sure. If he—

Othello: Did he confess to an affair? First the handkerchief, then a confession?

Narrator 1: Othello is so distraught, he passes out.

Iago: And now my medicine works. . . .

Narrator 2: Cassio, unsuspecting, enters the room looking for Iago.

Cassio: What's wrong with my lord?

Iago: He's had a fit of epilepsy. Don't touch him until it runs its course. He might become savagely mad. Leave us, then return later.

Narrator 1: Cassio departs. A moment later, Othello wakens.

Othello: I want to hear Cassio confess.

Iago: Cassio was to meet me here shortly. Hide yourself in the closet and watch his gestures. I will make him tell me all about it—when, how often. If you hold your tongue and temper, you will see his sneers. Can you be patient?

Othello: I'll be cunning and hide to see that.

Iago: *(to himself)* I'll really ask Cassio about his tart Bianca, a strumpet that sells her favors. He'll laugh at her, and his smiles will drive Othello mad. He will think Cassio scorns Desdemona.

Cassio: *(returning)* I don't know if this business with Desdemona is going to work.

Iago: *(quietly)* Too bad Bianca's not working on it. Then things would move quickly!

Cassio: Ha! Poor rogue. She loves me! Ha-ha!

Othello: *(to himself, as he watches)* He laughs at my wife!

Iago: I heard she wants to marry you.

Cassio: Marry her? I never promised that. She follows me wherever I go. She hangs on me, lolls on me. . . .

Othello: *(watching)* He gestures that she drapes herself all over him!

Narrator 2: Suddenly, Bianca enters the room.

Cassio: What do you want?

Bianca: Why did you give me this hankie? To taunt me with some other minx's token?

Othello: *(to himself)* That's *my* handkerchief!

Bianca: Come to my place tonight or else. . . .

Iago: *(to Cassio)* You should go after her. . . .

Narrator 1: As Cassio follows Bianca from the room, Othello emerges from his hiding place.

Othello: *(seething)* How shall I murder him?

Iago: Did you see how he laughs at your wife? He thinks so little of the token she gave him, he gave it to his whore!

Othello: My heart is turned to stone! My wife was so sweet, so fine. Now I wish she would perish and rot!

Iago: That doesn't sound like you.

Othello: Hang her! She sang so sweetly. . . . O the pity of it!

Iago: It is foul of her.

Othello: I will chop her into a mess! Or get me some poison, Iago. I will end it tonight.

Iago: Not poison. Strangle her in your marriage bed.

Othello: Excellent. That would be justice.

Iago: As for Cassio, leave him to me. I shall be his undertaker.

Scene 10

Narrator 2:	That night, Desdemona's cousin Lodovico arrives with a message.
Lodovico:	Othello, you have been recalled to Venice. Cassio will take over in Cyprus.
Othello:	I will return. But Cassio should not be left in charge!
Desdemona:	*(to Lodovico)* Cousin, Othello and Cassio have had a falling out. Can you set things right? I bear much love for Cassio.
Narrator 1:	At the mention of Cassio's name, Othello strikes Desdemona in a rage.
Othello:	Fire and brimstone, you devil! Get out of my sight!
Desdemona:	Why do you say that, husband? Why do you strike me?
Narrator 2:	Desdemona's eyes fill up with tears, and she runs from the room. Othello storms out after her.
Lodovico:	*(to Iago)* What? Strike his wife? Is this the same unshakeable Moor we knew?
Iago:	I don't know what's wrong with him.
Narrator 1:	Othello seeks his wife's maid.
Othello:	Has Desdemona ever been alone with Cassio?
Emilia:	No, sir. Never. I've been there to listen to every word that's ever passed between them.
Othello:	That's strange....
Emilia:	I swear I'm telling you the truth. I'll lay my soul on it. If anyone has told you otherwise, he is a wretch.
Othello:	Go bring my wife here.
Narrator 2:	Emilia nods and goes to find Desdemona. A few moments later, she enters the room, looking fearful.
Desdemona:	What is it, my lord?
Othello:	Look directly in my eyes, and swear to me that you are faithful!
Desdemona:	Why are you angry? Heaven knows I am faithful.
Narrator 1:	He erupts into tears of frustration.
Othello:	Heaven knows you are false!
Desdemona:	Why do you weep, my lord?
Othello:	I could stand all kinds of afflictions—sores, shame, poverty, captivity. But to be discarded when I have given my heart! I thought you were a lovely flower, but you are no more than a weed!
Desdemona:	*(in horror)* What sin have I committed?

Othello:	I can hardly speak it. The wind is hushed within the earth and will not hear it! My wife is . . . a shameless hussy.
Desdemona:	I have never been touched by anyone other than my husband! Heaven forgive us!
Othello:	Yes, cry for mercy from heaven—you who'll guard the gates of hell!
Narrator 2:	As Othello storms off, Emilia returns.
Emilia:	Alas, Madam, what ails him?
Desdemona:	*(tearfully)* He accused me of being a hussy.
Narrator 1:	Iago comes looking for Emilia.
Iago:	What is the matter, Desdemona?
Emilia:	*(angrily)* Some slanderous villain has put false notions in the Moor's head. He has been abused by a scurvy fellow. If I had a whip, I'd lash him from east to west!
Desdemona:	Good Iago, what shall I do? I don't know how I lost him! I have never trespassed against his love.
Iago:	Affairs of state have him in ill humor. Don't cry; all shall be well.
Narrator 2:	But Desdemona has a haunting feeling that all will *not* be well.
Desdemona:	Emilia, if I should die before you, please shroud me in my wedding sheets.
Emilia:	Why do you talk so?
Desdemona:	My mother had a maid who died singing a heartbroken song. Tonight that song will not leave my mind. It's all I can do not to go hang my head and sing it.
Emilia:	Let me help with your nightgown.
Desdemona:	I wouldn't wrong my husband for the whole world.
Emilia:	If you did, who would blame you? It's husbands' faults if wives fall. They break out in jealousies and strike us for no reason. Whatever ills we do, we have learned from their ills.
Desdemona:	Heaven help me not to return bad with bad, but to mend the bad I find. . . .

Scene 11

Narrator 1:	Iago has promised Othello that he will destroy Cassio. He convinces Roderigo that "removing" Cassio will keep Othello in Cyprus and improve the foolish nobleman's chances with Desdemona.
Roderigo:	But how shall I "remove" Cassio?

Iago:	By knocking out his brains!
Narrator 2:	Under cover of night, Roderigo gets ready to attack Cassio, who is walking home from Bianca's. Iago hides to watch.
Roderigo:	*(springing out)* Villain, you die!
Cassio:	Who attacks me?
Narrator 1:	Striking back, Cassio stabs Roderigo.
Roderigo:	O, I am slain!
Narrator 2:	In pitch darkness, Iago rushes forward to strike Cassio. He slashes him deeply in the leg, then flees before he is seen.
Cassio:	I am maimed! Help!
Narrator 1:	Othello has heard Cassio's cry.
Othello:	Good. Iago has done what he promised. Now I must take care of my wife. . . .
Narrator 2:	Lodovico and Iago run to Cassio's aid.
Iago:	Cassio, who did this to you?
Cassio:	I don't know. He's here in the dark, hiding somewhere.
Narrator 1:	Roderigo is not dead yet, and Iago knows he must silence him. Iago finds Roderigo—and stabs him.
Iago:	Die, murderous villain!
Narrator 2:	Meanwhile, Bianca has heard the shouts in the street and runs up to try to help the wounded Cassio. Iago blames her for the attack.
Iago:	This trash is mixed up in this. Where did Cassio dine tonight?
Bianca:	At my house. Why?
Iago:	Guilt makes you look pale.
Bianca:	I had nothing to do with this!
Iago:	We shall see. Lodovico, bear Cassio inside and dress his wounds. *(to himself)* This night will either make me or undo me.

Scene 12

Narrator 1:	Inside the castle, Othello goes to Desdemona's bedroom and locks the door. He watches her sleep.
Othello:	Her skin is so white and smooth. I will not scar her or shed her blood. Yet she must die. I must put out the light. . . .
Narrator 2:	He begins to weep.
Othello:	Ah, cruel tears. Sorrow strikes where it loves.
Desdemona:	*(muttering, half asleep)* Come to bed, my lord.

Othello: Have you said your prayers? I would not kill your spirit unprepared.

Desdemona: *(suddenly fully awake)* Why do you talk of killing?

Othello: You are to die. Think on your sins.

Desdemona: All I have done is love you!

Othello: Then why did you give Cassio the handkerchief I gave you?

Desdemona: I never gave him a token of love!

Othello: Don't lie. I saw it in his own hand!

Desdemona: He must have found it. By my soul, I never loved Cassio or offended you! Send for him.

Othello: My revenge has silenced him.

Desdemona: O fear! Is he dead?

Othello: Iago is taking care of it.

Desdemona: *(crying)* Then Cassio is betrayed—and I am undone!

Othello: Do you weep for him in front of me? Then die, you whore!

Desdemona: Oh, banish me, but don't kill me! Just let me say one prayer!

Othello: It's too late.

Narrator 1: Othello begins to smother Desdemona with a blanket. As Emilia bangs on the door, Desdemona struggles, then lies still.

Emilia: Open up! I must speak to you, sir!

Narrator 2: When Desdemona has stopped moving, Othello lets Emilia into the room.

Emilia: Foul murder has been done, my lord! Cassio has killed Roderigo.

Othello: *(to himself)* What? Cassio's still alive?

Narrator 1: Suddenly, Desdemona begins to move, making pitiful moaning sounds.

Desdemona: *(moaning)* O falsely murdered!

Narrator 2: Emilia rushes to Desdemona's side.

Emilia: My lady? O sweet mistress, what is wrong? O help!

Desdemona: *(weakly)* I die a guiltless death. . . .

Emilia: Who has done this?

Desdemona: *(dying)* No one. I did it myself.

Emilia: Why would she do this?!

Othello: As she was a whore, I killed her.

Emilia:	She was true as heaven—and an angel for taking the blame. You're a devil!
Othello:	She was false, with Cassio. Just ask your husband.
Emilia:	My husband? What would he know? He lies to the heart! May his soul rot for this!
Othello:	Silence yourself!
Emilia:	I will not. I'm not afraid of you. Ignorant dolt—to have done this deed. *(yelling)* Help! The Moor has killed my lady!
Narrator 1:	At the sound of her screams, Iago and Montano run in.
Montano:	How now, general? What is it?
Emilia:	How dare you, Iago! Othello says you told him his wife was false. Did you say that?
Iago:	I did.
Emilia:	That's a wicked, odious lie!
Iago:	Hold your tongue, woman.
Emilia:	I will do no such thing! My mistress has been murdered in her bed!
Montano:	O monstrous act!
Othello:	O! O! O!
Narrator 2:	Othello collapses onto the bed, his head in his hands.
Emilia:	Yes, lay thee down and roar. You killed the sweetest innocent that ever lifted an eye.
Othello:	She was foul. My hands stopped her breath. She was with Cassio and gave him a pledge of her love—her hankie—
Emilia:	Power of heaven, no! She never did!
Iago:	*(angrily to Emilia)* Say no more I tell you! Go home!
Narrator 1:	Iago raises his dagger over his wife.
Montano:	Hold, sir! Would you use your weapon on a woman?
Emilia:	That handkerchief—my husband urged me often to steal it. When I found it, I gave it to him.
Iago:	You filthy liar!
Narrator 2:	Iago rushes at Emilia and stabs her. Then he bolts from the room. Still alive, Emilia throws herself after him, but he escapes.
Montano:	Guards! After him!
Emilia:	*(faintly)* She loved you, Moor. She was chaste. I speak true....
Narrator 1:	Emilia dies. Othello howls in anguish, taking Desdemona's body in his arms. He realizes he has been all wrong.

Othello: *(in a distraught tone)* O, my ill-starred love! Here is my journey's end. But where should I go? O Desdemona! When we meet in heaven, one look from you will cast me to the fiends. Let them whip me and wash me in gulfs of fire! O dead! O! O! O!

Narrator 2: As Othello writhes in remorse, the injured Cassio comes in with Lodovico, who has captured Iago.

Lodovico: This wretch Iago has confessed.

Othello: You villain! You viper!

Narrator 2: Othello leaps up, grabbing a sword. He stabs Iago.

Othello: You trapped me, body and soul!

Iago: *(faintly)* Say what you like about me. I will never speak another word.

Lodovico: *(to Othello)* He said he conspired with you to kill Cassio.

Cassio: *(to Othello)* General, I have never wronged you.

Othello: I know that now. Forgive me. . . .

Lodovico: We found some letters on Roderigo that prove the conspiracy. Othello, you must come with us. Cassio I put you in charge of Cyprus. As for this slave, Iago, imprison him!

Othello: A word before we go. When you write of these deeds, speak of me as one who loved not wisely but too well . . . as one whose hand threw away a pearl . . . as one whose eyes drop great tears. . . . Tell them, I once took the enemy by the throat and killed him like this—

Narrator 2: Othello stabs himself and falls by his wife. He puts his lips to Desdemona's in a final kiss.

Othello: I die upon a kiss!

Lodovico: O bloody tragedy!

Cassio: I was afraid of this.

Lodovico: This is all your work, Iago, you dog. I sentence you to torture. And now I must go abroad and relate to the state this heavy act with a heavy, heavy heart.

Simply Shakespeare: Readers Theatre for Young People is from *Read* magazine, a Weekly Reader publication, in collaboration with Teacher Ideas Press. Edited by Jennifer Kroll. www.weeklyreader.com. www.lu.com/tips. 1–800–541–2086.

CHAPTER 10

Romeo and Juliet

By William Shakespeare

Adapted by Kate Davis

162 \ Chapter 10: Romeo and Juliet

 ## Summary

Two families of Verona, Italy—the Montagues and Capulets—have a long-running feud that has resulted in much bloodshed. Despite the hatred between their families, young Romeo Montague and Juliet Capulet fall in love and secretly marry. However, their bliss is short-lived. When Juliet's cousin kills Romeo's friend, Romeo avenges the death. In punishment, he is banished from Verona. Meanwhile, Juliet's parents, unaware of their daughter's marriage to Romeo, pressure her to marry another man and also inform her that they are having Romeo poisoned while in exile. Juliet seeks the assistance of a monk named Friar Laurence. He helps her avoid the unwanted marriage by giving her a potion that makes her seem temporarily dead. Friar Laurence then sends a messenger to Romeo, telling him of Juliet's action and the attempt to be made on his life. However, the messenger does not reach Romeo before he hears of Juliet's death and hurries back to Verona. Romeo breaks into the Capulet family crypt to give his presumably dead wife one last kiss, then kills himself. When Juliet comes to, she sees her dead husband and kills herself. The deaths of the lovers bring peace between the two warring families.

 ## Presentation Suggestions

Cluster the Montagues and friends—Benvolio, Lord Montague, Lady Montague, Romeo, Mercutio, and Balthasar—on one side of the room. Angle these readers so that they are partially facing the Capulets—Tybalt, Lord Capulet, Lady Capulet, Nurse, and Juliet—who are on the other side of the room. Place the narrators, Friar Laurence, and the Prince of Verona in the center and toward the back. You may also wish to place two empty chairs front and center and have Romeo and Juliet move to these chairs when they are interacting with each other in Scenes 5, 6, 9, 13, 17, 18, and 19.

 ## Props

The Prince can wear a crown. Juliet and Romeo can wear white. Romeo, Mercutio, and Benvolio might wear masks during the masquerade party. Friar Laurence can wear a blanket or sheet wrapped around him and tied with a cord in front. Romeo can have a vial or small container of some kind from which to drink in Scene 17. A plastic knife or ruler can be used as Juliet's suicide weapon in Scene 18.

Cast of Characters

(main parts in boldface)
Narrators 1, 2, 3
Benvolio, *Romeo's cousin, a Montague*
Tybalt, *Juliet's cousin, a Capulet*
Lord Capulet, *head of a prominent Verona family*
Lady Capulet
Lord Montague, *head of a rival Verona family*
Lady Montague
Prince of Verona, Italy
Romeo, *son of Montague*
Nurse, *to Juliet*
Juliet, *daughter of Capulet*

Mercutio, *Prince's kinsman*
Romeo's friend
Friar Laurence, *a monk*
Balthasar, *Romeo's servant*

Romeo and Juliet

By William Shakespeare

Adapted by Kate Davis

Scene 1

Narrator 1: The crashing sound of metal against metal echoes off cobblestones. Two feuding households—the Capulets and the Montagues—cross swords again. Fighting explodes in the streets of Verona.

Narrator 2: Youths dressed in their families' colors slash at one another. Market stalls are overturned. Screaming mothers and children flee.

Narrator 3: Benvolio, a young Montague, rushes in to prevent more bloodshed. He beats his sword down on top of two youths' weapons.

Benvolio: Part, you fools! Haven't you learned yet what this fighting will lead to?

Tybalt: Dog of the house of Montague! Prepare to die!

Benvolio: Put away your sword. I am trying to keep the peace.

Tybalt: You expect me to believe that? Coward!

Lord Capulet: *(to Lady Capulet)* What noise is this? Here comes Montague swinging his blade! Give me my sword!

Lady Capulet: No, I beg you!

Lord Montague: Villain! Stand forth!

Lady Montague: Stop! Not again!

Narrator 1: As the fighting grows more intense, Verona's people cry out:

All Readers: Down with the Capulets! Down with the Montagues!

Narrator 2: The prince comes riding through the town on horseback.

Prince of Verona: Rebellious subjects, enemies of peace! You men, you beasts! Throw your weapons to the ground!

Narrator 3: The prince angrily warns Lords Capulet and Montague.

Prince: This ancient grudge your families bear has too often brought bloodshed to our town. Hear me! If you disturb Verona's peace one more time, you will pay with your lives. Now, on pain of death, all men depart!

Scene 2

Narrator 1: The Montagues bring in their wounded.

Lady Montague: Where is Romeo? Was he involved in this fight, Benvolio?

Benvolio: No, I don't think so. I saw him early this morning, wandering in the woods with tears in his eyes.

Lord Mont.ague: He's depressed all the time—even locking himself in dark rooms. What's wrong with him?

Benvolio: He won't say.

Lady Montague: Hush. Here he comes.

Benvolio: You go on. I'll see what I can find out. *(to Romeo)* Good morning cousin.

Romeo: Is it still morning? The hours seem so long.

Benvolio: What makes them long, friend? What's the matter?

Romeo: Love.

Benvolio: You're in love?

Romeo: Out of it. She won't have me.

Benvolio: She who?

Romeo: What difference does it make? She's beautiful, wise and fair, but she keeps it all to herself.

Benvolio: Then forget her. There are plenty of other beauties. Take a new one to your eye, and the poison of your sadness will die.

Romeo: You think that will cure me?

Benvolio: Sure. Listen: I hear Lord Capulet is having a party tonight. All the prettiest girls in Verona will be there. Let's invite ourselves.

Romeo: Montagues at Capulet's house will never be tolerated.

Benvolio: It's a masquerade. We'll wear masks, like everyone else.

Romeo: My heart's not in it.

Benvolio: Come on. You've got to snap out of this. Before the moon is low, the maid you thought a swan you'll find is really just . . . a crow!

Romeo: I doubt it. But, yes, I'll go.

Scene 3

Narrator 2: The Capulet household bustles with preparations for the party. Lady Capulet enters Juliet's room.

Lady Capulet:	Juliet, come, I must speak with you. Tell me, nurse, do you know my daughter's age?
Nurse:	Of course! Juliet was the prettiest babe I ever cared for. She's nearly fourteen. I'd bet fourteen of my teeth that's how old she is—but then, I have only four teeth left!
Lady Capulet:	Fourteen years. Juliet, have you thought of marrying?
Juliet:	*(anxiously)* It is an honor I haven't dreamed of, Mother.
Lady Capulet:	Well, dream, my dear. Count Paris, kinsman to the prince, has asked for your hand!
Nurse:	Paris! A handsome man!
Juliet:	But I don't even know him!
Lady Capulet:	Your father wants to promise you to him. Marry Paris, and you'll share all he has!
Narrator 3:	Juliet continues to frown.
Lady Capulet:	Well, Count Paris will be at the party tonight. Look and see if you can love him.
Juliet:	*(grimly)* If you wish it, I'll try.

Scene 4

Narrator 1:	That evening, Romeo and Benvolio are joined by their friend Mercutio. All three head toward the Capulets' for the masked dance.
Benvolio:	Come on, cousin. Stop dragging your feet.
Romeo:	I'm not up for this.
Mercutio:	The eternal lover not up for a party full of young women? Borrow cupid's wings and fly, man.
Romeo:	My heart is like lead.
Benvolio:	Lighten up, Romeo! We're almost there. Put on your mask.
Narrator 2:	Romeo stops suddenly.
Romeo:	I really shouldn't go. Misgivings hang in the stars.
Benvolio:	Now what's bothering you?
Romeo:	I had a dream.
Mercutio:	Dreams are the children of an idle brain. They often lie.
Romeo:	*(insistently)* No, really, I fear some . . . untimely death.
Benvolio:	Shake it off. You're depressing us.

Romeo: For your sakes, I'll try. But may he that steers my course direct my sail.

🔊 Scene 5

Narrator 3: In his great hall, Lord Capulet seeks to undo the ill humor of the day's street brawl.

Lord Capulet: Welcome, all! Musicians, play. Turn the tables up. Let's dance!

Narrator 1: While Benvolio and Mercutio flirt with the young women, Romeo stands alone in one corner.

Narrator 2: Suddenly he notices Juliet—dancing. Romeo is instantly taken with her beauty.

Romeo: *(to himself)* That lady teaches the torches to burn bright! Has my heart ever loved till now? I never saw true beauty till this night.

Narrator 3: Romeo secretly follows Juliet all evening. She is intrigued by his stares and is drawn to him.

Narrator 1: Tybalt, a hotheaded Capulet youth, notices Romeo's flirting. Furious, he alerts Lord Capulet.

Tybalt: Uncle, a foe is here, a villain Montague. He comes to scorn us!

Lord Capulet: It looks like Romeo. He's well enough behaved. Leave him alone. I don't want to start anything.

Tybalt: I'll not endure him!

Lord Capulet: What? *I* am the master here. *I* decide what you will endure!

Tybalt: *(under his breath)* This trespass burns inside of me.

Narrator 2: Later, Romeo catches Juliet alone for a moment. "Accidentally," he brushes her hand.

Romeo: Forgive me. If my hand offends yours, I would smooth my rough touch with tenderness.

Juliet: *(flirting back)* Good pilgrim, you do wrong your hand too much. Even saints have hands that pilgrims' hands do touch. Why, palm to palm in prayer, hand and hand seem to—kiss.

Romeo: Then, by all means, let your palm touch mine—

Narrator 3: Romeo and Juliet reach out, tenderly placing the palms of their hands together, but are suddenly interrupted by Juliet's nurse.

Nurse: Juliet! Your mother wants a word with you.

Narrator 1: Reluctantly, Juliet goes. The nurse starts to follow her but is stopped by Romeo.

Romeo: Madam, who is her mother?

Nurse: Why, the lady of the house.

Romeo: *(quietly)* A Capulet?

Benvolio: Romeo, we've got to leave! They know who we are. Come quickly!

Narrator 2: As the three young men slip out, Juliet turns to her Nurse.

Juliet: Nurse, who is that man?

Nurse: *(sorrowfully)* His name is Romeo—the only son of Lord Montague.

Juliet: And my only love. *(seemingly crushed)* Son of my enemy? No, it cannot be!

Scene 6

Narrator 3: Romeo cannot forget Juliet. Like a man possessed, he roams outside the Capulets' villa. Boldly, he climbs a wall and lands in an orchard.

Narrator 1: Suddenly he spies a balcony door opening.

Romeo: *(talking to himself)* But soft, what light through yonder window breaks? Why, it is the East, and Juliet is the sun! It is my lady! Look how she leans her cheek on her hand. I wish I were a glove upon that hand.

Juliet: *(from balcony)* Ah, me.

Romeo: *(quietly)* She speaks. Speak again, bright angel!

Juliet: *(daydreaming, not knowing he is there)* Romeo, oh Romeo. Why must you be named Romeo? Refuse your father's name. Or if you cannot, swear your love to me, and I'll no longer be a Capulet.

Romeo: *(to himself)* Shall I speak?

Juliet: *(still dreaming aloud)* It's only your name that's my enemy. But what's in a name? A rose by any other name would smell as sweet. Be rid of your name and come to me!

Romeo: *(aloud)* I take you at your word! Call me your love, and I'll no longer be a Montague.

Juliet: *(in alarm)* Who's there?

Romeo: How can I tell you who I am? My name is an enemy to you.

Juliet: I haven't heard a hundred words from you, yet I know your voice. Romeo! How did you get in here? If my relatives find you, they'll murder you!

Romeo: Night will hide me. Even so, if they find me, I'd rather die by their hate than live without your love.

Juliet: I blush to think you heard what I said before. I should have been more reserved, but in truth, I am too fond of you. Do you love me? Say so, and I'll take you at your word.

Narrator 2:	Romeo instantly scrambles up a tree to be closer to Juliet.
Romeo:	*(eagerly)* I swear by the moon—
Juliet:	Oh, don't swear by the moon. It changes constantly. Unless, of course, your love is as changeable.
Romeo:	Never, my lady. But what shall I swear by?
Juliet:	Your self, which I worship.
Romeo:	*(trying again)* My heart is—
Juliet:	No, wait. On second thought, this is too sudden. When next we meet, *then* our love can bloom as a flower. Good night. Sweet dreams.
Romeo:	*(in exasperation)* You're going?
Juliet:	What more would you—?
Romeo:	Exchange your faithful vow for mine!
Juliet:	*(coyly)* I gave you mine before you even asked for it.
Romeo:	*(in confusion)* So now you want to take it back?
Juliet:	Only to give it to you again!
Narrator 3:	Romeo is relieved.
Juliet:	My love is a boundless as the sea. The more I give, the more I have, for both are infinite!
Nurse:	*(calling from inside)* Juliet?
Juliet:	*(to nurse)* Madam! *(to Romeo)* Stay here. I'll be right back.
Romeo:	Tell me I am not dreaming.
Juliet:	*(returning)* If your intentions are honorable, if your purpose is marriage, then send me word tomorrow. Tell me where and when the ceremony will be. I'll meet you, and we'll run away.
Romeo:	I will arrange it all.
Nurse:	Juliet! Where are you?
Juliet:	Now good night! Parting is such sweet sorrow that I could say good night till it be tomorrow.
Narrator 1:	Juliet rushes inside.
Romeo:	Sleep well. I'll go see Friar Laurence. Surely he will marry us.

Scene 7

Narrator 2:	Friar Laurence is in the monastery garden, picking herbs for remedies. Romeo approaches.
Friar Laurence:	Good heavens, Romeo. You look as if you've been up all night.

Romeo:	I have been, Father—feasting with my enemy. And I fell in love with the daughter of Capulet. She loves me, too! We exchanged vows. And we want to be married.
Friar:	This is so sudden, my son. I thought you loved another?
Romeo:	I did. But meeting Juliet has changed all that. Will you do it, Father? Will you marry us today?
Narrator 3:	The monk hesitates, thinking. Then suddenly he is resolved.
Friar:	Yes. I will be your assistant in this. Perhaps a marriage will turn your warring houses' hatred to love.
Romeo:	*(with joy)* Thank you, Father. We'll return this afternoon.

Scene 8

Narrator 1:	Romeo's friends are hanging out in the town square.
Benvolio:	Tybalt recognized Romeo last night. I hear he's looking for him and wants to settle his grudge.
Mercutio:	I hope Romeo can handle him. Tybalt is always hot for a duel.
Benvolio:	Here comes Romeo now.
Mercutio:	*(in annoyance)* Well, look who it is—the disappearing lover. You sure gave us the slip last night.
Romeo:	Give me pardon, friends. My business was great.
Mercutio:	You could at least have—
Narrator 2:	Juliet's nurse enters the square and calls to the young men.
Nurse:	I say, can any of you tell me where I might find the young Romeo?
Romeo:	I am he.
Nurse:	*(loudly)* I'd like to have a word with you.
Mercutio:	*(teasingly)* Ooo! The old biddy wants to ask you out.
Nurse:	*(angrily to Mercutio)* You scurvy knave!
Narrator 3:	Romeo leaves his friends and goes to speak with Juliet's nurse.
Romeo:	Ignore them.
Nurse:	Romeo, listen to me. I hope your intentions with Juliet are pure.
Romeo:	Only the best. Tell my lady to meet me at Friar Laurence's cell this afternoon. There we will marry.
Nurse:	Bless you! She'll be there.

Scene 9

Narrator 1: Romeo anxiously awaits Juliet's arrival at the monastery.

Friar: I hope heaven smiles upon your marriage—and that sorrows stay away from your door.

Romeo: After you join our hands, sorrow can't touch me. One minute's joy with Juliet as mine will be worth whatever death may dare!

Friar: Don't tempt fate. And love moderately—or it will flame up and out as quickly as fire. Now cool off a bit. Here comes your bride.

Romeo: Juliet! Tell me, with your sweet breath—are you as happy as I am?

Narrator 2: Juliet and Romeo dive for each other, but the friar throws himself between the eager lovers.

Juliet: *(to Romeo)* My love is grown so much, I cannot contain it!

Narrator 3: Romeo and Juliet can't keep their hands off each other.

Friar: Come with me quickly. We'll make short work of this. I dare not leave you two alone.

Narrator 1: Romeo and Juliet kneel to receive the sacrament of matrimony.

Scene 10

Narrator 2: It is late afternoon. Romeo's friends once again are in the square.

Benvolio: Let's go to my father's for dinner, Mercutio. It's hot. And the Capulets are roaming about.

Mercutio: Are you afraid of a brawl?

Benvolio: I fear *you'll* brawl. Oh, no. It's too late. Here comes Tybalt.

Tybalt: *(with hostility)* Well, whom do we have here—Romeo's buddies?

Mercutio: *(provokingly)* What of it?

Benvolio: *(to Mercutio and Tybalt)* Men, please, find a private place. Everyone is looking.

Narrator 3: Romeo approaches the group.

Tybalt: Here comes the party crasher himself. Romeo, you villain!

Narrator 1: Romeo is giddy, having just married Juliet. He thinks only of the night, when they will run away.

Romeo: Tybalt, I am no villain. In fact, I have much reason to love you.

Mercutio: Has he lost his mind?

Tybalt: Do you mock me? Another injury? Turn and draw your sword!

Romeo: I've never injured you. I hold your name as dear as my own.

Mercutio: Don't grovel at his feet!

Benvolio: *(to Mercutio)* Stay out of it, friend.

Mercutio: Tybalt—King of Cats—give me one of your lives, rat catcher!

Narrator 2: Mercutio and Tybalt brandish swords. Mercutio lashes out, his sword gleaming. Tybalt jumps free.

Romeo: Cousin, friend! The prince has forbidden such fighting. Hold off!

Narrator 3: But as Tybalt returns Mercutio's thrust, Romeo gets in the way. Mercutio, thrown off guard, is gouged deeply by Tybalt's blade. Mercutio stumbles as Tybalt flees.

Mercutio: *(with false bravado)* It's nothing. A mere scratch. *(quietly)* Get a doctor. I feel faint.

Benvolio: He's hurt!

Mercutio: *(shouting)* A plague on both your houses! *(weakly)* They have made worm's meat of me.

Narrator 1: Romeo bends over his fallen friend, a look of horror on his face.

Romeo: What—dead? Oh, blackest fate!

Benvolio: Vile Tybalt returns!

Romeo: *(under his breath)* Until this moment, Juliet's beauty held me in its spell. But now my fury swells. *(to Tybalt)* Tybalt, *you* are the villain! Mercutio's soul hovers just over our heads. Now I will have you join him!

Tybalt: No, wretch! It will be you!

Narrator 2: They fight ferociously. Then Romeo trips. His sword goes flying.

Narrator 3: Tybalt rushes at him. Romeo rolls and gropes for his sword. Just as Tybalt lunges, Romeo runs him through. Tybalt staggers—and falls.

Benvolio: Romeo! Be gone! Away! The prince will doom you to death!

Narrator 1: Romeo flees the scene in panic.

Scene 11

Narrator 2: Juliet is in her orchard, impatient for the nightfall and her new husband's return. Suddenly, her nurse approaches, wailing.

Nurse: Oh, lady! He's dead!

Juliet: *(in alarm)* Dead? Who? What are you saying?

Nurse: Romeo! Whoever would have thought it?

Juliet: What? Romeo is slain?

Nurse:	Tybalt! Tybalt was killed!
Juliet:	Tybalt *and* Romeo are dead?
Nurse:	Tybalt was slain, and Romeo is *banished*. There was fighting. Tybalt slew Mercutio, so Romeo killed Tybalt. The prince has exiled Romeo.
Juliet:	Romeo's hand shed my cousin's blood?
Nurse:	Shame to Romeo.
Juliet:	*(in outrage)* Blisters on your tongue, woman! Romeo is my lord!
Nurse:	Do you speak well of him that killed your cousin?
Juliet:	Should I speak ill of my husband? Oh, Romeo is banished? I'd rather die!
Nurse:	There, sweet Juliet. Go up to your room. I'll find Romeo to comfort you. I think I know where he'll hide.

Scene 12

Narrator 3:	Romeo has taken refuge with Friar Laurence. The realization of his deed has struck him.
Romeo:	*(hysterically)* I never meant to do it, but it was my life or his! Now the prince will take my life.
Friar:	He has banished you.
Romeo:	Banished! Death would be more merciful.
Friar:	Don't be so thankless. The world is broad and wide.
Romeo:	But Juliet is here in Verona!
Friar:	It's not as bad as you think.
Romeo:	If you could feel what I do, maybe you would understand.
Narrator 1:	A knock comes at the door.
Friar:	Get up, Romeo, and hide. *(calling out)* Who's there?
Nurse:	I come from Lady Juliet.
Friar:	Come in, woman. There is Romeo, drunk with his own tears.
Romeo:	*(to the nurse)* What does Juliet say? Does she think I am a murderer?
Nurse:	She weeps constantly.
Romeo:	My name has murdered her. Now let me kill it.
Narrator 2:	Romeo desperately draws his dagger and points it toward his own heart.

Friar: Stop it, Romeo! Be a man. Juliet is alive, and you would kill her with your death? Pull yourself together! Now listen. Go to Juliet and comfort her. But leave before dawn. Then you can go to Mantua and live there until we win the prince's pardon.

Romeo: Your words revive me.

Friar: I'll see to it that your servant brings you word in Mantua from time to time. Now go. Farewell.

Scene 13

Narrator 3: The next morning in Juliet's chamber, Romeo awakes to birdsong. Alarmed, he jumps out of bed.

Romeo: The morning lark! It's dawn. I must go or stay and die.

Juliet: *(drowsily)* It was the nightingale. It can't be dawn. Stay awhile.

Romeo: I have more desire to stay than will to go.

Narrator 1: Romeo returns to Juliet's arms. But a few minutes later, the bird sings again. This time, both Romeo and Juliet leap out of bed.

Juliet: It *is* the lark! Oh, Romeo, you must go. It grows light.

Narrator 2: Suddenly, a knock sounds on the door.

Nurse: *(knocking)* Your mother comes!

Narrator 3: As Romeo prepares to climb out the window, Juliet gazes deeply into his eyes once more.

Juliet: My eyes must fail me, for I see you pale, as one in a tomb.

Romeo: It is only sorrow, draining my blood. Fear not. Now, farewell.

Narrator 1: As Romeo climbs out the window and disappears, Juliet throws herself back on her bed and weeps.

Lady Capulet: *(from the hallway)* Daughter, are you up?

Juliet: I am not well.

Narrator 2: Lady Capulet enters Juliet's room.

Lady Capulet: Still grieving for your cousin? You should grieve instead for the villain that killed him. We're going to have Romeo poisoned in Mantua.

Juliet: *(weeping even louder)* Ohhh!

Lady Capulet: Come, Juliet. Too much weeping for Tybalt is not good for you. Here's something to bring you joy. Your father has arranged for you to marry Paris on Thursday!

Juliet: Paris? I'll not wed him! I'd sooner marry Romeo, who I'm supposed to hate.

Lord Capulet:	*(entering)* What's all this?
Lady Capulet:	She won't marry Paris.
Lord Capulet:	Won't do it? Count your blessings, girl. He's a worthy man.
Juliet:	No, please I beg you!
Lord Capulet:	*(in anger)* Is this the thanks I get for making a princely match? You are too proud. Next Thursday, you'll get your joints to church and be wed, or I'll drag you there myself!
Narrator 3:	Juliet sinks to her knees before her father.
Juliet:	Father, I'm on my knees—!
Lord Capulet:	Disobedient wretch!
Narrator 1:	Lord Capulet raises a hand, about to strike his daughter. His wife stops him.
Lady Capulet:	My lord!
Lord Capulet:	I try to marry her off well, and the whining fool says, "I can't." *(angrily to Juliet)* You'll marry Paris or leave my house!
Narrator 2:	Juliet's parents stride out. The nurse arrives.
Juliet:	*(hysterically)* Mother, please! Nurse! What can I do?
Nurse:	Here's what I think: Romeo is banished and dares not come back. Considering the circumstances, I think it best you marry Count Paris.
Juliet:	*(feeling betrayed)* What, you too? Some comfort!
Narrator 3:	Juliet, realizing she is totally on her own now, begins to plot.
Juliet:	Then amen. Go tell my parents I've gone to say confession. And tell my father I will be ruled by him.
Nurse:	That's better. I'll tell them.
Narrator 1:	The nurse leaves to convey Juliet's message to her parents.
Juliet:	*(after her)* Traitor! Now you and I are forever parted.

Scene 14

Narrator 2:	Juliet, in tears and despair, arrives at the monastery.
Juliet:	Father, come weep with me, past hope, past cure, past help!
Friar:	I know of your grief. Paris has been here this morning.
Juliet:	But you joined my heart to Romeo's. Now tell me of a remedy, for I long to die.
Narrator 3:	The friar rubs his brow. Then suddenly he stares at his herbs.

Friar:	I spy a kind of hope. If you are ready to die, would you be willing to . . . *pretend* to die?
Juliet:	I'd rather be chained up with snakes than marry Paris! I'll do anything to stay faithful to Romeo.
Friar:	Then listen well. Take this vial of liquid. Tomorrow night when you are alone, drink it. Presently, drowsiness will run through all your veins. Your pulse will stop; your breath will halt. For forty hours you will appear to be dead.
Narrator 1:	Juliet is fascinated.
Friar:	When your family comes to wake you in the morning, they will think you are dead. Meanwhile, I'll send a letter with one of my monks to Romeo. When you wake in the tomb, your husband will be there to bear you to Mantua.
Juliet:	Father, I thank you. Give me the vial. And God give me strength.

Scene 15

Narrator 2:	On the morning of Juliet's wedding, the nurse tries to wake her. But she finds her cold and stiff.
Nurse:	Lady. Lady! Help, my lady's—dead! *(screams)* Aaiieehh!
Narrator 3:	Lord and Lady Capulet rush in.
Lord Capulet:	What noise is this?
Lady Capulet:	My child!
Lord Capulet:	*(darkly)* O wretched day! Let me see my daughter. Death lies on her like frost upon the sweetest flower.
Lady Capulet:	*(hysterically)* O accursed, wicked day!
Lord Capulet:	*(in grief)* Bridal flowers must now serve her corpse. With my child, all my joy will be buried.

Scene 16

Narrator 1:	Romeo's servant Balthasar sneaks into the Capulet grounds to deliver a love letter to Juliet. Hearing commotion, he hides behind a bush. Shocked, he sees Juliet's body carried into the Capulet crypt.
Balthasar:	What? Dead? My master will be devastated. I must get back to Mantua and tell him before he hears it from someone else.
Narrator 2:	Balthasar mounts his horse and rides quickly to Mantua. When he arrives, Romeo runs up to him.
Romeo:	What news from Juliet, man? Is she well? I dreamt as much.
Balthasar:	Pardon, sir . . . How can I say this? I have terrible news. I saw Juliet's dead body laid in the Capulet family tomb.

Romeo: Juliet is dead? How? Why?

Balthasar: I don't know, sir. But her spirit now lives with the angels.

Romeo: Then I defy you, stars! Balthasar, go hire me a fast horse. I will ride to Verona tonight.

Narrator 3: In sadness, Balthasar goes.

Romeo: And I know a merchant who will sell me poison.

Scene 17

Narrator 1: At nightfall, Romeo steals back to Verona. On the road, his swift horse passes a monk walking with a slow donkey toward Mantua.

Narrator 2: In the saddlebag is the friar's undelivered letter to Romeo. A little later, Romeo arrives at the Capulet cemetery.

Romeo: Now I will descend into this bed of death.

Narrator 3: He draws a crowbar from his horse's bag and begins to pry loose the door to the crypt.

Romeo: Open your rotten jaws, tomb. And lend me your torch.

Narrator 1: Romeo passes dusty, cobwebby corpses and skeletons. Then he sees Tybalt's body.

Romeo: Forgive me, cousin. I can do you no better favor than to sever the life of the one who slayed you.

Narrator 2: Romeo looks past Tybalt and spies Juliet's body. He approaches her and pulls back her shroud.

Romeo: Oh, my love, my wife. Why, your cheek still bears the blush of life. Death has no power over your beauty. And sorrow shall have no power over us! Eyes, look your last. Arms, take your last embrace.

Narrator 3: Romeo takes Juliet's body in his arms.

Romeo: Come bitter poison, guide me to my love.

Narrator 1: Romeo pulls out the potion he has bought and drinks it. Then he bends his face to Juliet's.

Romeo: Thus, with a kiss, I die.

Scene 18

Narrator 2: Friar Laurence sneaks to the crypt to be with Juliet when she wakes.

Friar: *(to himself)* Why didn't Romeo come to my monastery, as I wrote? What if my monk was delayed? Oh, I fear something dreadful. But there—a horse. Maybe Romeo rode directly here.

Narrator 3: The friar takes a torch from the doorway and proceeds inside the tomb. Soon he spots Romeo, sprawled on the stone floor, dead.

Friar:	O what unkind hour!
Narrator 1:	Juliet begins to stir.
Juliet:	Friar. Where is Romeo?
Friar:	Lady, some greater power has foiled our plan. There lies Romeo.
Juliet:	No! Romeo—dead?
Friar:	Listen, lady! A noise! The watchman comes. We must go!
Juliet:	No, I will *not* go!
Narrator 2:	Friar Laurence tries unsuccessfully to drag Juliet from the crypt. He finally gives up and flees. Alone, Juliet bends over Romeo's dead body.
Juliet:	What's this in my true love's hand. A vial of poison? Let me drink the last and join him.
Narrator 3:	She tries to drink the poison but finds the vial already emptied.
Juliet:	No friendly drop left to help me? Then I'll be brief.
Narrator 1:	Juliet grabs Romeo's knife.
Juliet:	O happy dagger. Let me die!
Narrator 2:	She plunges the dagger into her heart.

Scene 19

Narrator 3:	As morning breaks, word spreads through Verona's streets that Romeo and Juliet are dead. The friar, found in the orchard, has explained all to the prince.
Narrator 1:	Capulets and Montagues—both families—converge solemnly in the square. They bear the bodies of the star-crossed lovers to the palace.
Prince:	Capulet, Montague—see what a scourge is laid upon your hate! Heaven has found a way to kill your joys with love. Because of you, even I have lost kinsmen. Now all are punished!
Lord Capulet:	Brother Montague, it is time we laid our feud to rest. My daughter would have wished it. Give me your hand.
Lord Montague:	I will do more. I'll have a statue of Juliet made in pure gold.
Lord Capulet:	And I one of Romeo. They shall stand side by side—poor sacrifices to our ill will.
Prince:	*(to Lords Montague and Capulet)* Go and talk this out further. Much must be mended. Never was there a story of more woe than this of Juliet and her Romeo.

Simply Shakespeare: Readers Theatre for Young People is from *Read* magazine, a Weekly Reader publication, in collaboration with Teacher Ideas Press. Edited by Jennifer Kroll. www.weeklyreader.com. www.lu.com/tips. 1–800–541–2086.

CHAPTER 11

Taming of the Shrew

By William Shakespeare

Adapted by Kate Davis

Summary

A rich gentleman named Baptista has two single daughters of marrying age. A number of suitors vie for the hand of the sweet, beautiful younger daughter, Bianca. However, Baptista refuses to marry her off until her older sister, Katharine, is married. The problem is that Katharine has a very disagreeable temperament and doesn't want to marry. When Baptista announces that he's looking for a tutor for Bianca, two romantically interested gentlemen pretend to be tutors to gain the opportunity to get close to her. Meanwhile, a good-natured, fortune-seeking gentleman named Petruchio decides to marry Katharine and claim her sizable dowry. He thinks he has a plan by which he can "tame" her, making her into a kind, polite person and a pleasant wife. But can he really change the most ill-tempered woman of all time?

Presentation Suggestions

Place Katharine and Bianca front and center, with their father, Baptista, just behind them. Cluster Bianca's suitors—Lucentio, Hortensio, Tranio, and Gremio—to the side of Bianca. Place Vincentio and Stranger behind them. Place Petruchio, his servant Grumio, Tailor, and the narrators to the side of Katharine. Place Servant in the back row, behind them and near Baptista.

Props

Bianca and Katharine can wear skirts or dresses. The pretend tutors, Lucentio and Hortensio, can be dressed to represent their roles. Lucentio can wear a graduation mortarboard cap and scholarly glasses. He can carry serious-looking books. Hortensio can hold a musical instrument and sheet music. Petruchio can be wearing nice clothing, then throw on an old shirt during Scene 6. He can hold a food item, such as a bag of chips, with which to tease the hungry Kate in Scene 8.

Cast of Characters

(main parts in boldface)
Narrators 1, 2
Lucentio, *from Pisa, in love with Bianca*
Baptista, *a rich man from Padua*
Katharine, *the shrew, older daughter of Baptista*
Hortensio, *suitor of Bianca*
Tranio, *servant of Lucentio*
Bianca, *younger daughter of Baptista*
Gremio, *another suitor of Bianca*
Petruchio, *from Verona, suitor to Katharine*
Grumio, *servant of Petruchio*
Servant
Tailor
Stranger
Vincentio, *Lucentio's father, from Pisa*

Taming of the Shrew

By William Shakespeare
Adapted by Kate Davis

Scene 1

Narrator 1: A young man named Lucentio arrives with his servant Tranio to study in Padua, Italy. While looking for lodging in town, they overhear an argument.

Lucentio: What's this ruckus?

Narrator 2: Lucentio and Tranio listen as an older man fends off his daughters' suitors in the square.

Baptista: *(to suitors)* Gentlemen, don't ask again. I will *not* give my daughter Bianca to any man until a husband is found for her older sister, Katharine.

Katharine: Father, do you mean to pawn me off on these mates, like barter?

Hortensio: "Mates"? Ha! You'll have no mate until you become a gentler, milder sort.

Katharine: Don't worry, fool! If you *did* care for me, I'd comb your head with a three-legged stool!

Hortensio: Deliver us from such a devil!

Tranio: *(quietly to Lucentio)* What a show! That maid is stark-raving mad.

Lucentio: *(in entrancement)* Look at her sister. She is quite the opposite—mild and beautiful!

Baptista: Go home, Bianca, and stay inside until your sister is wed. I'm sorry if this displeases you. You know I love you.

Bianca: Father, I humble myself to your wishes. I'll keep to my books and music.

Katharine: *(to Bianca)* Papa's pretty pet! I could stick a finger in your eye!

Gremio: *(to father)* Sir, why lock up Bianca for her sister's fiendishness?

Baptista:	My mind is made up. *(to suitors)* If either of you knows a good tutor for Bianca, send him to me. Bianca, go inside. Katharine, stay here.
Katharine:	Now you tell me when to come and go? I'll go where I like!
Narrator 1:	Katharine storms off.
Gremio:	*(to Hortensio)* For Bianca's sake, I'm going to try to find her a fit tutor.
Hortensio:	Me too. But let's also look for a man who will marry that shrew.
Gremio:	What fool would marry a devil?
Hortensio:	There are plenty of fellows who would take her—with her father's money.
Gremio:	Personally, I'd rather be whipped!
Lucentio:	Is this love at first sight? I burn, I pine for beautiful Bianca! Will you help me win her, Tranio?
Tranio:	If love has captivated you, then we must free the captive. But it won't be easy. Didn't you hear the crux of the matter?
Lucentio:	I only saw Bianca's coral lips. Her sweet breath perfumed the air.
Tranio:	Wake up, sir. If you love the maid, you'll have to use your wits to win her. Her father has shut her away till he's rid of her shrewish sister.
Lucentio:	Cruel father! But wait—didn't he say he's looking for a tutor?
Tranio:	If you were the maid's teacher, you could move in! Except—your father expects you to entertain his guests while you're here. How can you be in two places at once?
Lucentio:	I can't. But—my father's friends here don't know what I look like. *You* can be Master Lucentio, and I'll be the tutor. Switch clothes and trade places with me.
Tranio:	I'll do it! I promised your father I would be of service to you. Although, I think he had something else in mind!

Scene 2

Narrator 2:	Another newcomer has arrived in Padua. Petruchio of Verona has come to visit his friend Hortensio—and to find a wife.
Narrator 1:	Petruchio and his servant Grumio knock at Hortensio's gate.
Hortensio:	Who's there? Petruchio, my old friend! What brings you to Padua?
Petruchio:	The wind that scatters young men in the world to seek their fortunes. My father died, and I decided to travel. I have a little money and I plan to wive and thrive!

Hortensio:	If you seek a wife, I know a shrewish young woman who's available. She's rich, too. But I don't wish her on you.
Petruchio:	"Rich," you say? I tell you flat out, wealth is the aim of my wooing. I don't care if she's foul, rough, cursed, or worse. I've come to wive it wealthily in Padua.
Grumio:	Give him enough gold, and he'll marry a toothless old trot!
Hortensio:	I was only joking. But if you're serious, I can help you to a beautiful, rich wife. She was raised as a gentlewoman, and she only has one fault—she's *intolerable!* I wouldn't marry her for a gold mine.
Petruchio:	You don't know how gold affects me. I don't care if she nags as loud as thunder. Tell me who she is, and I'll woo her.
Hortensio:	Her name is Katharine. She's known all over Padua for her scolding tongue. Her father is Baptista Minola.
Petruchio:	My father knew Signor Minola! I'm going to his place at once. I won't sleep until I meet her.
Hortensio:	Wait and I'll go with you. For in Baptista's house is *my* treasure, his other daughter, Bianca, the jewel of my life. Her father is going to keep her inside until Katharine the Cursed is wed.
Grumio:	Katharine the Cursed? For a maid, that title's the worst!
Hortensio:	I'll introduce you to her father, Petruchio, if you will do me a favor. Baptista is looking for a tutor. Help me disguise myself as a music master. Then, when I am inside the house, I can court Bianca!
Narrator 2:	On the way to Baptista's house, they meet Bianca's other suitor, Gremio, talking with Lucentio, who is dressed as a scholar.
Narrator 1:	Lucentio has promised to disguise himself as a tutor to try to sway Bianca's affections toward Gremio. But he secretly intends to court Bianca himself.
Gremio:	*(to Petruchio)* Read her plenty of love poetry, and perfume these papers for her.
Lucentio:	*(lying)* Whatever I read, I will plead *your* case to her, as if you were there.
Gremio:	Well, Hortensio— Remember how we agreed to find a tutor? I've found a scholar of literature.
Hortensio:	What a coincidence. I too recently found a music tutor for Bianca, who is so beloved of me.
Gremio:	She is beloved of *me*!
Hortensio:	Let's not argue that now. I have more important news. This gentleman, Petruchio, has agreed to court Katharine and *marry* her if the dowry pleases him.
Gremio:	Would you woo a wildcat?

Petruchio: A little din won't daunt my ears. I've heard lions roar and the alarms of war. I fear no woman's tongue. Leave her to me!

Gremio: As the labors were left to Hercules!

Scene 3

Narrator 2: In Baptista's house, Katharine is tormenting Bianca.

Bianca: Good sister, untie me! I'll give you my jewels, my clothes—anything you ask!

Katharine: First tell me whom you love best. Which suitor?

Bianca: I haven't yet seen the face of the man I fancy most.

Katharine: Liar! It's Hortensio, isn't it?

Bianca: If *you* like him, you can have him.

Katharine: Perhaps it's Gremio you prefer. He is richer and will keep you in style.

Bianca: Is that why you envy me? Untie me and stop joking around—

Katharine: Is everything I do a joke to you?

Narrator 1: Katharine slaps her sister, as their father enters the room.

Baptista: *(to Katharine)* Stop that, you insolent dame! Why do you wrong her, you worthless, devilish spirit?

Narrator 2: Baptista unties his youngest daughter, who immediately starts crying and runs out of the room. Katharine rushes at the fleeing Bianca.

Katharine: She insults me with her silence. I'll get back at her for it!

Baptista: She has never crossed you. That poor girl!

Katharine: She's your little treasure, isn't she? Bianca must have a husband, while I must dance at her wedding—and lead apes around! I'll marry when I'm ready to marry, and not before!

Baptista: Has any man ever had such grief?

Narrator 1: Soon the hopeful lovers and tutors arrive at Baptista's. They are joined by one more suitor—Tranio, posing as Lucentio.

Petruchio: Good day, sir. Have you a fair and virtuous daughter named Katharine?

Baptista: I have a daughter Katharine, period.

Petruchio: I've heard so much of her beauty, wit, and mild behavior that I'd like to see her for myself. To show my good faith, I present you with a music tutor.

Narrator 2: He gestures to Hortensio.

Baptista: You are both welcome. *(to Petruchio)* But I must tell you, I doubt Katharine is for you.

Petruchio: You don't like my company?

Baptista: It's not that.... But who are you and where are you from?

Petruchio: I'm the son of Antonio of Verona.

Gremio: Ahem! The rest of us would like to speak. *(to Baptista)* Signor, I too present you with a tutor, a scholar clever with the Classics. Please accept his services.

Baptista: Thank you. *(seeing Tranio)* What—are you yet another suitor?

Tranio: Pardon, sir, I'm a stranger to this city, but I come to court your fair, virtuous daughter Bianca. My name is Lucentio; my father is Vincentio. I hope to gain your favor. In faith, I offer this gift, a musical lute for your daughter's enjoyment.

Narrator 1: Tranio hands Baptista the instrument.

Baptista: Thank you. I know of your father.

Narrator 2: He gives the lute to Hortensio, then has a servant take the tutors to his daughters.

Petruchio: Pardon me, sir, a word.... My father was quite wealthy, and I am the heir to his lands and goods. I don't have a lot of time to come wooing, so I was wondering: If I can win Katharine, what dowry do you offer?

Baptista: To take her off my hands, one-half of my land and twenty thousand crowns. But you'll have to win her love first. Be prepared for angry words.

Petruchio: We'll be like two raging fires. I will be as coarse with her as she is with me, and thus shall I squelch her ire.

Baptista: Well, good luck.

Narrator 1: Hortensio comes back and is rubbing his head.

Baptista: How now, sir? Weren't you able to break Katharine in on the lute?

Hortensio: No—she broke the lute in on *me*! I simply tried to show her the correct way to finger the strings, and she struck me on the head with it! While my head was sticking through the lute, she called me "Twangling Jack" and twenty other vile terms.

Petruchio: Well, there's a lusty wench! I love her ten times more now than I did before!

Baptista: *(leaving)* I'll send her to you.

Petruchio: *(to himself)* I have a plan for handling Katharine. I'll be more contrary than she is, but smother her with kindness. If she rails, I'll tell her she sings as sweetly as a nightingale. If she frowns, I'll tell her she looks as gay as dew-dappled roses. If she tells me to get lost, then I'll thank her for asking me to stay!

Scene 4

Narrator 2:	Katharine marches into the room where Petruchio is waiting.
Petruchio:	Good morrow Kate. That's your name, I hear.
Katharine:	Then you're hard of hearing, for my name is Katharine.
Petruchio:	You lie, for I've heard you called Plain Kate and Kate the Cursed. But I think you are the prettiest, daintiest Kate in the world. Your virtue and mildness are praised in every town. So much so that I am moved to woo you for my wife.
Katharine:	Let whoever "moved" you here *re*move you!
Petruchio:	My pet, come sit on my lap.
Katharine:	Donkeys are made for sitting on.
Petruchio:	Come, come, little wasp.
Narrator 1:	Katharine swats at him.
Katharine:	If I'm a wasp, then you better beware my sting.
Petruchio:	Listen Kate, I am a gentleman—
Katharine:	We'll see about that.
Narrator 2:	She swings at him with a mighty arm—and just misses him!
Petruchio:	Strike me and I'll cuff you.
Katharine:	Then you are *not* a gentleman!
Petruchio:	Don't look so sour, Kate.
Katharine:	That's how I look at a crab!
Petruchio:	Listen to you! I was told you were rough and sullen, and yet I find you pleasant, courteous, and sweet as spring flowers. Why, the world slanders you, Kate.
Narrator 1:	Katharine opens the door for him.
Katharine:	*(stamping feet)* Go away, fool!
Petruchio:	Look how graceful you are!
Katharine:	Where did you get all this talk?
Petruchio:	I had a witty mother.
Katherine:	Well she had a witless son!
Petruchio:	I'm wiser than you know. For I've won the consent of your father. Like it or not, you shall be my wife. For I am born to turn you from Wild Kate to Kind Kate. Will you or nill you, I will marry you!
Narrator 2:	Baptista returns.

Baptista:	How is it going, Petruchio?
Petruchio:	Fine, fine! She is modest as a dove, patient, and even-tempered. In fact, we agree so well, we'll be married next Sunday.
Katharine:	I'll see you *hanged* on Sunday!
Petruchio:	*(to father)* Don't pay attention to her. She's just pretending to be cross. Privately, she said she loves me. Ready the feast; invite the guests. For we will be wed!
Baptista:	Then give me your hands, for it's a match. God grant you joy!
Narrator 1:	Katharine is dumbstruck.
Petruchio:	*(to Katharine)* The wedding day will be here before you know it. I'm off to Venice to buy rings and things and fine array. And kiss me Kate, for we will be married on Sunday!

Scene 5

Narrator 2:	Now that Katharine is betrothed, the suitors return to compete for Bianca's hand.
Baptista:	*(to Gremio and Tranio)* Whoever can make Bianca the best offer will win her.
Gremio:	I can give her six oxen, a sailing ship, and a home filled with gold, ivory, fine linen and tapestries.
Tranio:	*I* offer four houses, two thousand gold coins a year, countless acres of land, and a *fleet* of ships!
Baptista:	Lucentio, your offer is the best. If your father can guarantee it, you shall marry Bianca on the Sunday after Katharine's wedding. If he can't, then Bianca is Gremio's.
Gremio:	*(quietly to Tranio)* Your father will never grant you that! You'll soon be the loser!
Narrator 1:	Baptista and Gremio leave.
Tranio:	*(alone)* That's what he thinks. If I can "suppose" to be Lucentio, I can find someone to be my "supposed" father!
Narrator 2:	A few days later, the tutors are busy with their wooing of Bianca.
Narrator 1:	Lucentio, disguised as a scholar, and Hortensio, as a musician, vie for time alone with Bianca.
Bianca:	Music master, go tune your instrument in the other room. I'll listen to a lecture till you are done. Be gone.
Narrator 2:	Lucentio recites Latin phrases to her.
Lucentio:	*Hac ibat Simois; hic est Sigeia . . .*
Bianca:	How does that translate?

Lucentio: *(playfully)* "I am Lucentio, disguised to get your love, and the Lucentio that is fooling your old man, is my servant!"

Bianca: Let me see if I've got this right . . .

Narrator 1: She repeats the same Latin back.

Bianca: In other words, "I know you not. I trust you not. *(winking)* But do not despair."

Narrator 2: Hortensio keeps coming in, and they keep sending him out, saying he's out of tune.

Narrator 1: Finally, it's Hortensio's turn to be with Bianca, but when he tries to woo her, a servant calls her away. Bianca clearly prefers the handsome scholar.

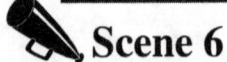 Scene 6

Narrator 2: On the morning of Katharine's wedding, Petruchio is nowhere to be found.

Baptista: Where is the bridegroom? The priest and guests are waiting at the church!

Katharine: It's not bad enough that I'm forced to marry against my will. Now the mad-brained fool doesn't even show up! I wish I'd never seen him!

Narrator 1: She runs crying from the room.

Baptista: I can't blame her. This would vex a saint let alone an impatient shrew.

Narrator 2: Finally, a servant runs in with news.

Servant: Petruchio's coming! But he looks so odd. He's wearing a ragged cloak and breeches, boots covered with wax, and an old rusty sword. And he's riding a diseased and staggering swaybacked mare.

Tranio: Petruchio's usually dressed so fashionably. He must be in a strange humor.

Petruchio: Anybody here? Where is my lovely bride? Why are you all staring at me?

Baptista: You *do* know this is your wedding day, don't you? We feared you wouldn't show up, and now you come dressed like an eyesore!

Petruchio: Where is Kate? I've come to take her to church.

Tranio: Don't let her see you. Go to my room and put on some better clothes.

Petruchio: No—I'll see her like this.

Baptista: Then I trust you will not marry her.

Petruchio: She's not marrying my clothes. Say no more. I go to find my bride and seal that title with a kiss!

 Scene 7

Narrator 1: While others go off to the chapel, Tranio and Lucentio stay behind. After the wedding, Gremio is first to return.

Tranio: Are they bride and groom?

Gremio: They are, and she was a lamb compared to him. You should have seen him! When the priest asked if Katharine would be his wife, Petruchio swore so loudly, the priest dropped his book. When he bent to pick it up, Petruchio cuffed him, and the vicar fell over!

Tranio: What did the bride say?

Gremio: She stood there trembling as the madman stamped and swore. When the ceremony was over, he yelled for wine like a lout, drank it down, then threw the dregs in the sexton's face. After that, he smacked Katharine on the lips so loud, it echoed through the church!

Narrator 2: The whole wedding party arrives home. Kate is NOT happy.

Petruchio: Gentlemen, ladies, friends, and guests, I know you all expected to dine with me today, but I must take my leave.

Baptista: What? You're leaving *now*?

Petruchio: If you knew my reason, you'd understand. As it is, I thank you all for coming to see me and my sweet wife. Drink health to us, and now farewell!

Katharine: I'm not going anywhere—not until I please! Here's the door, and there's your way. Go if you will. I will stay.

Petruchio: Kate, my dear, don't be angry.

Katharine: I *will* be angry. Why shouldn't I? Friends, let's go in to the bridal dinner. I see this man will make a fool of a woman unless she has the strength and spirit to resist.

Petruchio: Obey the bride, all of you. Go into the feast and be merry. *(grabbing her)* But as for you, bonny Kate, you must go with me.

Narrator 1: Katharine tries to wrestle herself away.

Petruchio: Don't stamp your feet or fret. I will be master of what is mine! Grumio, is my horse ready?

Grumio: Aye, if the oats haven't eaten him.

Petruchio: Then let's go. Now get back, all of you. Don't touch my wife. Draw your sword, Grumio. Help me rescue this mistress. We are beset by thieves! Fear not, sweet wench, I'll protect you!

Baptista: Let them go. He's crazy.

Tranio:	Never have I seen such a mad match.
Bianca:	She is mad herself and madly mated.
Gremio:	And Petruchio now is madly Kated!

Scene 8

Narrator 2:	Petruchio leads Kate back to his country house. On the way, her horse stumbles and tosses her into a swamp.
Narrator 1:	As Petruchio rides off, she wades through the mud, swearing at him.
Narrator 2:	When they reach his home, the servants are waiting at the door. Petruchio had warned them to be ready for strange behavior.
Petruchio:	*(pretending not to see them)* What, no man at the door to take my horse? Where are those knaves?
Servant:	Here we are, sir!
Petruchio:	*(yelling at them)* You loggerheaded grooms, do your duty! Peasants, go fetch my dinner! *(to Kate inside)* Sit down, dearest Kate, and be merry!
Narrator 1:	The servants quickly bring dinner in.
Petruchio:	What, no water? Go get it, you rogues. Take off my boots. Ouch! *(kicking servant)* Watch it! Bring me my slippers! *(sweetly)* Come, Kate, and wash up, dear.
Narrator 2:	The servant drops the pitcher.
Petruchio:	You villain! Will you drop it?
Katharine:	Be patient. It was an accident.
Petruchio:	He's a beetle-headed knave! Come eat, Kate, you must be starving.
Narrator 1:	The servant brings a perfect meal.
Petruchio:	What's this? Burnt mutton? *(thowing it)* You heedless jolthead!
Katharine:	*(hungrily)* Pray husband, it's fine!
Petruchio:	We can't eat it like that! It'll give us cholera! I forbid you to touch this over-roasted flesh. Let's go to the bridal chamber! *(to servants)* Show Kate the way.
Narrator 2:	Puzzled, a famished Kate is led away.
Petruchio:	*(alone)* Now I will tame her tantrums. She'll not eat or sleep until she becomes agreeable. I'll rail and brawl, then kill her with kindness until it curbs her headstrong manner. That's the best way to tame a shrew!

Narrator 1: That night, Petruchio finds fault with the way his bed is made and flings the covers on the floor. When Kate tries to doze off in a chair, he keeps her awake with complaints.

Narrator 2: The next day, she is even more tired and hungry than before. She tries to convince Petruchio's servant to bring her some food.

Katharine: Did Petruchio marry me to starve me? Beggars do better at my father's door. Instead I'm fed on brawling, and he does it to spite me in the name of love. Grumio, I pray, bring me a meal. I don't care what it is.

Grumio: How about a cow's foot?

Katharine: That'll do. Let me have it.

Grumio: Actually, it's rotten. How about some broiled tripe?

Katharine: Fine, fine. Fetch it.

Grumio: No, that's rancid, too. Perhaps you'd prefer a piece of beef with mustard?

Katharine: A dish I love to feed on! Bring it!

Grumio: I think the mustard is too hot.

Katharine: Then just bring the beef.

Grumio: No, you'll have both or none.

Katharine: Then both, or one, or anything!!

Grumio: Then I'll just bring the mustard.

Katharine: *(at the end of her rope)* A plague on you! Get out of here!

Narrator 1: Petruchio now enters with food.

Petruchio: Sweetness, how are you, Kate?

Katharine: Cold and hungry.

Petruchio: Here, love. See how much I love you? I've fixed this meat just for you.

Narrator 2: She lunges for it, but he takes it away.

Petruchio: Tut, tut. Not a word of thanks?

Katharine: *(clenching teeth)* Thank you, sir.

Petruchio: That's better. Now eat, and may it do thy heart good. I've decided we will return to your father's house. We'll celebrate the wedding in silk coats and gold rings. I've had a fine gown and cap made for you.

Narrator 1: A haberdasher brings in a little cap.

Petruchio: This is too small! This paltry thing is no bigger than a walnut shell!

Katharine: But I like it. Petite is the fashion these days for gentlewomen.

Petruchio: When you are gentle, you shall have one, but not till then.

Katharine: Now, listen to me. I am no child or dummy. Better men than you have endured me speaking my mind, and if you can't, then stop up your ears. I tell you I like the cap, and I will have it!

Petruchio: What? You say you want to see the gown? Bring it here!

Narrator 2: A tailor brings in a beautiful new dress.

Petruchio: Mercy! This sleeve is carved like an apple tart! Here's a snip and a slash!

Tailor: You told me to make it fashionable.

Petruchio: I didn't tell you to ruin it!

Katharine: But it's a very pleasing gown!

Tailor: I made it just as instructed.

Petruchio: You lie—you thimble, you thread, you half a yard! You've butchered it. Take it away, you flea, you nit, you rag!

Narrator 1: Grumio takes the tailor aside.

Grumio: Ignore his unkind words. Take the gown and I'll pay you for it tomorrow.

Petruchio: We'll have to go to your father's in the clothes we're wearing. It's the mind that makes us rich, not our garments. Is the jay more precious than the lark because his feathers are more beautiful? No, good Kate. Let's go to the feast. It's seven o'clock now; we can be there by noon.

Katharine: I dare say, it's two, and we'll not get there until suppertime.

Petruchio: Are you still crossing me? Then we won't go till tomorrow—at whatever o'clock I say!

Scene 9

Narrator 2: Meanwhile, back at Baptista's, Hortensio convinces Tranio that the scholar is trying to steal Bianca.

Tranio: It's not true. I'm sure she fancies *me*.

Hortensio: Don't be so sure. Listen to them.

Lucentio: *(as they eavesdrop)* Mistress, I wish to teach you the story the "Art of Love."

Bianca: May you prove master of your "art"!

Lucentio: You are mistress of my heart!

Tranio: *(faking hurt)* Oh, unkind woman!

Hortensio:	I told you! She makes a god of that fellow! I will not wear this disguise anymore. I am not a musician; I am Hortensio. And I forswear Bianca!
Tranio:	Now I've seen it with my own eyes, I too forswear Bianca!
Hortensio:	I'm going to go marry a wealthy widow. Kindness, not beauteous looks, wins my love. Good-bye.
Narrator 1:	Bianca returns with Lucentio.
Tranio:	*(coming out of hiding)* Mistress, the music teacher has forsworn you.
Bianca:	Good, then we are rid of him!
Tranio:	Lucentio, a watchman has seen a stranger on the road who might fill the bill as your father, Vincentio. He even looks like a father.
Lucentio:	Good, then go enlist him.
Narrator 2:	Tranio concocts a story for the man.
Tranio:	You are unsafe in Padua, sir. I can protect you in my home if you're willing to pose as a wealthy merchant.
Stranger:	If it is a matter of life and death, then I will do it.
Tranio:	You must play the part of a man named Vincentio. Baptista is expecting him to arrive soon to assure the marriage of his daughter. Come; I'll explain all.
Narrator 1:	Later, Tranio invites Baptista to his home to work out the dowry deal with the supposed Vincentio. Tranio sends a servant to warn Lucentio.
Servant:	Sir, Baptista is nearing an agreement to give Bianca away to Tranio. He says that if you want to marry Bianca yourself, you better do it *now!*
Lucentio:	How can I?
Servant:	He said there is a priest ready at St. Luke's Church. Take her there and marry her. When Baptista finds out the deal with Tranio and the stranger is a sham, he'll be glad to let you have her.
Lucentio:	I'll do it, if she will agree. Now, happen what may!

Scene 10

Narrator 2:	Katharine and Petruchio are traveling during the day back to her father's house.
Petruchio:	How brightly the moon shines.
Katharine:	It's not moonlight; it's the sun!

Petruchio:	*(stopping)* Are you still crossing me? If I say it's the moon, it's the moon. It shall be whatever I say, or we'll turn back.
Katharine:	No please, we've come so far. It *is* the moon if you say so.
Petruchio:	You lie. It is the sun.
Katharine:	Then it is the blessed sun!
Narrator 1:	Kate is finally realizing that she can get much further by agreeing with him.
Katharine:	Whatever you name it—sun, moon, or *candle*—so it shall be for me.
Petruchio:	Good, then forward we shall go.
Narrator 2:	Soon they see an old man on the road.
Petruchio:	Tell me, Kate, have you ever seen a more lovely maid? Her eyes are like stars spangling the skies.
Kate:	*(to old man)* Young fair maiden, where are you going?
Petruchio:	Are you crazy, Kate? This is a faded, wrinkled man, not a maid.
Katharine:	Pardon my mistake, sir. The sun dazzled my eyes.
Petruchio:	Which way are you going, sir? You are welcome to join us.
Vincentio:	Your strangeness amazes me—but I am Vincentio from Pisa. I'm bound for Padua to visit my son, Lucentio.
Petruchio:	Then we are practically related. For your son may have married my wife's sister Bianca by now. Bianca is a well-born gentlewoman with a sizeable dowry.
Vincentio:	Is this true, or are you jesting?
Petruchio:	Come along and see for yourself.

Scene 11

Narrator 1:	Petruchio and Katharine escort Vincentio to Lucentio's house, the very place where Baptista is working out financial arrangements with the false father.
Narrator 2:	The real Vincentio knocks on the door, and a window opens above. Out pops the pretend Vincentio.
Stranger:	Who is it, beating down the gate?
Petruchio:	Tell Lucentio his father is at the door
Stranger:	You lie! His father is here looking out the window. *I* am Vincentio.
Vincentio:	Knave, you steal my name!
Stranger:	*You* are pretending to be *me*! Help, son! Baptista, help!

Narrator 1:	As Petruchio and Kate watch, Tranio, Baptista, and the stranger come to the door.
Tranio:	*(to Vincentio)* Who are you, old man?
Vincentio:	Nay, what are *you*? Wearing silk jacket and velvet stockings!
Tranio:	My father can afford it.
Vincentio:	*Your* father is a mere sailmaker! And you are my son's servant!
Stranger:	No, he is Lucentio—my only son and heir to my lands.
Tranio:	Police! Take this man to jail!
Vincentio:	O immortal gods! *(to Tranio)* Have you murdered my son?
Narrator 2:	Just as officers are about to drag Vincentio away, the real Lucentio arrives. Tranio and the stranger quickly run away.
Lucentio:	*(kneeling before Vincentio)* Pardon, sweet Father.
Vincentio:	Oh, my son! You're alive!
Bianca:	*(kneeling before Baptista)* Pardon, dear Father.
Baptista:	What's going on?
Lucentio:	I am Lucentio, the right son to the *real* Vincentio, here. While those false fellows were clouding your eyes, I married your daughter.
Baptista:	I thought you were the tutor.
Lucentio:	Love has wrought miracles! Bianca's love has caused me to change places with my servant.
Vincentio:	Where is that villain? I'll slit his nose for trying to send me to jail!
Lucentio:	Don't. I forced him to pose as me.
Baptista:	Did you say you married my daughter? Without asking my consent?
Vincentio:	Do not worry, sir. I will make sure you are compensated.
Narrator 1:	The two fathers, Lucentio, and Bianca all go inside to settle their affairs.
Katharine:	*(laughing)* Shall we join them to see the outcome, dear husband?
Petruchio:	First give me a kiss, sweet Kate. Better once than never, for never is too late.
Narrator 2:	Smiling, she kisses him.

Scene 12

Narrator 1:	Later, a party is held in Lucentio's house for all the newly married couples—including Hortensio and the wealthy widow.

Lucentio:	At last our jarring notes agree. Welcome to my house! Feast with the best!
Narrator 2:	Much later, Bianca decides to retire and takes Katharine and the widow with her.
Baptista:	*(to Petruchio)* Well, good son, I thank you for marrying Katharine, but I lament you had to take a shrew.
Petruchio:	She is not shrewish anymore. And I will prove it with a friendly bet. Let each man summon his wife, and whosoever comes first, that man will win one hundred crowns.
Lucentio:	I'll go first. Grumio, call my wife.
Grumio:	*(returning)* Sir, she sends word that she is busy and cannot come.
Petruchio:	Intolerable!
Hortensio:	Grumio, go entreat *my* wife.
Grumio:	*(returning again)* She thinks you jest and says you should go to *her*.
Petruchio:	Not to be endured! Grumio, go tell Kate I command *her* to come to me.
Hortensio:	I know she will not.
Baptista:	Good heavens, here she comes!
Katharine:	What is your will, sir?
Lucentio:	Amazing!
Hortensio:	I wonder what it means.
Petruchio:	It means peace and love and a quiet, happy life! Kate, where are your sister and Hortensio's wife?
Katharine:	Sitting by the fire, chatting.
Petruchio:	Then go fetch them.
Baptista:	Good Petruchio, I will add twenty crowns to your winnings, for Katharine is like another daughter and deserves another dowry!
Narrator 1:	Katharine returns with the other two.
Bianca:	Fie! What foolishness calls me?
Lucentio:	You have cost me one hundred crowns.
Bianca:	If you were betting on my acting dutiful, then you are a fool.
Petruchio:	Katharine, tell these women what they owe their husbands.
Katharine:	Unknit your brows, ladies. For scornful glances don't only wound your lords, they blot your beauty. Your husband is your life, the one who cares for you. He will endure the cold and storms of night for your safety. He craves no other tribute from you than your love. If

	you would have the same, then why not offer him an agreeable nature? When you are peevish, sullen, and sour, you are graceless. My mind was once like yours. I had more than enough reasons to frown. But now I see our lances are but straws. Pleasing my husband gives me new strength—and joy.
Petruchio:	Why, there's a lass! Come kiss me, Kate.
Narrator 2:	They kiss.
Petruchio:	And to you all, I bid goodnight.
Hortensio:	Go well, for you have tamed a shrew, one Katharine named.
Lucentio:	It's a wonder that she was ever tamed!

Simply Shakespeare: Readers Theatre for Young People is from *Read* magazine, a Weekly Reader publication, in collaboration with Teacher Ideas Press. Edited by Jennifer Kroll. www.weeklyreader.com. www.lu.com/tips. 1–800–541–2086.

CHAPTER 12

The Tempest

By William Shakespeare
Adapted by Jennifer Kroll

Summary

Prospero, a learned man and powerful magician, was the duke of Milan until his younger brother Sebastian stole his title and position, with the help of Alonso, the king of Naples. Set afloat by his enemies in a ship without masts and sails, Prospero nevertheless survived, and he now lives with his only daughter, Miranda, on a deserted island. When a ship carrying Sebastian, Alonso, Alonso's son Ferdinand, and others, sails near Prospero's island, the magician concocts a powerful storm and shipwrecks the group on the island. Using his magical powers and cunning, Prospero brings about a love match between Miranda and Prince Ferdinand and manipulates the others into seeing the error of their ways.

 ## Presentation Suggestions

Seat or stand Prospero front and center, with Miranda on one side of him and Ariel on the other. Seat or stand Ferdinand off to the side of Miranda, and Sebastian, Antonio, Gonzalo, and Alonso off to the side of Ariel. Narrators, Boatswain, and Sailor may be situated in a row behind the other characters or on the far side of Ferdinand.

 ## Props

Prospero may carry a yardstick or other item as a sorcerer's staff. He might also wear a pointed magician's hat. Ariel might wear natural colors such as green and brown. He might don a black shirt or scary mask during Scene 5. He can have a flute, recorder, or other wind instrument to play. Sailor and Boatswain might wear sailor's or fishing hats. Gonzalo, Sebastian, Antonio, Ferdinand, and Alonso should wear dressy clothing, as they are returning from a wedding. Each of these characters might also sport some type of sword. Miranda might wear a skirt, or flowers in her hair. Other possible props are a piece of firewood for Ferdinand to carry in Scene 4, food items or a tray of food for Scene 5, and a chess set for Ferdinand and Miranda to use at the end of the play.

Cast of Characters

(main characters in boldface)
Narrators 1, 2
Boatswain, *ship's officer*
Alonso, *king of Naples*
Sailor
Miranda, *Prospero's daughter*
Prospero, *rightful duke of Milan, a sorcerer*
Ariel, *a spirit, servant to Prospero*
Ferdinand, *Alonso's son*
Gonzalo, *an old adviser*
Sebastian, *Alonso's brother*
Antonio, *Prospero's brother, unlawful duke of Milan*

The Tempest

By William Shakespeare

Adapted by Jennifer Kroll

Scene 1

Narrator 1: Rain pours down, thunder roars, and lightning bolts rip across the sky. On board a sailing ship, the crew battles against a storm-tossed sea.

Boatswain: Take in the topsail, men! Quickly! Quickly!

Narrator 2: A number of passengers make their way up to the deck. Among them is Alonso, the king of Naples, and Antonio, duke of Milan.

Alonso: Boatswain, where's the captain?

Boatswain: You're getting in the way. You must go back to your cabin immediately.

Alonso: Do you know to whom you're speaking? I am the king of Naples!

Boatswain: All right then, King. If you can command the storm to die down, make yourself useful. If not, go back to your cabin! *(to sailors)* Down with the topmast! Lower! Lower!

Sailor: The ship's going to capsize!

Boatswain: Turn her around! Set out to sea again!

Sailor: It's too late! The ship is splitting! We're going down!

Scene 2

Narrator 1: Meanwhile, in a cave dwelling on a nearby island, the sorcerer Prospero and his 15-year-old daughter, Miranda, watch the ship's struggles by means of magic.

Miranda: Father, if you've used your magical powers to create this storm, please make it stop at once! I feel so sorry for those poor people on board! Look! They're terrified! Are they going to die?

Prospero: Calm down, Miranda. No harm will be done to anyone, I promise. Yes, I have caused the storm. But I did it for you.

Miranda: For me? How can that be?

Prospero: My dear daughter, do you remember anything of the time before we came to live on this island?

Miranda: It's like a dream, but I think I remember having four or five serving women who looked after me.

Prospero: I'm amazed that you can remember. You were no more than three years old. Do you remember how we came to be here?

Miranda: I don't.

Prospero: Well, then, I shall tell you our story. Twelve years ago, I was the Duke of Milan, a prince of power. You my dear, were a princess.

Miranda: Can it be true? And if it is, what foul play brought us here? Or was it by good fortune that we came to be on this island?

Prospero: It was a combination of foul play and good fortune that brought us here.

Miranda: Explain yourself, Father.

Prospero: My younger brother, your uncle, is named Antonio. Twelve years ago, he was the person I loved most, next to yourself. Alas! He proved himself undeserving of my great love.

Miranda: What did he do?

Prospero: When I first came to power as duke, I was more interested in my books and my magic studies than I was in practical matters of government. I let my brother, Antonio, take over many of my duties. I was so wrapped up in my studies that I didn't notice how much Antonio, the brother I trusted, was changing.

Miranda: How did he change, Father?

Prospero: Antonio became ambitious and no longer loyal to me. He decided that since he was doing the work of a duke, he should also have a duke's full power. But to become the duke of Milan, he needed to get rid of me.

Miranda: Get rid of you?

Prospero: Yes. My brother called on my enemy, the king of Naples, for assistance in achieving this goal. The two of them had you and me captured and removed from the city in the dead of night. You were only a very young child.

Miranda: I am amazed we survived!

Prospero: I guess Antonio didn't want our blood on his hands. Rather than kill us outright, he had us set afloat on a leaky old boat without masts or sails.

Miranda: I must have been such a bother to you then.

Prospero: No, no. You were no bother. You were the angel who preserved me. When I was ready to give up, you made me want to stay alive.

Miranda:	How did we come ashore?
Prospero:	By luck or divine providence, as well as by the kindness of a friend. We had some food and fresh water on our boat because a noble man, Gonzalo, left it there for us. He also left us some garments and supplies, as well as some beloved volumes from my library.
Miranda:	I wish I could see that man and thank him! . . . But, Father, you still haven't told me why you created the tempest.
Prospero:	Our enemies have been travelling by ship through this part of the world on their way back from the wedding of the king's daughter in Tunis. This I discovered with my magic powers. I conjured up the storm in order to bring the king's party ashore here. That is all you need to know at the moment. Now sleep, Miranda. You must be feeling sleepy. . . .
Narrator 2:	Miranda is enchanted by Prospero's words and immediately falls asleep. As she lies sleeping, an elfin spirit appears in the cave.
Prospero:	Come here, Ariel.
Narrator 1:	The spirit approaches Prospero and bows deeply before him.
Ariel:	Hail, great master! I am here to do your bidding.
Prospero:	Have you, my spirit, carried out my orders?
Ariel:	Every single one. I boarded the king's ship and whirled about, causing turmoil. I created flashes of lightning and dreadful thunderclaps. Ferdinand, the son of the king of Naples, was the first to panic and jump ship. The king and the rest of his party followed soon after. Only the captain and crew remained on the ship.
Prospero:	Well done, Ariel. Is everyone from the king's party safely ashore?
Ariel:	Not a hair on any head was harmed. All of them, except Ferdinand, are wandering around the island together. I landed Ferdinand by himself, and the last time I saw him, he was sitting alone, sighing and staring out to sea.
Prospero:	What have you done with the ship and sailors?
Ariel:	All are safely in a hidden corner of the harbor. The sailors are charmed and sleeping below deck.
Prospero:	Then you've performed your task exactly as I asked. But there's still more work to do. What time is it?
Ariel:	It's past noon.
Prospero:	Well past noon, I'd say. We'll have to make good use of the next few hours, if my full plan is to be carried out.
Ariel:	More toil?
Prospero:	*(scolding)* Now, now. No grumbling. Must I remind you how I saved you from that evil sorceress, Sycorax, who had imprisoned you in the trunk of a pine tree?

Ariel: She commanded me to do terrible things. I couldn't obey.

Prospero: You would still be stuck in that tree trunk if it weren't for me. Keep that in mind.

Ariel: Yes, master. But you promised my freedom. . . .

Prospero: And you shall have it, after two days' time. Go now, and carry out the rest of our plan.

Narrator 2: Ariel turns and disappears.

Prospero: *(to Miranda)* Wake up, dear heart. You have slept well.

Miranda: Your strange story made me feel so sleepy. . . .

Prospero: Shake it off. I believe we are about to have a visitor.

Narrator 1: Meanwhile, out on the beach, Ferdinand, Alonso's son, sits moping, with his knees tucked up under his chin.

Ferdinand: Alas! I fear my father is drowned and all the rest are gone as well. I am the last one of our party left alive, and I am trapped on this uninhabited island.

Narrator 2: Ariel, who is invisible, comes and stands near Ferdinand. He begins to play a little flute.

Ferdinand: *(glancing around wildly)* Who's there? Where is that music coming from? Oh, it's gone now. . . . Ah, there it is again. . . .

Narrator 1: Ferdinand gets up and follows the sound of the music. Still invisible, Ariel leads Ferdinand down the beach and then inland, until he approaches the dwelling of Prospero and Miranda.

Prospero: Miranda, look over there. What do you see?

Miranda: What is that? See how it looks about! What a beautiful form it has! It must be a spirit.

Prospero: No, daughter. It eats and sleeps and has the same senses that we have. This young man that you're looking at was in the shipwreck. He has lost his friends and wanders around looking for them.

Miranda: He must be a god or angel. Nothing natural was ever so noble in appearance!

Prospero: *(gleefully, to himself)* It's all working out just as I planned!

Narrator 2: Ferdinand suddenly sees Miranda.

Ferdinand: You must be the goddess of this island. Instruct me, lady, how I should act here in your realm. Your wish is my command.

Miranda: I'm a mortal maiden, sir, not a goddess.

Ferdinand: *(to himself)* She speaks my language as if she were in Naples!

Prospero: *(to Ferdinand, harshly)* What is your purpose here, sir? How do we know that you come in peace and mean us no harm?

Miranda:	Father, why do you speak to him so harshly? This man stirs my heart. For my sake, show pity.
Narrator 1:	Ferdinand stares at Miranda, completely smitten.
Ferdinand:	If you are not promised to someone else, I'd like to make you queen of Naples.
Prospero:	*(to Ferdinand)* You're a spy! I know it. *(to Miranda)* Don't speak to him! He's a traitor!
Miranda:	But Father! Nothing bad on the inside could look so handsome on the outside.
Prospero:	*(harshly, to Ferdinand)* Come, young man. I'll put chains around your feet. You'll drink seawater and eat withered roots and husks for dinner.
Narrator 2:	Ferdinand draws his sword.
Ferdinand:	I don't think I would enjoy such entertainment.
Narrator 1:	Prospero brandishes his wizard's staff. Ferdinand's sword falls from his hand.
Prospero:	You are under my command now. Come.

Scene 3

Narrator 2:	Meanwhile, on another part of the island, Alonso, the king of Naples, wanders about with his brother, Sebastian. Accompanying them are Gonzalo, an honest old adviser, and Antonio, Prospero's villainous younger brother, who reigns as duke of Milan.
Gonzalo:	Although we have lost much, it is a miracle that we are still alive. We should be grateful.
Sebastian:	*(to Antonio)* The old fool keeps going on and on about how lucky we are.
Antonio:	*(sarcastically, to Sebastian)* Just wait. He's getting ready to come out with some more gems of wisdom.
Gonzalo:	What a beautiful place! The air here is remarkably sweet!
Narrator 1:	Sebastian and Antonio sniff the air and laugh.
Sebastian:	*(to Antonio)* Who is he kidding? It smells disgusting.
Gonzalo:	Everything needed for life is here. The grass is thick and green.
Sebastian:	*(to Antonio)* No, wait. I see a tiny patch of green over there.
Narrator 2:	They both laugh again, at Gonzalo's expense.
Gonzalo:	*(turning to King Alonso)* The thing that astonishes me the most, Sire, is this: Our clothes are just as fresh and bright as they were when we wore them at the marriage of your daughter, Claribel, the new queen of Tunis.

Alonso:	*(in distress)* The marriage! Don't remind me! I wish I had never sent my daughter to live so far from home. If we hadn't made such a long voyage, I would not have lost my son in that storm. Alas! I fear I will never see either my son or daughter again.
Sebastian:	*(to Alonso)* It's your own fault that you've lost them both. You could have married Claribel to somebody who lives closer to Naples.
Gonzalo:	Lord Sebastian! There is no need to pour salt into the wound. You are only making matters worse.
Sebastian:	As if you make things better with your endless jabbering!
Narrator 1:	Ariel approaches and begins playing solemn music. He remains invisible to the men.
Gonzalo:	I feel sleepy.
Alonso:	I cannot keep my eyes open a minute more.
Narrator 2:	Gonzalo and Alonso slump to the ground and sleep.
Antonio:	They fell asleep suddenly! Both at once! How strange.... Hmm.... Perhaps it is fate acting on your behalf, Sebastian. Guess what I'm picturing right now. I'm picturing your brother's crown on your head.
Sebastian:	Are you fully awake? Did I hear you right?
Antonio:	You heard me. Is it not true that King Alonso's son, Ferdinand, is drowned?
Sebastian:	There doesn't seem to be much hope that he is still alive.
Antonio:	Then who is the next heir of Naples?
Sebastian:	Claribel.
Antonio:	She is queen of Tunis. She lives far from Naples. Sebastian, your time has come. Act, and advance your position. You can become the king of Naples once your brother is dead.
Sebastian:	You mean for me to act as you did when you supplanted your brother, Prospero, as duke of Milan?
Antonio:	Yes. Just look how well I suit the role!
Sebastian:	But doesn't your conscience bother you?
Antonio:	Conscience? What part of the body is that? I'm sure I don't have one of those inside me anywhere Come now. Here lies your brother, the king, sleeping so soundly that he looks as if he might be dead. All you have to do is put your sword in him, and he *will* be dead. I can do the same to the old windbag who sleeps beside him.
Narrator 1:	They draw their swords and stand above their sleeping companions, ready to strike. Suddenly, Ariel's music begins again. Alonso and Gonzalo wake up and see the drawn swords.

Gonzalo:	Heaven preserve the king!
Alonso:	Why do you have you swords drawn? What's the matter?
Sebastian:	We were standing here, guarding you while you slept, and we heard a noise like the bellowing of some wild beast. Didn't it wake you, Your Majesty?
Alonso:	I heard nothing.
Antonio:	But it was a terrible noise! It was like the roar of a whole herd of lions.
Alonso:	Did you hear it, Gonzalo?
Gonzalo:	Sir, all I heard was a strange humming sound that woke me up. When I opened my eyes, I saw their weapons drawn.
Alonso:	That's strange.... Well, in any case, we had better be cautious and leave this place. Let's go in search of Ferdinand.
Narrator 2:	As the king's party sets off to search for Ferdinand, Ariel heads off in another direction, to tell Prospero what has been done.

Scene 4

Narrator 1:	Back at the dwelling of Prospero and Miranda, Ferdinand is hard at work carrying firewood for Prospero.
Ferdinand:	*(to Miranda)* I would normally consider this a very unpleasant task. With you close by me, though, I am enjoying myself. These thousands of logs seem like nothing at all.
Miranda:	Please don't work so hard! I can't bear to watch. My father is away in his study right now. Sit down and rest a minute.
Ferdinand:	I can't stop now, or I'll never get this task done before nightfall.
Miranda:	If you sit down, I'll carry the logs for you. Let me have the load you're carrying....
Ferdinand:	No, no. I can't sit by lazing around while you work, fair lady.
Miranda:	Please. Just let me help.
Narrator 2:	Ferdinand and Miranda do not realize that Prospero is watching them from a distance.
Prospero:	Wonderful, wonderful. They are both completely smitten with each other. This hardship that I've inflicted on Ferdinand is having exactly the effect that I intended.
Ferdinand:	Miranda, Miranda. I've met many women of beauty and virtue before now, but none compares to you.
Miranda:	If I had my choice, I would rather have you for a companion than any other. But I shouldn't be saying that. My father would be angry.

Narrator 1: As Prospero listens from a distance, smiling, Ferdinand and Miranda express their love for each other. They talk about how much they would like to get married.

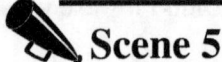 Scene 5

Narrator 2: Alonso, Sebastian, Gonzalo, and Antonio have been walking around looking for Ferdinand for several hours.

Gonzalo: I can go no further, sir. My old bones ache, and I'm hungry.

Alonso: I'm weary, too, and my heart is heavy. I fear that my son is drowned and we will never find him.

Narrator 1: Alonso and Gonzalo sit down to rest. Meanwhile, Antonio and Sebastian speak quietly together.

Antonio: Don't lose your resolve. We will soon get another chance to do away with your brother.

Sebastian: We will take advantage of the very next opportunity.

Narrator 2: Suddenly, all four men hear strange music.

Alonso: What's that?

Narrator 1: Several strange, elfin figures enter, carrying a banquet table heaped with food. The figures set the table down and dance around it, beckoning the men to eat.

Gonzalo: This is amazing! It can't be real! Imagine what they would say back in Naples if we described this!

Alonso: We must be careful. Let's approach cautiously.

Narrator 2: As the men approach the table, thunder roars and lightning flashes. The table vanishes, and Ariel appears, dressed all in black. He looks very frightening as he points a long finger first at Antonio, then at Sebastian and Alonso.

Ariel: You three men of sin! The heavens know what you have done!

Narrator 1: Alonso, Sebastian, and Antonio draw their swords.

Ariel: You are fools to think you can hurt me. You might as well try to wound the wind or kill the water.

Narrator 2: The three men suddenly find their swords too heavy to lift. Their weapons drop to the ground.

Ariel: My business here is to remind you of a deed done twelve years ago. Remember how you took Prospero from Milan and left him exposed on the open sea, all alone with his innocent child? The powers of the universe have not forgotten that vile deed, and now you are being punished for it!

Narrator 1: With a clap of thunder, Ariel vanishes.

Alonso:	This is horrible! Horrible! Did that creature, that thing, speak of Prospero? After that creature! We must chase and destroy it and save ourselves!
Narrator 2:	Alonso, Sebastian, and Antonio run off with their swords drawn. Gonzalo follows.

Scene 6

Narrator 1:	It is late afternoon. Ferdinand and Miranda are sitting near the woodpile, having a conversation with Prospero, who has finally stopped being unkind to Ferdinand.
Prospero:	If I've punished you too severely, Ferdinand, I am sorry. I hope that you both will forgive me when you realize that these trials have only made your love grown stronger. *(turning to Miranda)* I no longer object to your friendship with this man. I support it wholeheartedly.
Miranda:	Father! This is truly wonderful!
Ferdinand:	Sir, I don't know how to thank you.
Prospero:	*(to Ferdinand)* Just be a good husband to her. *(to both)* Be happy together. I gladly give you my blessing.
Narrator 2:	Prospero leaves the two young people alone. He heads off into the woods to the place where Ariel is holding Alonso, Sebastian, Antonio, and Gonzalo frozen in a magic circle.
Prospero:	How are things progressing with our visitors, Ariel?
Ariel:	Here they all are, my lord, just as you requested.
Prospero:	Excellent. Soon you shall have your freedom, Ariel. Once our goals are accomplished, I will command no more spirits. Nor will I ever again control the weather and the natural elements. In fact, I plan to bury my magic books and break my magic staff in two.
Narrator 1:	Prospero looks at the king and the other men frozen in the magic circle. Suddenly, he recognizes Gonzalo, the man who saved his life twelve years before. Tears come to his eyes.
Prospero:	Oh, good Gonzalo! I will always be in your debt.
Narrator 2:	Prospero Looks at each of the other men in turn.
Prospero:	Alonso, you evil man, you greatly wronged my daughter and me. Sebastian, you are no better, for you assisted your brother, the king, in the plot to end my life.
Narrator 1:	Prospero turns at last to look at his own brother, Antonio.
Prospero:	There you are, my brother. Your ambition was so great that it destroyed your ability to feel remorse and natural affection. I don't feel anger toward you anymore, only sadness. I forgive you for everything.... *(to Ariel)* Go and wake the sleeping captain and crew and bring the ship close by. Then you may have your freedom.

Ariel: I'll be back in a heartbeat!

Narrator 2: The enchanted men begin to wake up and move around.

Gonzalo: What's going on?

Prospero: Behold Prospero, the wronged duke of Milan. I bid a hearty welcome to you, Alonso, and to your company.

Narrator 1: Prospero opens his arms and embraces King Alonso.

Prospero: See, I am solid, not a spirit or ghost.

Alonso: I'm afraid I must be going crazy!

Narrator 2: Prospero embraces Gonzalo.

Prospero: Noble friend, your honor is beyond words.

Narrator 1: Finally, Prospero steps back and addresses Sebastian and Antonio quietly.

Prospero: If I wanted to, I could tell the king about your recent conversations. I know what treachery you have been planning. However, if you promise to repent of your evil ways, I'll keep my mouth shut.

Sebastian: *(to Antonio)* How can he know what we have plotted? Is he some devil?

Prospero: *(to Antonio)* Although you, my brother, do not deserve that name, still I forgive you. I now take back my title and my dukedom.

Alonso: If you are Prospero, tell us the story of how you survived all these years. Tell us how we came to meet you here after our shipwreck and the loss of my son, Ferdinand.

Narrator 2: Tears come to Alonso's eyes as he speaks of Ferdinand.

Alonso: *(quietly)* Alas! For a moment, I had almost forgotten my tragedy. *(to Prospero)* Recently, I lost my son.

Prospero: And recently, I lost my daughter.

Alonso: You did? I am so sorry. Truly I am. If only they could both be alive and living in Naples as king and queen. I'd give up my own life to make it so. When did you lose your daughter?

Prospero: In this last tempest. Come with me, and you will learn the details.

Narrator 1: Prospero leads Alonso and the others to the entrance of his dwelling. He pulls a curtain aside. Inside, Ferdinand and Miranda are sitting at a table, playing chess. They look up.

Prospero: It seems that I have recently lost my daughter to your son.

Alonso: Is this a vision?

Sebastian: It's a miracle!

Narrator 2: Ferdinand jumps up to embrace his father.

Alonso: My son! Who is this maiden?

Ferdinand: She is Miranda, Prospero's daughter and my fiancée. We're getting married.

Gonzalo: This is unbelievable! Who would ever have thought that the Duke of Milan would be cast out of Milan, only to have his grandchildren and great-grandchildren become kings and queens of Naples?

Narrator 1: The boatswain and captain come rushing up.

Boatswain: We have good news and more good news! Not only have we found our king and company, but our boat is still intact. In fact, it has never been in better shape. We are ready to sail.

Prospero: Now that wrongs have been righted and failings forgiven, let us return to Naples. There is a wedding to plan.

Simply Shakespeare: Readers Theatre for Young People is from *Read* magazine, a Weekly Reader publication, in collaboration with Teacher Ideas Press. Edited by Jennifer Kroll. www.weeklyreader.com. www.lu.com/tips. 1–800–541–2086.

CHAPTER 13

Twelfth Night

By William Shakespeare

Adapted by Kate Davis

Summary

Viola and Sebastian, a twin brother and sister traveling together, are separated during a shipwreck. Coming to on a beach, Viola assumes that Sebastian is dead. She finds out that she is in Illyria, a country ruled by Duke Orsino, who is in love with a beautiful countess named Olivia. Unfortunately for Orsino, Olivia is busy mourning the deaths of her father and brother and wants nothing to do with him. Viola disguises herself as a young man and gains employment from Duke Orsino, who sends her to bring his messages of love to Olivia. Olivia promptly falls in love with Orsino's new messenger—Viola—who has, in fact, secretly fallen in love with her employer, Orsino. Things become even more tangled when Sebastian shows up on the scene and is mistaken for his twin sister in her masculine disguise.

Presentation Suggestions

Seat or stand the players in a row. Viola should be located front and center, between Orsino and Olivia. Place Malvolio to the side of Olivia, then Maria on the other side of him. Next to Maria, place Sir Toby, Sir Andrew, and Feste. On the other side of Duke Orsino, seat Sea Captain, Sailor, Sebastian, and Narrators.

Props

Because the play takes place during the Christmas season, it might best be performed when the classroom is decked out for the holidays. Viola and Sebastian should wear matching shirts and hats or at least clothes of the same color, to indicate that they're twins. Viola should have a hat on that she can remove to let her hair down at the end. Feste can wear a jester's hat or other funny hat to indicate that he is a jester. Alternatively, he might wear a Groucho Marx–style mustache or some other evidence of his jokester's status. Sir Toby and Sir Andrew should have bottles and glasses for pouring and tasting. Sailor and Sea Captain can wear sailor caps. Maria can wear an apron or a maid's cap. She might hold a letter of some kind to drop in front of Malvolio. Olivia should have a ring to give to Viola.

Cast of Characters

(main parts in boldface)

Narrators 1, 2

Viola, *sister of Sebastian; also masquerades as Cesario*

Sebastian, *brother of Viola*

Sea Captain

Duke Orsino, *ruler of Illyria*

Maria, *Olivia's maid*

Sir Toby Belch, *Olivia's uncle*

Sir Andrew Aguecheek, *Belch's friend*

Feste, *a jester*

Olivia, *a countess*

Malvolio, *Olivia's steward*

Sailor

Twelfth Night

By William Shakespeare
Adapted by Kate Davis

Scene 1

Narrator 1: A violent storm whips the seas on which Viola and her twin brother, Sebastian, are sailing.

Narrator 2: Suddenly, a huge wave splits the ship in two! Sebastian is thrown into the sea.

Viola: My brother! Come back!

Sebastian: Viola! My sister! *(fading)* God save you! . . .

Narrator 1: The next morning, Viola lies washed ashore in a strange land. She awakes on the sand near the captain of her ship. Viola looks around.

Viola: What country is this, friend?

Sea Captain: By my charts, it is Illyria.

Viola: Illyria. Such a name sounds like paradise. But paradise is where the sea has taken my brother.

Captain: Be comforted, lady. Chance has saved you. By that same chance, Sebastian may not be drowned. After our ship split, I saw him clinging to a floating mast. As if riding a dolphin's back, he was cresting the waves.

Viola: If I had gold, I'd give it to you for saying so. You give me hope. Now what do you know about this Illyria?

Captain: Illyria is ruled by Duke Orsino, a melancholy soul. He pines for the love of Olivia, a beautiful countess. But she will not have him. She is mourning for her father and brother, who both died a year ago.

Viola: *(sadly)* Lost a brother? Just like me. I wonder if she would let me work for her until I find a way home.

Captain: I doubt it. Olivia will not admit the company of anyone, especially suitors, *especially* Orsino.

Viola: Perhaps then I can earn protection by working as *his* servant.

Captain: As a woman, you'd have little chance of that.

Viola: Suppose I dress as a boy? I can sing and teach the duke about poetry. Will you help me hide what I am and introduce me to him?

Captain: I will. If my tongue blabs of your true nature, let me fall blind.

Viola: Good friend, lead on!

Scene 2

Narrator 2: At the duke's palace, Orsino is surrounded by musicians as he broods over his love of Olivia.

Duke Orsino: If music be the food of love, play on. Give me more of it, so that my lovesickness will die.

Narrator 1: Viola, now disguised as a boy and calling herself Cesario, has been with the duke only three days. Yet Orsino is so impressed with his new servant that he confides in "him."

Orsino: I have opened the book of my secret soul to you, Cesario. My passion for Olivia grows daily, yet she vows not to leave her house for *seven* years. I am heartsick and depressed. Will you go and speak to her for me?

Viola: If she is as deep in mourning as people say, she'll never let me in.

Orsino: Stand at her door and say your foot will root there until the servant lets you see her. Be persistent.

Viola: And if I am let in, then what?

Orsino: Then tell her how deeply I am in love with her! Speak poetically about how faithful I'll be, how miserable I am without her. She will listen to you better than she will to me.

Viola: I don't know why.

Orsino: Your lips are as smooth as a goddess's and your voice as high. Olivia is more apt to listen to a youth who resembles a woman than to a man as lovesick as myself.

Viola: I'll do my best to persuade this lady to join you in life . . .

Narrator 2: However, there is one small problem. . . .

Viola: *(quietly, to herself)* . . . but in truth, I would be your wife.

Narrator 1: Viola herself has fallen in love with Orsino!

Scene 3

Narrator 2: While Olivia mourns her days away, her fat uncle drinks and parties his nights away in her garden. Olivia's maid is sent to quiet him.

Maria:	Sir Toby, pipe down and come in! You are disturbing my lady.
Sir Toby Belch:	But Twelfth Night is a time for celebration. What a plague, that she should take her brother's death so seriously! Surely care is an enemy to life. *(hiccups)* Let's live!
Maria:	Can't you confine yourself to more modest limits?
Toby:	But I am already confined— *(stumbling)*—in these tight clothes.
Maria:	My lady fears this quaffing will undo you. And she's not happy about that knave you've brought to court her.
Toby:	Who? Sir Andrew? He's a good man—brilliant! He plays the viola, speaks four languages. . . .
Maria:	He's a fool.
Toby:	He's rich!
Maria:	He keeps you in drink. He is a coward with a gift for whining. Many wish he had the gift of a grave!
Sir Andrew Aguecheek:	*(entering)* How now, Sir Toby? *(to Maria)* Bless you, fair shrew.
Toby:	Bless whom? She's done nothing but pester me. Accost her, Sir Andrew!
Andrew:	What's that?
Toby:	*(drunkenly)* My niece's maid. Accost!
Andrew:	*(to Maria)* Glad to meet you, Miss Accost.
Toby:	No, you dummy! *Accost* means attack her!
Andrew:	It does? I knew that.
Maria:	*(as she leaves)* Brilliant, is he? *(laughing)* Good night, fools!
Andrew:	I mustn't eat too much beef; it harms my wit. Sir Toby, I've come to tell you I'm leaving tomorrow.
Toby:	Why, dear knight?
Andrew:	Your niece will not see me. The only men she pays any attention to are her dead father and brother.
Toby:	Aw, don't go. The holidays are not spent until Twelfth Night is over. We have more singing and dancing to do yet. You *can* dance, can't you?
Andrew:	I can cut a fine caper. Watch!
Narrator 1:	Aguecheek begins to dance . . .
Narrator 2:	. . . and falls flat on his face.

Scene 4

Narrator 1: The next day, Feste, Illyria's jester, returns to Olivia's house after having visited the duke. Maria spies him in the great room.

Maria: Where have you been, fool? No excuses. My lady will hang you if she knows you've been with Orsino.

Feste: *(jesting)* Many a good hanging prevents a bad marriage!

Maria: That's wisdom for a fool.

Feste: God gives wisdom to those that have it. And those that are fools, let them use their talents.

Maria: And your talents are . . . ?

Feste: A quick wit. What else? For better a witty fool than a foolish wit.

Narrator 2: Olivia enters with her steward, Malvolio. Someone knocks at the door, and Maria goes to answer it.

Narrator 1: Swaggering with self-importance, Malvolio swings a long key chain to remind everyone he is keeper of her keys and money. The countess sees Feste but tells Malvolio she is in no mood for the jester's antics.

Olivia: Take the fool away.

Feste: *(to Malvolio)* You heard her. Take the lady away.

Olivia: *(taking offense)* Your wit runs dry.

Feste: Good lady, give me permission to show that *you* are the fool.

Olivia: Me? How can you prove that?

Feste: With a question: Tell me, Countess, why do you mourn so?

Olivia: For my brother's death.

Feste: I think your brother's soul is with the devil.

Olivia: No, his soul is in *paradise!*

Feste: Aha! If that were so, then he has no need of being mourned, does he?

Narrator 2: Olivia considers, then laughs.

Olivia: Well done. You make a good point—and cheer me besides!

Feste: *(triumphantly)* Ta-da! *(to Malvolio)* Like I said, take the fool away!

Malvolio: Madam, how can you abide this rascal? His mind is decayed.

Olivia: Oh, don't take yourself so seriously. You make a cannonball out of birdshot. A true fool cannot slander anyone; it's his job.

Narrator 1: Maria, the maid, returns.

Maria:	Madam, a gentleman is at the gate, insisting he speak with you.
Olivia:	Let me guess—he's sent by Orsino. Now I'm depressed again. Malvolio, go tell him I'm sick, or whatever you must to get rid of him.
Narrator 2:	Malvolio does as asked, relishing his task. But the caller will *not* go away.
Malvolio:	*(to Olivia)* He refuses to depart, Countess.
Olivia:	What kind of man is this who wants to see me?
Malvolio:	He is not yet old enough for a man, nor young enough for a boy. Yet, he speaks very convincingly.
Olivia:	Hmmm. Interesting. I'll humor him and hear what he has to say.

Scene 5

Viola:	*(as Cesario)* Most radiant, unmatchable beauty—you *are* the lady of the house? I'd hate to throw my speech away if you're not. I took pains in creating it, and 'tis poetical.
Olivia:	Truly? I heard you were saucy while at my gate. You began your speech rudely.
Viola:	I learned to be rude from the way I was treated there.
Olivia:	Well, tell me the hideous matter you've come to deliver.
Viola:	Lady—your beauty is painted by nature's sweet hand. If you were never to marry or leave a copy behind, you'd be the cruelest she alive.
Olivia:	*(conceitedly)* Don't worry. I can make a list of my beauty and send it out to the world. Two lips, one neck . . .
Viola:	I see what you are; you are too proud. But my master still loves you.
Olivia:	How does he love me?
Viola:	With tears, with groans that thunder love, with sighs of fire.
Olivia:	I suppose you will say he is noble, learned, valiant, and gracious.
Viola:	All those things and more.
Olivia:	His love bores me. Your master knows my mind. I cannot love him and told him so long ago.
Viola:	If *I* loved you as intensely as he, I couldn't understand your denial.
Olivia:	And if you loved me . . . ?
Viola:	I'd camp outside your doors. Write love songs till your heart soared. I'd holler your name and not be still till "Olivia" echoed off every hill.
Narrator 1:	Olivia is moved by the youth's passion and poetry.

Olivia: You would do that all for me?

Viola: That and more.

Olivia: Go tell Orsino, "Send requests to me no more."

Narrator 2: Olivia smiles flirtatiously at her visitor.

Olivia: *(coyly)* Unless *you* come back to tell me how he takes it.

Viola: My master's heart is like flint, waiting for your spark. Yet you treat him so poorly. Farewell, fair cruelty.

Scene 6

Narrator 1: As soon as Viola leaves, Olivia's heart begins racing for the bright young man who just visited.

Olivia: *(dizzily)* His face, his speech, his spirit! His soul catches me as quickly as one catches the plague!

Narrator 2: The countess fans herself.

Olivia: *(longingly)* If only the master were the messenger! I've got to see that young man again! *(calling)* Malvolio!

Narrator 1: Olivia removes a small ring.

Malvolio: At your service, madam.

Olivia: Quick, run after that young man. *(fibbing)* Tell him to take his master's ring back; I am *not* for the duke. *(slyly)* But tell the duke's messenger to come back tomorrow and I'll explain why.

Narrator 2: Malvolio hurries off, catching up at last with the disguised Viola.

Malvolio: Ho! You forgot to take the duke's ring back. *(in a huff)* Thanks for making me chase after you.

Viola: *(puzzled)* I gave Olivia no ring.

Malvolio: Oh sure. I'll bet you threw it at her. I'll return it the same way; I doubt it's even worth stooping down to pick it up.

Narrator 1: Malvolio dashes the ring to the ground and stomps off.

Viola: What a milk-livered measle. *(shaking head)* What can Olivia mean, giving me this ring? Oh, heaven forbid—don't tell me she's been charmed by my disguise! She *did* look longingly at me. This must be a ploy to bring me back.

Narrator 2: Viola considers what she has gotten herself into, posing as a man.

Viola: Disguise, you are wicked! Orsino loves Olivia dearly. I am fond of Orsino. And Olivia dotes on me. As a man, I have no chance for my master's love. As a woman, Olivia might as well love a dream. Time, you will have to untangle this one. It's too hard a knot for me to untie.

Scene 7

Narrator 1: But other knots of confusion are busy tying themselves.

Narrator 2: In another part of Illyria, a sailor and a foreign gentleman have made their way from the shore to town.

Sailor: Let me stay with you and serve you.

Sebastian: No, you've already done so much for me. I cannot let my sadness rub off on such a good man.

Sailor: What sadness?

Sebastian: I had a sister, my double. But before you pulled me from the sea, my sister drowned.

Sailor: How awful! She was your twin?

Sebastian: Yes, though far more beautiful and fair of mind. Now the salty sea has claimed her. . . . *(choking up)* Forgive me, but I am so near to tears, the memory of her will drown me with more salt water. Farewell.

Sailor: Where will you go?

Sebastian: To find lodging. Then I'll go to the duke's to plan my return home.

Scene 8

Narrator 1: In Olivia's kitchen, Sir Toby, Sir Andrew, and Feste are celebrating the end of the holidays—again.

Toby: The best of life is eating and drinking!

Andrew: Give us a love song, fool!

Feste: *What is love? 'Tis not hereafter, Present mirth hath present laughter, What's to come is still unsure, Youth's a stuff will not endure.*

Toby: Shall we rouse the night owl in a round or two? Come, let's sing!

All: *On the twelfth day of December, the roguish knaves did dance—*

Narrator 2: The ruckus rouses Maria, who goes to the kitchen to quiet the men.

Maria: What caterwauling! I warn you. Malvolio is going to come and scold you.

Narrator 1: Malvolio enters the kitchen

Malvolio: *(angrily)* Are you men mad? Do you make an alehouse of my lady's house? Have you no manners but to gad about at this time of night? Have you no respect for persons, place, or time? Now keep quiet, or the countess and I will make you leave.

Toby:	Oh, go hang yourself. Do you think that just because you are virtuous, there shall be no more cakes and ale? *(to Maria)* Bring us more wine, Maria.
Malvolio:	*(to Maria)* If you prize my lady's favor, you won't condone this behavior. If you allow it, I'll have to tell on you.
Narrator 2:	Malvolio struts off.
Maria:	*(shouting after him)* Oh, go shake your ears!
Andrew:	Go challenge him, Toby.
Maria:	I've got a better idea. Let's trick him into making a fool of himself.
Toby:	Good, good! Tell us how.
Maria:	His head is crammed so full of his own excellencies, he thinks anyone who looks at him loves him.
Toby:	So how can we bait him?
Maria:	I'll drop a love letter in his path, doting on how a certain man walks, speaks, looks. My handwriting is identical to my lady's. When Malvolio reads the letter, he'll be convinced Olivia is writing about *him*.
Toby:	He'll think Olivia loves him!
Maria:	I'll hide you three in the bushes so you can watch. Now get to bed—and dream about tomorrow.
Narrator 1:	She leaves.
Andrew:	She's a good wench.
Toby:	One that adores me. Come on; let's get to sleep. You have to send for more money in the morning.

Scene 9

Narrator 2:	The next morning, Feste returns to the duke's palace and finds him still moaning about his sorry love life.
Orsino:	What was that sad song you gave us the other night?
Feste:	*(singing) Come death; I am slain by a fair cruel maid.*
Orsino:	Yes, that's the one. It eased the pain of my passions. What did you think of that tune, Cesario?
Viola:	It echoed perfectly of love.
Orsino:	You speak as if you know of love, boy. Do you?
Viola:	I am devoted to *you*, master.
Orsino:	Yes, yes. But I'll bet someone special has caught your eye. What kind of woman is she?

Viola:	Actually, she is like you.
Orsino:	And how old is she?
Viola:	Well . . . about *your* age.
Orsino:	Then she is too old for you. Fool, give me your song again.
Feste:	May the god of melancholy protect you. I'll sing, but lovesick men do better to sail on a sea of change than to make a voyage of nothing.
Orsino:	My love for Olivia is worth all I suffer. *(to Viola)* Cesario, go to the countess again, and ask her to be mine.
Viola:	Master, suppose for a moment that some *other* woman loved you—
Orsino:	No other woman's heart could ever hold as much love as mine does.
Viola:	That may not be so. My father had a daughter who loved a man. . . .
Orsino:	And what happened to her?
Viola:	She never told of her love, but pined away, smiling at grief.
Orsino:	Did this sister die of her love?
Viola:	*(riddling)* I don't know. I am all the daughters of my father's house.
Narrator 1:	When Orsino looks confused, Viola quickly changes the subject.
Viola:	I'll be off to see the countess now.
Orsino:	Beg her not to deny my love.

Scene 10

Narrator 2:	In the garden at Olivia's, Malvolio is about to fall into a trap.
Maria:	*(to Feste, Sir Toby, and Sir Andrew)* Quick, hide in the shrubbery.
Toby:	I'll be glad to see that pompous, pribbling pumpion put to shame.
Maria:	Here he comes. I know this letter will make an idiot of him.
Narrator 1:	Maria lets the letter fall.
Malvolio:	*(talking to himself)* Olivia knows I have more scruples than any other man. She admires me for this. One day I shall become *Count* Malvolio.
Toby:	*(quietly)* Did you hear that?
Malvolio:	And when I am count, I shall call my servant Toby forth and chide him for his drinking.
Toby:	*(muttering angrily)* His "*servant*"? That scab! I'll put him in bolts and shackles!
Feste:	*(whispering)* Shhh! You'll give us away.

Narrator 2: Malvolio discovers the letter.

Malvolio: What's this? Why, it's written in my lady's hand. *(reading aloud)* To my unknown beloved— the gods know whom I love. M, O, A, I doth sway my life. *(to himself)* Who is M, O, A, I?

Andrew: *(whispering gleefully)* Maria pens a pretty poison!

Malvolio: M, O, A, I? Why—all those letters are in *my* name!

Feste: Now she's won him.

Malvolio: *(reading on)* I am above thee, but do not be afraid of greatness. Some are born great, some achieve greatness, some have greatness thrust upon them. If you love me, smile constantly. Wear long yellow stockings, and crisscross your garters over them. Such a fashion drives me wild. I will be yours, my steward. *(to himself)* She means me! I'll do whatever she asks!

Narrator 1: Malvolio is starry-eyed as he walks away. The watchers come out of the bushes.

Feste: Ha-ha! I wouldn't have missed that for a pension of thousands!

Toby: I could marry Maria for this!

Narrator 2: Maria returns to the scene.

Maria: Did it work?

Andrew: You have put him in such a state, when it leaves him, he'll run mad!

Maria: Wait till he struts before my lady. She's bound to be annoyed.

Narrator 1: Olivia enters the garden, dreaming of Cesario.

Olivia: That man has captured my soul. I must send for him. Maria, call my steward to run a message.

Maria: I'll bring him to you in the hall. But I warn you, he is acting possessed.

Olivia: *(to herself)* That makes two of us. For Cesario has possessed *me*.

Narrator 2: At Orsino's request, Viola has returned to Olivia's. Sirs Toby and Andrew open the gate to her.

Olivia: *(blushing)* What a coincidence. I was just sending for you.

Viola: May heaven rain favors on you, fair princess.

Olivia: Hearing your poetic voice again is like music from the spheres. Uncle, please let us be alone now.

Narrator 1: After they go, Viola bows.

Viola: *(to Olivia)* I am your servant, and Orsino would be yours as well.

Olivia: Please, speak of him no more. Let us discuss other matters.

Viola: Such as?

Olivia:	I'm sorry I forced my ring on you. You must have seen through my shameful cunning.
Viola:	So it *was* a ploy. I pity you.
Olivia:	Well, pity is related to love. What do you really think of me?
Viola:	That you are not what you think you are.
Olivia:	Maybe I think that of you.
Viola:	*(riddling)* Then you would be right. For I am not what I am.
Olivia:	And I would have you be other than what you are—*(lunging after Viola)*—my husband! By the roses of spring, Cesario, I love thee!
Narrator 2:	Olivia begins to chase Viola around the bushes.
Olivia:	I can no longer hide my passion behind my pride! I know you do not seek it, and I cannot understand it—still, I must tell you, *I love thee!*
Viola:	*(trying to escape)* I swear, I have one heart and one truth, and no woman shall have them except me!
Olivia:	Give your love to me! Or at least tell me what I can do for you.
Narrator 1:	Viola continues to dodge Olivia. They finally come face to face at the garden gate.
Viola:	You can give your love to my master. Now good-bye!
Olivia:	*(desperately)* Please come again! Maybe someday you will move my heart enough to make me tolerate Orsino.

Scene 11

Narrator 2:	Later, Sir Andrew is fuming.
Andrew:	I'll not stay here a jot longer!
Toby:	Tell me your reason.
Andrew:	Your niece gives more time to a serving boy than she has ever given to me. "May heaven rain favors" indeed! And did you see the way she looked at Cesario?
Toby:	Maybe she did it to strike fire in your heart. Fire back, man! *(egging him on)* Show the youth what you are made of. Bang him into dumbness and change Olivia's impression of you.
Andrew:	*(whining)* How can I do that?
Toby:	Challenge Cesario to a duel.
Andrew:	Must I? I'm no swordsman.
Toby:	Do it! Olivia will be impressed by your bravery. I'll set it up.
Narrator 1:	Maria interrupts them.

Maria: Good sirs, if you want to laugh yourself into stitches, follow me. Malvolio is in the hall with my lady. He looks so ridiculous, Olivia will probably hurl things at him!

Narrator 2: Malvolio, transformed into the likeness of the letter, struts by. He smiles a dumb smile at Olivia.

Malvolio: Ho, lady. How is my sweet?

Olivia: What's wrong with you? I'm as sad as can be, and all you can do is stand there smiling?

Malvolio: You may be black in the mind, but I am yellow in the legs. Get it? *Yellow* in the legs . . . ?

Narrator 1: He displays his socks.

Olivia: Nice garters. They must be obstructing the blood to your brain.

Malvolio: *(still smiling)* The only obstruction I know of is that we are not in each other's arms.

Olivia: WHAT?

Maria: How dare you speak so boldly?

Malvolio: "Do not be afraid of greatness," she said. "Some are born great—"

Olivia: Ha!

Malvolio: "Some achieve greatness—"

Maria: Who? *You?*

Malvolio: "and some have greatness thrust upon them."

Olivia: Heaven restore your mind! *(privately to Maria)* Lock this fellow in a dark room! I would not have a madman on the loose!

Scene 12

Narrator 2: Sir Toby catches up to Viola, dressed as Cesario, returning to Duke Orsino's palace.

Toby: Hold, sir! My man has a quarrel with you and would like to settle it.

Viola: You must be mistaken. I have no quarrel with anyone.

Toby: He sends you this letter. *(reading)* Youth, thou art a scurvy fellow. Olivia uses thee kindly, yet you lie in the throat. I challenge you! Your sworn enemy, Andrew Aguecheek.

Viola: What is this about?

Toby: The offense doesn't matter anymore. Be on your guard. This fellow is skilled and full of wrath—a devil in a brawl. You'd do best to strip your sword naked and engage him.

Viola:	*(to herself)* It wouldn't take much now for me to tell them I'm not a man! *(aloud)* Where is he?
Narrator 1:	Belch yanks Sir Andrew out of the bushes.
Toby:	Right here. Go to it, man!
Andrew:	*(quietly to Toby)* Couldn't we just let the matter slip?
Toby:	*(to both)* Lift your swords.
Andrew:	*(whining)* Pray, God save me!
Narrator 2:	But as they begin to clash swords, a passing sailor suddenly takes it upon himself to try to break up the fight.
Sailor:	*(to Sir Andrew)* Put down your sword. No one shall harm my master!
Viola:	*(to the sailor)* Your master? Who is that?
Sailor:	Why, *you*, of course, sir.
Viola:	But I've never seen you before.
Toby:	*(to the sailor)* Get out of the way, swabbie!
Narrator 1:	The noise attracts some officers.
Toby:	*(pointing to the sailor)* Arrest that man for obstructing justice!
Narrator 2:	They pin the sailor's arms.
Sailor:	*(to Viola)* Now would be a good time to repay the kindness I showed by saving you at sea, sir! Will you vouch for me?
Viola:	I have no idea who you are.
Narrator 1:	As officers drag the sailor away, Viola runs off.
Sailor:	*(calling after Viola)* Will you deny you know me—after all I have done for you?

Scene 13

Narrator 2:	Sir Andrew and Sir Toby chase Cesario, but "he" gives them the slip.
Narrator 1:	Just outside the countess's house, they spy Sebastian, who is on his way to see the duke. Mistaking Sebastian for his twin sister in disguise, they confront him.
Toby:	There's Cesario! Get him!
Andrew:	Why don't we just let him go?
Toby:	Don't be such a coward!
Narrator 2:	Sir Andrew reluctantly smacks Sebastian with his gloves.
Andrew:	So, we meet again, eh?

Narrator 1: Sebastian hits him back.

Sebastian: *(to Sir Andrew)* What are you talking about? Take that! *(to Sir Toby)* And who is this lumpish hedgepig?

Narrator 2: Belch raises his sword.

Toby: *(taking insult)* Give me an ounce of your blood!

Narrator 1: Sebastian whacks Sir Toby's head with the flat of his sword. Hearing the fight, Olivia appears.

Olivia: Uncle—hold off! Disturbing the peace again? Get thee gone!

Narrator 2: Sirs Toby and Andrew flee as the countess fawns over the young man she believes to be Cesario.

Olivia: If they'd have hurt you, dear man, my heart would break. Come inside. Let me make you feel better.

Narrator 1: Sebastian is amazed by her forwardness—and her beauty.

Sebastian: *(in confusion)* If this is a dream, then let me still sleep!

Olivia: This is no dream. For I loved you the minute I laid eyes on you.

Sebastian: Lady, I wrangle with my reason, but this accidental meeting has wrapped me in good fortune.

Olivia: So you feel as I do? Forgive me for being hasty, but let us celebrate our love. Are you willing?

Sebastian: Good lady, I swear, you shall always have my faith.

Olivia: Heaven, shine on us then! Go to the priest and come back to tell me when the ceremony will be!

Scene 14

Narrator 2: Fleeing from Sir Andrew, Viola returns to the safety of Duke Orsino's house.

Orsino: How fares it with Olivia?

Viola: I can say no more to sway her mind to you, sir. But believe me when I say her mind has swayed.

Orsino: What do you mean?

Viola: I don't think Olivia is in mourning anymore. Maybe you should visit her yourself.

Orsino: Will she admit me?

Viola: It's worth a try.

Orsino: Then to Olivia's we go!

 **Scene 15**

Narrator 1: As the duke and Viola approach the countess's house, officers pass with a sailor under custody. The sailor tries to get Orsino's attention.

Sailor: I beseech you, Duke, hear my case! These men wrongly arrested me. I drew my sword to defend that ungrateful boy by your side. I saved him at sea, but now he denies me.

Orsino: *(to Viola)* Do you know him, Cesario?

Viola: He did kindly defend me, but I'd never seen him before that.

Sailor: Of course you have, Sebas—!

Orsino: Silence! We will deal with this later. Look, here comes the countess. Now heaven walks on Earth. *(in awe, to Olivia)* Gracious lady—!

Narrator 2: Olivia ignores the duke.

Olivia: *(to Viola)* Dearest Cesario, did you make our plans?

Viola: What plans? Listen, the duke would speak to you.

Olivia: *(impatiently)* Now what? Still harping on the same old tune, Orsino?

Orsino: *(feeling hurt)* Still so cruel, Olivia?

Olivia: Still so *boring,* sir?

Orsino: Why you uncivil lady! Out of devotion, I have sent you countless tender offerings. Yet all you show is ungratefulness. What shall I do now?

Olivia: Do whatever you like.

Orsino: You totally disregard me? If I had the heart to do it, I would kill what I love. But that is a savage jealousy. No, instead, I'll remove Cesario from your sight. For I see you hold more affection for him than for me. Come man. She has a raven's heart.

Viola: I go with you willingly.

Olivia: Why do you leave, Cesario?

Viola: I love this man more than life.

Olivia: Oh, I am deceived!

Viola: Who has deceived you?

Olivia: Why, you, husband.

Viola: *Husband?*

Olivia: Of course. Do you deny it?

Orsino: *(to Viola)* HUSBAND!? Are you her *husband?*

Viola:	No, my lord, not I.
Olivia:	But you have sworn your faith to me! Have you changed your mind about the wedding already?
Orsino:	*(angrily, to Viola)* Wedding? Why, you crafty, lying sneak! Have you wooed her behind my back? Go—take her! But now direct your feet where you and I will never meet again!
Viola:	But my lord, I swear—
Narrator 1:	Andrew and Toby wander back. Toby is holding his head.
Andrew:	A doctor. Send for a doctor.
Orsino:	What ails you?
Narrator 2:	Sir Toby points to Viola.
Toby:	*(moaning)* That young knave has broken my head!
Orsino:	Another insult, Cesario?
Viola:	No. They drew their swords on *me*. I never touched them!
Toby:	Run him out of town!
Narrator 1:	But luckily, just as they are about to do so, Sebastian shows up on the scene. He kneels before Olivia.
Sebastian:	Forgive me for hurting your kinsman, but they set upon me first. Anyway, I have good news. You and I will soon take our vows. . . . Why do you look at me so strangely?
Narrator 2:	Everyone stares back and forth at Viola and Sebastian.
Orsino:	One face, one voice, two persons!
Sebastian:	*(seeing sailor)* Ah, good man, we meet again! How are you?
Sailor:	Have you cut yourself in two?
Narrator 1:	Viola can't believe her eyes.
Viola:	Wonderful sight! Brother?
Narrator 2:	Sebastian studies Cesario.
Sebastian:	I never had a brother. Only a sister, but the waves devoured her. *(to Viola)* Who are you?
Viola:	*(in shock)* My father was Sebastian. My brother too, but he is in a watery tomb. Are you his spirit?
Sebastian:	If I am, then I must be in another world. And if you were a woman, I would say tearfully, "Welcome, drowned Viola!"
Narrator 1:	Viola whips off her cap and lets her hair down.
Viola:	Then let me make us all happy. For when I change these masculine clothes for maiden ones, you will see that I *am* Viola!

Sebastian: *(embracing her)* Sister!

Viola: To confirm my identity, I will bring to you a captain who helped me gain service with this noble count.

Sebastian: *(to Olivia)* My lady, see, you have been mistaken. You would have married a maid! But I tell you; you are promised to a man—to me!

Narrator 2: Olivia embraces Sebastian.

Orsino: *(to Viola)* Now, boy, I too shall have a share of this happy moment. You have told me a thousand times no one could love me as you do.

Viola: Every word of that was true.

Orsino: Then give me your hand. Your service to me is done. Since you called me master for so long, from this time forward, I shall call you mistress.

Olivia: *(to Belch)* Where is Malvolio? I want him to send for Viola's clothes.

Toby: Dear niece, you had the steward locked away.

Olivia: God save him—I forgot!

Scene 16

Narrator 1: Finally released from the dark room, Malvolio rushes to Olivia, with Feste and Maria following.

Malvolio: Lady, you have done me wrong.

Olivia: But you were acting insanely.

Malvolio: I am as well in my wits as any fool and only acting as you commanded me in this love letter.

Narrator 2: Malvolio hands Maria's letter to Olivia.

Olivia: *(reading)* Indeed, this looks like my hand . . . but it is Maria's!

Maria: *(to Olivia)* I admit that your uncle and I played a trick on Malvolio. But let's not tarnish the joy of this hour. The joke deserves laughter, not revenge.

Olivia: Dear Malvolio, you have been most notoriously abused.

Malvolio: And I will be revenged on the whole pack of you!

Narrator 1: Malvolio stomps off.

Orsino: *(to Maria)* Go beg him to find some humor in this. *(to Viola, Sebastian, and Olivia)* Now we all have golden vows to make. For Viola, when in woman's clothes you shall be seen, then I shall make of you Orsino's queen!

Feste: *A great while ago the world began. With a hey, ho, the wind and rain. But that's all one; our play is done, For love reigns in Illyria again!*

Simply Shakespeare: Readers Theatre for Young People is from *Read* magazine, a Weekly Reader publication, in collaboration with Teacher Ideas Press. Edited by Jennifer Kroll. www.weeklyreader.com. www.lu.com/tips. 1-800-541-2086.

Index of Scripts

As You Like It, 1
Hamlet: Prince of Denmark, 17
Julius Caesar, 33
King Lear, 51
Macbeth, 69
Midsummer Night's Dream, A, 91
Merchant of Venice, The, 107
Much Ado About Nothing, 121
Othello, 139
Romeo and Juliet, 161
Taming of the Shrew, 179
Tempest, The, 199
Twelfth Night, 213

The Comedies
As You Like It, 1
Merchant of Venice, The 107
Midsummer Night's Dream, A, 91
Much Ado About Nothing, 121
Taming of the Shrew, The, 191
Twelfth Night, 213

A Romance
Tempest, The, 199

The Tragedies
Romeo and Juliet, 161
Julius Caesar, 33
Hamlet: Prince of Denmark, 17
King Lear, 51
Macbeth, 69
Othello, 139

www.ingramcontent.com/pod-product-compliance
Lightning Source LLC
Chambersburg PA
CBHW082035300426
44117CB00015B/2495